French Country Kitchen

Geraldene Holt trained as a potter and later qualified as a teacher. She and her family live in a sixteenth-century thatched farmhouse in Devon and in London. Whenever possible she travels widely and especially enjoys cooking abroad, particularly in France.

Geraldene Holt's first book *Cake Stall* (Penguin Books, 1983), was written as a result of running a market stall in Tiverton selling cakes, biscuits, cookies and scones, using recipes that were tried and tested during twenty years of family cooking and entertaining. Her second book was *Travelling Food*, a guide to picnics, packed lunches and away-day food. As a result of her frequent radio broadcasts she followed this with the *Devon Air Cookbook*. Her *Budget Gourmet* was published in Penguin in 1985.

Through her regular contributions to *Homes and Gardens* and *Taste* magazines, her food columns for two West Country newspapers and her broadcasting on television and radio in the south-west, Geraldene Holt has become a well-known and influential food writer. In 1984 she was invited to become a founder member of the Guild of Food Writers.

Geraldene Holt

French Country Kitchen

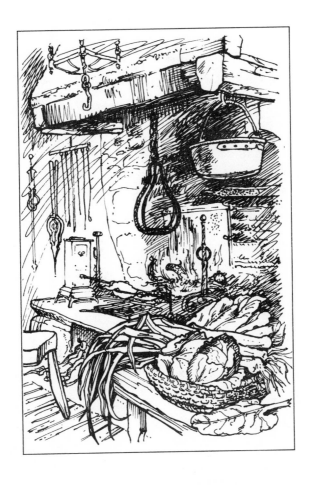

PENGUIN BOOKS

Penguin Books Ltd, 27 Wrights Lane, London w8 5tz (Publishing and Editorial)
and Harmondsworth, Middlesex, England (Distribution and Warehouse)
Viking Penguin Inc., 40 West 23rd Street, New York, New York 10010, USA
Penguin Books Australia Ltd, Ringwood, Victoria, Australia
Penguin Books Canada Ltd, 2801 John Street, Markham, Ontario, Canada L3R 1B4
Penguin Books (NZ) Ltd, 182–190 Wairau Road, Auckland 10, New Zealand

First published 1987

Copyright © Geraldene Holt, 1987
Illustrations by Alan Barlow
All rights reserved

Made and printed in Great Britain by
Richard Clay Ltd, Bungay, Suffolk
Phototypeset in Linotron Aldus by
Rowland Phototypesetting Ltd,
Bury St Edmunds, Suffolk

FOR MY FATHER AND MY DAUGHTER
WITH LOVE

CONTENTS

ACKNOWLEDGEMENTS

Most authors have an impossible task in attempting to record the extent of their debt to those who have influenced them. I am no exception.

My gratitude goes to both Elizabeth David and M. F. K. Fisher and their publishers: to Robert Hale/Jill Norman for permission to quote from *An Omelette and a Glass of Wine* by Elizabeth David, and to the Hogarth Press for permission to quote from *Two Towns in Provence* by M. F. K. Fisher.

I should, also, like to thank those friends and acquaintances who have given particular advice and help in the preparation of this book. In addition to those mentioned in the text I am specially grateful to, in France, Suzanne and Jeannette Doize, Yvette, Brigitte and Jean Marquet, Bernard and Marie-George Perrier, Susan and Harry Beazley, Pierre and Henriette Kieny, Hubert Laurent and his parents, Isabelle Jaine, Abel Broc, Marc Ryan and his grandfather Pierre Rolland, Geneviève Roux in her bookshop in Boulieu and Monique Génis.

In England I have received much kindness and encouragement from Pamela Todd, Eleo Gordon, Marie-Pierre Moine, Derek Cooper, Axel Nesme, Nicholas Dimbleby, Melvyn Ramsden and my local bookseller, John Lyle.

It has been a delight to work with Alan Barlow on the illustrations for the book, and I am grateful to Alan and his wife, Grace, for much generous hospitality. My thanks also go to Judy Gordon and Esther Sidwell at Penguin Books for such cheerful cooperation.

Finally I should like to record my limitless thanks to my daughter, Madeleine, who introduced me to the Ardèche, and to my father, who first taught me to love France when he started to teach me the language at meal-times when I was very young.

Introduction

If it is true that everyone belongs to two countries, their own and France, then for many of us, to land in France is to come home, if not legally then spiritually.

Quite when you cease to count how many times you've stayed there is usually hard to recall. For me, it must be nearly twenty years ago. Perhaps it was the time we were staying – long before its name became so familiar in wine lists – in Beaumes de Venise, near Orange in northern Provence. The village nestles against the foothills of Mont Ventoux and lies on the easterly edge of the plain that stretches, flat and hazy, past Carpentras to the Rhône; and the place is now once again, as in the time of Pliny, well known for its honeyed and beguiling muscat wine.

One blisteringly bright morning that summer we were choosing cheese for lunch from the overflowing shelves in the Casino shop in the square. A French woman suddenly asked us, in perfect English, where we lived in England. We told her and a few moments later we were invited to join Anne-Marie and her family for dinner that evening.

As we sat on the terrace of her father's house, sipping pale yellow chilled muscat, we laid the foundations of a warm friendship with a charming family and confirmed, for ever, our deep affection for the south of France. The meal was simple and delicious: a salad of fresh tunny fish, local cheeses and a fruit tart; the atmosphere was happy and relaxed.

On the following day Anne-Marie took us to see one of the huge local caves, once occupied by Neanderthal man, and now marooned twenty feet above her father's vineyard on the valley floor.

Two days later we were all sad to leave Beaumes de Venise to continue our holiday on the other side of the Rhône valley near the beautiful town of Uzès in the Languedoc.

Today Uzès, which once supplied the water that flowed across the Roman Pont du Gard on its way to Nîmes, is a glamorous place. Smoked glass-fronted boutiques sport Paris clothes, and the arcaded

Place aux Herbes where I used to buy huge bunches of fresh basil to dry at home in England has been restored and paved. But Uzès is still a delightful country town and retains its reputation for good food which prompted Racine to write while living there in 1661, 'A man may starve here from lack of literature but he will assuredly eat well; this place prides itself on its table.'

Now there is a bookshop in Uzès and a music festival too, and a notable gastronomic event when the garlic fair is held each year towards the end of June.

Discovering France and remembering its food is always a pleasure. But for me the food that is prepared and eaten in unprepossessing homes, cafés and local restaurants is the most satisfying, the most revealing. I rarely seek out stars or *toques* at expensive restaurants – I normally find country cooking more appealing with its lack of pretension, its honest simplicity.

French country cooking embodies the spirit of the people and of the place. It would be a mistake to think of this food as without refinement. Its rusticity is due to its proximity to the countryside. It uses local produce and the freshest vegetables and herbs. These are the qualities everyone who enjoys eating values. These hall-marks of the food make for warm, welcoming dishes that are far more eloquent of a time and place than much modern fastidiously fashionable food. Good food never goes out of fashion.

As we cook, we each do so in an individual and unique way – an extra hint of a herb here, a little longer in the oven there. This is one of the joys of cooking. A dish has a slightly altered but no less enjoyable note every time it is prepared. To welcome this aspect of cooking and eating greatly increases the pleasure: detecting and appreciating these shades in flavour is rewarding to the discerning palate. And these variations happen when food is produced by hand, not on a mass scale by machines. It is important to celebrate such differences if we value a society designed not for unquestioning automatons but for ourselves.

In France, it is always inspiriting to rediscover that almost everyone has a firm view on what matters in eating, that is, its quality. This has little to do with price, and everything to do with respect for raw materials and how they are treated in the kitchen. There is a national and fiercely defended determination to enjoy the arts of the table. This is shared by the small farmer in the Ardèche who manages to live only modestly well from his few hectares of stony soil as well as by the prosperous lawyer from the north who spends August in his house in St Raphael.

I count myself fortunate that on most occasions in France I am able to live as part of a rural community, getting to know its inhabitants, shopping in markets and cooking in some temporary, maybe ill-equipped, but charming kitchens.

I remember a cool, dark kitchen in the basement of a farmhouse in Var with a particularly capricious cooker, another in a cottage in Vaucluse surrounded by fields of lavender, or the neat, bright kitchen that opens straight on to the garden in the presbytery in a hamlet in the Ardèche.

One's cooking is inspired by the local produce: the scented melons from the fields around Carpentras; rich hare and game of the Coiron which I cook with freshly gathered berries from juniper bushes clinging to the stony outcrops that border the Gorges de l'Ardèche; or concocting a dish around the local rice from the Camargue with spices from the vast and splendid market at Pierre-latte, perhaps not far from where Hannibal crossed the Rhône with raft-borne elephants; and sometimes cooking a local dish, first served by friends or in a restaurant, one chances on new tastes. The sole with grapefruit arrived like that.

One of the privileges of knowing France in this way is to be invited into neighbours' houses, and invariably into their kitchens. I can see Mme Marquet's: the wood-burning stove in one corner of her cosy shady kitchen where everything is burnished until it gleams in the grey light. She produces a trembling, soft omelette made with the dark, speckled eggs from her hens and we eat it on the vine-shaded terrace by the kitchen. As we eat and talk, I study the variety of fossils that her husband has brought home from the fields, now displayed on the low walls around the garden.

The food of these country regions of the south of France is good – uncomplicated but not unsubtle. Escoffier's dictum, *Faites simple*, rings true. And the cooks of the region are happy to illustrate it: a farmer's wife shows me how she cures her home-made *saucissons* in wood ash, a baker with a feeling for the past talks to me about his chestnut bread, and in the dairy next to the river meadow where all day goats' bells make haunting music, a young woman who has chosen an 'alternative' way of life invites me to sample the changes in flavour of goats' cheeses of varying maturity. How different these freshly made creamy discs taste from the well-aged *picodons* of Dieulefit, each neatly wrapped in chestnut leaves.

The best country cooking has an appropriateness which is peculiar to itself. The ingredients – their taste and texture – are in harmony. You eat and you sense the rightness of it. There is no need for the helter-skelter search for amazing flavour combinations which characterizes some present-day cooking. But, of course, this does not mean that French country cooking is unchanging. It evolves in the same way as do other aspects of a nation's culture, through considered thought, the acceptance and sometimes the rejection of new ideas. This questioning fashions the path of cultural change, leading us to believe that, as time passes, we make what we hope is progress. But perhaps only posterity can truly judge.

This book grows out of my own experience of cooking and eating in the south of France. It does not attempt to provide an encyclopaedic view of the food of the region. While its faults and omissions are due to its partiality and my own enthusiasms it owes much to the French men and women who introduced me to those experiences for which I am eternally grateful.

The late Tom Stobart wrote, 'There is no such thing as a good but impersonal cookery book.' I now realize that I see every food, every dish in a context. Each one with a story. All of them important in the narrative that amounts to a life. That is why I often record how and when and why I cook and eat. I'll tell one story from so many to illustrate how and why this book was written.

About seven years ago in Fréjus in Provence I picked up a piece of hedge clipping from a shrub growing near the ruins of the Roman theatre. Today this cutting is a tree and each spring it fills our conservatory with an overpowering and beautiful scent like that of orange blossom. But after looking through all my gardening books I still couldn't discover its name.

Last year I spent some time travelling alone in the Midi, drawing together my knowledge of France in preparation for this book. One Sunday afternoon I arrived in Hyères on the coast and as I walked down an avenue of palm trees I noticed a huge specimen of the shrub I'd grown at home. Seeing an elderly couple making their way gingerly down the street I stopped and asked them the name. 'Oh, it's a pittosporum,' answered Madame. And then, realizing that I was English, she asked me about Haywards Heath, and did I know it. She had stayed there fifty years ago. After a short time we all sat down on a nearby bench and they asked me what I was doing in France. I explained, and we talked about food. We discussed whether their lunch of *couscous*, which they had just enjoyed at the retired officers' mess, could now be considered to be as distinctly French as a Cheltenham curry was English. We parted and I spent the afternoon climbing the steep streets in the old part of Hyères up near the crusader fort.

In the early evening I returned to my hotel forty miles north. Within five minutes there was a telephone call from the charming Hyères couple inviting me to tea the next day. I drove back south through a cloudburst which temporarily flooded the vineyards. But in Hyères the sun burnt in an almost luridly blue sky. In their spacious apartment overlooking the Mediterranean, Mme and M. Kieny sat on each side of me and we talked about England and about Rupert Brooke and we recalled his poem about Grantchester. I gave them the English tea and the Devon honey which I had brought.

Then they led me across to a table on which lay an enormous book and they invited me to look at it. It was Prosper Montagné's *Le Grand Livre de la cuisine*, a wedding present from their closest friend fifty-five years earlier. How magnificent, I said, turning the pages. But how could I sit here, I wondered, reading the recipes and possibly taking notes while still their guest. At that moment M. Kieny turned from his desk and gave me a small envelope. He said, 'We didn't know if you would accept the book, so we wrote the card to give you if you did.' Feeling much moved by this unexpected kindness, I opened the card:

À Mme Geraldene Holt
cette édition de 1929 du *Grand Livre de la cuisine* en souvenir de notre rencontre fortuite ce dimanche 19 Mai 1985 près de l'église anglicane de l'avenue Beauregard à Hyères (Var) en espérant que sa lecture l'aidera dans ses recherches sur l'art culinaire des provinces françaises.

M. et Mme Kieny.

Some years ago when I was selling cakes an elderly gentleman leant across the stall and whispered to me 'Food is love.' I would not disagree. The food in this book records my love for France. I hope you will be able to share it.

Le Presbytère, and
Clyst William Barton, 1987

HERBS AND SPICES

Uzès

It is the feast of St Jean, the height of summer. As you approach Uzès across the *garrigue* you meet a few early risers already hurrying away from the centre of town, carrying bulging bags, a bundle or so, even a lacy sack of what is known as 'the stinking rose', *Allium sativum* or garlic. Today is the annual garlic fair. Growers from further south have brought some of their choicest produce to sell in the elegant streets and the arcaded Place aux Herbes of this charming town.

Huge pyramids of the papery bulbs – some white, some rosy pink – have been built on the pavements, in the streets, at the back of lorries and around the fountain. Bundles of garlic spill over tables, long garlands hang from the awnings of market stalls, others are worn round the necks of the sellers. Even the shops are selling garlic – but far dearer. Over everything hangs a perfumed cloud, not so much of garlic – more like a gentle aroma of leeks, closer to chives or young onions. This is freshly harvested garlic and the flavour, when eaten, has a creamy richness which gains its familiar pungency only as it dries during the summer. M. Charnas has arrived with his son and daughter, and they sit on sacks of garlic plaiting the stems to make long chains. He tells me that he grows his garlic in the sandy soil around Cavaillon in strips set between the melons for which the area is well-known. Each clove or *gousse* is planted in late September or October. Three hundred years earlier Olivier de Serres, the father of French agriculture, had found by accident that garlic must be planted in the autumn in order to produce a head of garlic, composed of separate cloves. If you plant the cloves too late in the season, the garlic will grow, but in the form of an onion – the head will not divide or become *daussé*, as he terms it in his classic work, *Le Théâtre d'agriculture et mesnages des champs*.

It's far easier to grow garlic in England than I expected, and not just in the south. A Swiss woman I know grows garlic most successfully on her allotment in Huddersfield. The trick though, as I discovered through trial and error before I'd read Olivier de Serres, is to plant it in the autumn.

In France the crop is harvested during May, and some is sold green straight away. Whenever I see it on sale – bunches can be found, even in northern France during May – I buy some. Green garlic tastes mild, like leeks, and it makes an excellent soup or sauce.

The main crop, though, is lifted and left on the ground to ripen in the sun like onions, until the stalks have shrivelled. Then it is gathered into bundles and is sold in markets and shops. Some is plaited (I can never resist making a few chains) but country people don't bother; it is hung up in bundles to continue drying. To keep garlic as long as possible or at least until the next season, store it in an airy, cool, dry place. Never leave it in the sun or in bright light.

Cooking with garlic can rarely be done secretly – the kitchen, even the whole house, will be filled with this essential scent of the south. Recently it has been discovered that it is the oils released in the aroma of the herb that are so valuable medicinally. Prosper Montagné recommends removing the pale green sprout that starts to grow in the centre of a clove when garlic is stored at room temperature. To crush garlic, peel a clove, place it on a board (ideally one kept specially for it) with a sprinkling of salt and flatten it with the blade of a heavy knife. Some people prefer to use a garlic press but Elizabeth David says that they coarsen the flavour and make it acrid; others find that a plastic garlic press does not have this effect whereas a metal one does. Or is it to do with the size of the holes? It seems that garlic can still mesmerize us with its magical powers, making definitive pronouncements hard to prove.

Long, slow-cooked, unpeeled cloves of garlic can give a gentle and well-rounded flavour to a dish. Of course, a whole head of garlic, roast or baked, is served in its true guise as a vegetable, when we normally regard this historic plant as a herb.

One of the most cheering aspects of the recent growth of interest in good food in Britain has been a rekindled enthusiasm for herbs. The French have never lost their fervour for the subtle and aromatic flavouring that these plants bring to a dish – *poulet à l'estragon, purée d'oseille à la crème, loup de mer au fenouil* – all classic dishes that have helped to ensure that herbs and their associations with the country play a central role in their cuisine.

In the south of France wild herbs grow far more profusely than we can ever manage in a well-tended garden here. During his travels in France in 1664, John Evelyn wrote, 'Sep: 30 we lay at Loumas, the next morning came to Aix; having pass'd that most dangerous and extremely rapid river of Durance: In this tract all the Heathes or Commons are cover'd with Rosemary, Lavander, Lentiscs and the like sweete shrubs for many miles together, which to me was then a very pleasant sight.'

It is no different today. To lie on a warm Provençal hillside in the evening sun, one's skin pressing against leaves of thyme and mint, marjoram and fronds of fennel until the fragrant oil is released into the hot, dry air, is to know this ancient, unchanged terrain as once the Romans and before them the Greeks knew it. And, later, to share with someone you love wine made from the vines in the valley below, and eat food cooked over a fire perfumed with stems of rosemary, is to savour to the full this Mediterranean France that speaks of the past. It is a country which, once it has entered your soul, you will never cease to long for.

To John Evelyn's rosemary and lentisc, or sage, are added wild thyme and marjoram, basil, fennel, and mint to make the mixture of dried herbs known as *herbes de Provence* which can be a useful addition to the spice cupboard and for cooking outside. But it must be said that there is a further delight to be had by using the herbs fresh. Even so, whether you are in the south of France or your own herb patch it is good to know how to preserve herbs for use all the year round.

Most herbs are at their peak for flavour just as they come into flower. This is the best time to pick them for drying. Collect each herb separately on a dry day and tie in bunches. If you can, hang them upside down in a warm place that is not too light, and they should retain their colour. When brittle-dry, crush the leaves in your hands and discard the stalks and tougher pieces. Then store in lightproof jars with screw tops.

Wild thyme or *serpolet* is worth picking for drying. But I also find the plant seems to grow quite well in my Devon garden, and so does wild marjoram. Obviously, though, all the southern herbs prefer conditions as close to those of the Midi as you can manage. If you can find a warm, dry spot at the base of a south-facing wall it is ideal. Or you might consider growing the herbs in pots so that they can be moved into a sheltered place – a greenhouse, cold frame or windowsill during the winter. If you live in a region with hard winters, it may be wise to treat tender herbs like tarragon and chives as you would a non-hardy geranium; in this way your perennial herbs will survive many years.

Aside from the pleasure of growing your own herbs, those you dry seem far superior in flavour to those bought in packets. Even basil, not normally a herb that dries well, can be coaxed, when dried at home, to retain some of the peppery sweetness which for most of us summons up the southern sun so successfully. The plant does quite well in Britain on a really sunny windowsill.

One of the nicest ways to preserve the flavour of basil and tarragon is to feed a stem or two into a bottle of olive oil, and leave it in a dark place for three to four weeks until the oil has absorbed the scent. Alternatively these herbs freeze well, but basil, in particular, should be used straight from the freezer in a sauce or soup instead of allowing it to thaw, as it may oxidize and blacken very quickly. It is better to freeze tender herbs like these in a plastic carton, covered with a layer of melted butter or oil. Or chop the herb finely and beat into some softened butter with a squeeze of lemon juice to make a savoury herb butter for melting over vegetables or fish, or for adding to soups during the winter. Herb butters store well in the freezer for up to six months.

Some years ago in Normandy I spent quite a time waiting to see what the seeds of 'sarriette' I'd been given would grow into. Had I been carrying Tom Stobart's invaluable *Herbs, Spices and Flavourings* (Penguin Books) there would have been no problem. (It turned out to be the piquant herb that goes so well with broad beans, summer savory.)

Courgettes à l'Oseille

COURGETTES WITH SORREL

In Jeannette's garden, surrounded by a low stone wall to keep out sheep and goats, everything grows with a luxuriance we rarely see here. This is her recipe for giving the bland taste of courgettes the welcome sharpness of fresh sorrel.

> **small courgettes**
> **salt**
> **olive oil or sunflower oil, or**
> **a mixture**
> **sorrel**

Slice the courgettes, not too thinly. Sprinkle with salt and leave in a colander for 15 minutes to draw out the water. Rinse in cold water, drain well and dry carefully in a clean cloth or on kitchen paper.

Fry the courgettes, in batches if necessary, in the oil, and drain on kitchen paper. Arrange the slices neatly on a serving dish and keep hot.

Shred the sorrel and sprinkle with a little salt. Leave for 10–15 minutes. Heat a tablespoon or so of oil and throw in the sorrel. Cook, stirring, for 4–5 minutes until the sorrel has collapsed and the water has been driven off. Spoon the sorrel over the courgettes and serve hot or cold.

Jeannette adds that should sorrel be unavailable you could prepare *courgettes au vinaigre* (courgettes with vinegar), as a pleasing alternative. Heat a little olive oil, stir in a chopped clove of garlic and some coarsely chopped parsley. Cook until soft but not coloured. Carefully add a little wine vinegar, taking care that it does not spit. Remove from the heat, and pour over the courgettes and serve hot or cold.

DINDONNEAU À L'AIL EN CHEMISE

TURKEY WITH WHOLE CLOVES OF GARLIC

When garlic, still in its papery covering, is roasted beside poultry or game the flavours enhance each other. In this recipe I find that the turkey, which can be rather bland these days, gains a more gamy taste from the garlic, which itself roasts to a sweet purée. If you can, cook the dish in the autumn with large cloves of the new season's garlic. And if you are a garlic devotee, provide one whole head of garlic for each person, and in that case don't separate the cloves – just detach a layer of the outside papery leaves.

4 legs of turkey, small or medium	16–20 cloves of garlic
30 g (1 oz) butter	1 wineglass French rosé wine
salt, milled pepper	½ wineglass light stock or water
8 slices of *lard fumé* or smoked streaky bacon	

Skin the meat and, if not already removed, cut and detach the scaly part of each leg at the first joint. Look for the tendon on each leg at this joint and detach. Sometimes it is necessary to grip it with pliers to be able to pull it free. In France where turkey is growing more popular the tendons have usually been removed.

Lightly brown the turkey legs in the butter. Season each with salt and pepper and wrap two slices of the bacon around each. Arrange the meat in a buttered roasting tin and add the cloves of garlic, tucking them in close to the turkey.

Roast in a moderate oven (Mark 5, 190°C, 375°F) for 45–60 minutes, basting the meat and the garlic from time to time with the cooking juices. The meat is cooked when only clear juices run from the thickest part of the leg when a knife is inserted.

Transfer the meat and the garlic to a hot serving dish and pour off all the surplus fat (reserve it for roasting potatoes) from the roasting tin. Add the wine and a little stock or water and boil fast, stirring in the pan juices until the sauce is reduced to half. Taste to check the seasoning and serve with the turkey and the garlic. Serves 4.

TAPENADE AUX OEUFS DURS

TAPENADE WITH HARD-BOILED EGGS

In the south, alongside the barrels of olives in brine, superb capers
are often available. Buy whatever you can afford or carry and store
them in their own brine in a lidded jar in the refrigerator. In
Provence there is a particularly fine variety known as *'non-pareil'*
and, if possible, these are the best for *tapenade*, whose name comes
from the Provençal *tapena* for caper. *Tapenade* is also very good
served with bread alone.

115 g (4 oz) black olives	55 g (2 oz) tuna fish
50 g (1¾ oz) anchovy fillets, brined or in oil	1 lemon
	about 100 ml (3½ fl oz)
4 tablespoons capers, drained	olive or sunflower oil
	hard-boiled eggs

Stone the olives and crush in a mortar. Gradually add the rinsed
fillets of anchovy, the capers, tuna fish and the juice of half the
lemon. Work all the ingredients together to make a fairly smooth
paste. Or purée everything in a processor, but not too smoothly.

Slowly add the oil to the paste as when making mayonnaise.
Check the flavour and add more lemon juice if required.

Spoon on to a serving dish and surround by sliced or quartered
hard-boiled eggs. Serves 4–6.

PURÉE D'AUBERGINE

AUBERGINE PURÉE

If there is one unifying vegetable of the countries bordering the
Mediterranean it is surely the bulging purple-skinned aubergine. It
is an amazingly accommodating creature, happily fried, baked,
stuffed or puréed. In a tiny restaurant in the Var I discovered this
aubergine purée flavoured with mint – a herb which is not widely

used in French cooking but is, of course, characteristic of the cuisines further east in the Mediterranean.

285 g (10 oz) aubergine	**salt**
2 tablespoons olive oil	**1 tablespoon finely**
juice of half a lemon	**chopped mint**

Halve the aubergine lengthways and place cut side down on a lightly oiled oven dish. Place under a hot grill and cook until the skin has blackened and blistered and the inside is soft.

Remove from the grill and cover the dish with an upturned bowl. Leave until the aubergine is cool enough to handle. Then scrape the flesh of the vegetable into the bowl of a blender or a processor. Mix in the oil, lemon juice and salt with sufficient chopped mint to flavour it lightly.

Spoon the purée into a dish and chill until ready to serve. Serves 3–4. This purée goes well with thinly sliced *saucisson sec*, especially the *jesu* of the Langedoc and the *rosette* of the Ardèche.

Conques

TURBOT CUIT À LA VAPEUR À LA CRÈME DE ROMARIN DE BERNARD PERRIER

BERNARD PERRIER'S STEAMED TURBOT WITH ROSEMARY-CREAM SAUCE

The real delight in this dish is the beautiful cream sauce with its delicate flavour of rosemary. Bernard Perrier at Barattero serves the sauce with turbot; I find it also goes well with scallops and I think sole would be good too.

680 g (1½ lb) turbot, filleted and cut into four (reserve the skin and bones)	½ wineglass dry white wine
lemon juice	1 shallot, finely chopped
a slice of onion, ½ stick celery, a bay leaf and a few peppercorns	4 sprigs of fresh rosemary
	1 wineglass dry vermouth
	150 ml (¼ pt) *crème fraîche*
	salt

Place the turbot on a plate and sprinkle with lemon juice; set aside until ready to cook.

Cover the skin and bones of the fish with water and add the onion, celery, bay leaf, peppercorns and wine. Simmer for 15 minutes. Strain and reduce to make 4 tablespoons.

In another pan simmer the shallot with the rosemary and the vermouth for 10 minutes. Add the fish stock, and strain it into the cream. Bring almost to the boil, season with salt to taste and keep hot over water while you steam the fish.

Serve the fish with the cream sauce spooned around it and garnish with a tiny sprig of fresh rosemary. Serves 4.

L'Aigo Boulido, ou l'Eau Bouilli

It is said that *l'eau bouilli* can save life. Certainly this authentically instant soup can revive one's flagging spirits and my friends Jeannette and Suzanne in the Ardèche serve it on Sunday evening to those who have over-indulged at midday. They declare that the books that tell you to boil the soup are wrong, the soup is made in the bowl.

per person:	salt
1 clove garlic	boiling water
1–2 slices of French bread	Gruyère cheese, finely
olive oil	grated

Crush the garlic into a soup plate, add the bread, torn into pieces. Dribble the oil over the bread and sprinkle in a little salt.

Pour on the boiling water and sprinkle the Gruyère cheese on top. Eat straight away.

In the Ardèche in the past *l'eau bouilli* was always served to a newly married couple just before they retired to bed. Perhaps it still is.

Oeufs en Cocotte à l'Oseille

COCOTTE EGGS WITH SORREL

I find that the sorrel purée freezes well for cooking with later in the year or when the frost has finished off my sorrel clumps until the spring.

85 g (3 oz) sorrel leaves	salt, milled pepper
30 g (1 oz) butter	4 dessertspoons *crème*
4 eggs	*fraîche* or single cream

Wash and drain the sorrel. Melt the butter in a small pan and when foaming add the sorrel. Cook over moderate heat, stirring all the time, for about 5 minutes until you have a thick, smooth purée.

Divide the sorrel between four cocotte dishes. Break an egg into each, season with salt and pepper and spoon the cream on top.

Place the eggs in a bain-marie filled with hot water and cook in a moderately hot oven (Mark 5, 190°C, 375°F) for 5–7 minutes, or cook on the hob until the white of egg only is set. Serve straight away. Serves 2–4.

PIGEONS AUX TROIS HERBES
SUR LIT DE RIZ
PIGEON WITH THREE HERBS ON A BED OF RICE

Plump harvest woodpigeons are at their best in August and September. I devised this dish in order to turn what I normally regard as the tediously long cooking time of brown rice to advantage, but when we came to eat the dish we found the combination of *riz complet* with pigeons unexpectedly good.

2 woodpigeons	1 shallot, finely chopped
fresh thyme, rosemary and	salt, milled pepper
marjoram	225 g (8 oz) brown
55 g (2 oz) butter	round-grain rice
1 slice of *lard fumé* or	about 300 ml (10–18 fl oz)
smoked streaky bacon	stock or water

Have the pigeons plucked and dressed for the oven. Tuck most of the herbs into the body cavities.

Melt the butter in a cast-iron casserole and cook the *lard fumé* and shallot in it for 2 minutes. Add the pigeons and turn them in the butter until browned all over. Transfer the pigeons to a plate and season with salt and pepper.

Stir the rice into the butter remaining in the casserole until completely coated. Pour in the stock, season lightly and bring to the boil.

Place the pigeons on top of the rice, tuck any remaining herbs around them and cover the casserole.

Cook in a moderate oven (Mark 4, 180°C, 375°F; this dish is

easy-going – cook for longer in a low oven if you prefer) for 1½–2 hours until the meat is tender and the rice has absorbed all the liquid. Serves 2–3.

TARTELETTES AU PIZZA

PIZZA TARTLETS

Sometimes a bread-based pizza is too substantial for a picnic on a hot day and the answer can be small filled tartlets.

Pâte brisée
115 g (4 oz) flour
55 g (2 oz) butter, slightly
  softened
1 egg yolk
¼ teaspoon salt
2 tablespoons ice-cold
  water

Pizza filling
1 onion, chopped
1 or 2 cloves of garlic, finely
  chopped

1 tablespoon olive oil
450 g (1 lb) fresh or tinned
  tomatoes, peeled
½ teaspoon sugar
marjoram or oregano
thyme or *serpolet*
a bay leaf
salt, milled pepper
anchovy fillets or olives or
  Parmesan cheese, finely
  grated

Make the pastry as explained on p. 78. Wrap in plastic and chill for about 30 minutes.

Meanwhile make the filling. Cook the onion and the garlic in the oil for 5 minutes until soft. Add the chopped tomatoes, sugar and herbs and a little salt and pepper. Simmer the mixture for 20–25 minutes until almost all the liquid has evaporated.

Purée in a blender or push through a sieve.

Roll out the pastry to line six lightly buttered 10 cm (4 in) tartlet tins. Do not stretch the pastry as you do this otherwise it will shrink too much during baking.

Prick the bases of the pastry cases and chill for 15–30 minutes. Bake in a moderately hot oven (Mark 6, 200°C, 400°F) for 10–15 minutes until lightly coloured.

Spoon the filling into the pastry cases. Add a crisscross of anchovy fillets or a few olives or a little cheese and replace in the oven for 10 minutes until piping hot. (The filling is also delicious left plain but given a generous dusting of coarsely ground black pepper.) Serve hot, warm or cold. Makes 6 tartlets.

LE GRAND AÏOLI

Aïoli is Provence; that is where it is best. And where when the sun shines on olive oil, egg yolks and garlic some mysterious culinary process traps everything that is warm and eternal in that mound of shining yellow cream. If you've eaten *le grand aïoli* in Provence under a clear blue sky with plenty of companions and a local wine you've been spoilt: it will never be as good in England. But each time, one hopes it might be. Outdoor food, definitely.

2–5 cloves of garlic   275 ml (½ pt) olive oil (if
**   (depending on their size)   very fruity replace with**
2 egg yolks   half sunflower oil)

Crush the peeled cloves of garlic in a mortar and mix in the egg yolks. Add the oil a drop at a time, beating continuously with a wooden spoon.

Once the *aïoli* has started to thicken the oil can be added in a thin stream but it is essential to keep beating as you do so. If the oil is high quality you may need to add a tablespoon or so of warm water to slacken the consistency of the *aïoli*. The classic version is made with olive oil, egg yolks and garlic, alone. If the olive oil is good the flavour will be superb. But you may prefer to add a dash of lemon juice and some salt and pepper.

To serve, spoon into a pottery or wooden bowl or serve in the mortar if you've used one. On a large platter make a vast display from the following, and serve with the *aïoli*:

soaked and poached salt cod
a selection of cold vegetables: boiled potatoes, *haricot verts*, artichoke bottoms, spring onions, radishes, lettuce hearts, Mangetout peas, olives, tomatoes.

GÂTEAU DE FOIES DE VOLAILLE AU BEURRE BLANC

CHICKEN-LIVER MOUSSE WITH BEURRE BLANC

In the Bresse region of Burgundy where some of the best chicken in France are reared, a particularly delicate mousse is prepared with the pale livers of these birds. Françoise Allirol, whose fine cooking distinguishes her Restaurant du Château in Annonay, serves her version with Ardéchois juniper berries and *beurre blanc*. Even made with the less subtle-tasting livers from English chicken this mousse is exceptionally pleasing.

225 g (8 oz) chicken livers
fingernail paring of garlic
4 eggs
4 egg yolks
425 ml (¾ pt) creamy milk
a little ground mace
salt, milled white pepper
a small knob of butter

Beurre blanc
2 shallots, very finely
  chopped

3 tablespoons white wine
  vinegar
3 tablespoons dry white
  wine
200 g (7 oz) butter
1 tablespoon cream
  (optional and not for
  purists)
18–24 juniper berries
1 tablespoon gin

Mince the livers finely in a processor or mincer. Mix in the crushed garlic, eggs, egg yolks and milk, and beat until incorporated. Strain through a sieve into a bowl and season lightly with the mace, and some salt and pepper.

Butter 6 small moulds and place a disc of buttered greaseproof paper in the base of each. Divide the mixture between the moulds and place on a layer of folded newspaper in a bain-marie, with warm water deep enough to come half way up the moulds.

Cook in a moderate oven (Mark 3, 160°C, 325°F) for 20–30 minutes or until set. Do not overcook or the custard will be spoiled. The *gâteaux* are cooked when the blade of a knife comes out clean from the centre.

To make the *beurre blanc*, simmer the shallots with the wine vinegar and the wine in a glass or enamel pan until the mixture measures just under a tablespoonful.

Remove the pan from the heat but replace it now and again to maintain the temperature. Gradually beat in the butter in small pieces never allowing the butter to melt totally. If you wish, finally beat in a little cream – I notice that chefs are increasingly doing so.

Soak the juniper berries in the gin and a tablespoon of hot water, and simmer for a few minutes; drain to serve. Sometimes I reduce the liquid further and add it to the *beurre blanc*.

Turn the chicken mousses out on to small plates. Place 3 or 4 juniper berries on top of each and spoon a little *beurre blanc* around each mousse. Serves 6.

If you have a mousse over it is very good served lightly chilled with hot toast.

OEUFS À L'AIL

EGGS WITH GARLIC

Hard-boiled eggs stuffed with a piquant garlic paste.

**about 10 cloves of garlic
5 anchovy fillets, rinsed
and chopped
1 teaspoon capers, chopped
2–3 tablespoons olive oil
2–3 teaspoons white wine
vinegar**

**salt, milled pepper
4 hard-boiled eggs, halved
sprigs of chervil or flat
parsley**

Peel the cloves of garlic, and cook in a little water for 10–15 minutes until tender.

Drain and pound the garlic with the anchovies, capers, oil and vinegar until fairly smooth. Season with salt and pepper and add the yolks from the eggs. Pound together or whizz in a blender or processor until smooth.

Spoon the mixture into the whites of eggs and place a sprig of chervil or parsley on each. Serves 2–4, or serve as part of a larger hors d'oeuvre.

SOUPE AU PISTOU

Most summers I find that growing basil in Britain is not as difficult as is often supposed. Under glass or in a sunny corner or windowsill just a pot or two (treat it like a busy-Lizzie) makes your summer cooking truly evocative of the south. In France two kinds of basil are grown: small-leaved, usually designated for sauces, and large-leaved, which is preferable for salads.

Those who make it know that home-made *pesto* really brings pasta alive and totally transforms this otherwise plain Provençal bean and vegetable soup. Dried haricot beans are optional – some nineteenth-century cook books omit them altogether. But if possible I like to include fresh white haricot beans, which are in the markets in the south during late July; they are added to the soup with the potatoes. (Fresh white haricot beans are added to hot water, dried white haricot beans are soaked and added to cold water.)

1 tablespoon olive oil
1 onion, finely chopped
115 g (4 oz) white haricot
   beans, fresh or, if dried
   then already soaked and
   cooked
2 potatoes, diced
1 stick of celery, chopped
salt, milled pepper
225 g (8 oz) green haricot
   beans, cut in short
   lengths

green part of a leek, finely
   sliced
2 tomatoes, peeled and
   chopped
55 g (2 oz) fine vermicelli

Pistou
2–3 cloves of garlic
a handful of basil leaves
3–4 tablespoons olive oil
finely grated Parmesan or
   Gruyère cheese

Heat the oil in a large pan and soften the onion. Add the white haricot beans, potatoes and celery with about 1½ litres (2½–3 pt) water and some salt and pepper. Simmer, covered, for 10–15 minutes.

Now add the green haricot beans, leek, tomatoes and vermicelli and cook for a further 10 minutes. Taste to check the seasoning.

Meanwhile pound the garlic with the basil, gradually adding the olive oil and just a tablespoon or so of the hot liquid from the soup.

Serve the soup in large bowls, spoon in some *pistou* and sprinkle in some grated Parmesan or Gruyère cheese. Serves 6.

SAUCE À L'AIL À LA PROVENÇALE

PROVENÇAL GARLIC SAUCE

This sauce is probably strictly for garlic lovers or those who believe, along with the ancients, that garlic purifies the blood and prevents rheumatism. In fact, it comes from the collection of doctors' recipes called *Le Trésor de la cuisine du bassin méditerranéen*, edited by Prosper Montagné.

45 g lean *jambon* or unsmoked bacon, diced	1 teaspoon flour
olive oil	up to 570 ml (1 pt) stock
1 onion, chopped	bouquet garni
1 carrot, sliced	grated nutmeg
2 or 3 heads of garlic, each clove peeled	milled pepper, salt

Cook the *jambon* or bacon in the oil with the onion, carrot and garlic until turning golden.

Stir in the flour and gradually pour in the stock, stirring all the time. (If the heads of garlic are small add rather less liquid.) Add the bouquet garni, the grated nutmeg, some pepper and probably very little salt.

Cover and cook over moderate heat until the garlic is softened. Press the sauce through a sieve and simmer longer if too thin.

Serve with roast veal, pork or *saucisses*.

MELON FARCI AUX CAPUCINES

MELON STUFFED WITH NASTURTIUMS

Here is a pretty dessert from Paul Reboux's *Plats nouveaux – essai de gastronomie moderne*, a charming book from the 1920s. Some English supermarkets now sell boxes of nasturtium flowers to add to salads, so even town-dwellers may care to try this delightful way of serving a melon. Use whichever fruits take your fancy – it is the idea that is so attractive.

a good-sized cantaloupe melon	225 g (8 oz) strawberries
½ small, fresh pineapple	70 g (2½ oz) caster sugar
2 bananas, peeled and sliced	1 wineglass fruit liqueur or champagne
	nasturtium flowers

Wipe the melon with a damp cloth. Cut across the top to make a round opening large enough to take a tablespoon. Remove all the seeds and discard. Then scoop out the flesh, making sure you don't make a hole in the skin, and cut into neat pieces in a bowl. Add the pineapple, diced, and the bananas and strawberries, and sprinkle in the sugar.

Spoon the mixed fruits back into the melon and pour in the liqueur or champagne. Replace the lid and keep the melon in a cold place for up to one hour before serving.

Tie the nasturtiums into a bunch and when ready to serve, remove the melon lid and tuck the flowers into the top of the melon. Surround the melon with chipped ice if available. If there are guests, serve the melon to the leading lady and present her with the bouquet. She can distribute nasturtiums to the other guests to nibble with the fruit salad. Serves 6–8.

SORBET DE LAVANDE EN TULIPES

LAVENDER SORBET IN BISCUIT TULIPS

I had always wanted to devise a lavender sorbet using the fresh flowers from my French lavender bushes. And one autumn when I returned from France I discovered that the Country Gentlemen's Association had published this recipe from John McGeever, head chef at Congham Hall in lavender-growing Norfolk. I love it but a friend said the taste reminded him of being in a nightclub at 3 o'clock in the morning! The sorbet is even more beguiling served in these fragile biscuits that resemble folded porcelain.

Sorbet
2 ripe Ogen or honeydew
  melons
1–2 lemons
115 g (4 oz) caster sugar
½ bottle champagne or dry
  sparkling wine
15 g (½ oz) fresh lavender
  flowers
2 egg whites
a few drops of blue
  colouring

Tulipes
2 egg whites
115 g (4 oz) caster sugar
a few drops of vanilla
  essence
45 g (1½ oz) flour
55 g (2 oz) butter, melted

Halve the melons, discard the seeds and scrape all the flesh into a blender or processor. Purée with the juice of the lemons and the sugar.

Gently warm the wine in a glass or enamel pan, remove from the heat and stir in the lavender flowers. Leave to infuse for 10–15 minutes and strain through a fine sieve, pressing to extract the oil. Cool and add to the purée.

Whisk the egg whites until stiff and fold into the lavender purée. Add a drop or two of blue food colouring if you wish, just to give the sorbet a pale lavender hue.

Turn into a lidded plastic container and freeze. Whisk lightly after 30 minutes to check that no liquid has separated out at the bottom. Freeze until firm. Serves 8–10.

To make the *tulipes*, whisk the egg whites lightly, add the sugar and vanilla essence and whisk again. Sift the flour on to the mixture and stir in the melted butter.

Place level tablespoons of the mixture, well-spaced, on buttered non-stick baking sheets. Bake in a hot oven (Mark 7, 220°C, 425°F) for about 5 minutes until each biscuit is pale yellow with a golden brown rim.

Remove from the oven, leave for 30 seconds, and then, using a palette knife, gently lift off each biscuit and place over an upturned glass or into a shallow dish or bowl, fluting the edge as you do so. After a few minutes when the *tulipe* has cooled and hardened, lift off and place on a wire rack. Store the *tulipe* in a lidded box in a dry place until required. These biscuits also freeze well for up to 2 months. Makes 8–10 biscuits.

TOMATES FARCIS

STUFFED TOMATOES

Clearly there are as many ways of stuffing a tomato as there are cooks. But the first essential is a good-quality tomato. No problem in France in the summer. But in England unless you grow your own it is best to buy Marmande or beefsteak tomatoes. I include the recipe mainly for the method. But it's worth bearing in mind that what one aims for, as in all cooking, is an enhancement of fine ingredients, not a disguise due to a confused over-indulgence of additional flavours. Here one is hoping with skill and flair to reveal the tomato-ness of a tomato. So that while not losing the simple charm of the raw fruit, its scent and sweetness, one hopes to add the round fat flavour and the melting quality, exciting yet comforting, of a perfectly baked tomato. When it happens it's a revelation. Overcooking makes a tomato taste acrid and watery, and something beautiful and unique to the fruit has been stolen by the oven and is lost for ever.

2 large ripe tomatoes
1–2 tablespoons olive oil
1 shallot, finely chopped
1 clove of garlic, finely
  chopped
2 tablespoons mixed fresh
  herbs – tarragon, chervil,
  parsley, basil, etc. –
  chopped

a few celery leaves,
  chopped
3 tablespoons fresh white
  breadcrumbs
1 large egg, beaten
salt, milled pepper

Cut a lid from each tomato and scrape out the seeds, membrane and juice. If you wish, discard the seeds and chop the rest. Drain the tomatoes upside down while you prepare the filling.

Heat the oil and cook the shallot and garlic until soft. Add the chopped tomato and cook, stirring, for 5–8 minutes until almost all the liquid has evaporated. Remove from the heat and stir in the herbs, celery leaves and almost all the breadcrumbs and egg. Season with salt and pepper.

Spoon the filling into the tomatoes and sprinkle each with the remaining breadcrumbs. Dribble a little olive oil over each and place the filled tomatoes in an oiled oven dish.

Cook in a moderate oven (Mark 4, 180°C, 350°F) for 25–30 minutes until the filling is cooked, when it will rise out of the tomatoes a little. Serve straight away or leave until cold. Serves 2.

CRÈME AUX CAPRES ET AUX POMMES

APPLE AND CAPER CREAM

I devised this as a sauce for serving with smoked fish. Ideally I like to arrange a curl of smoked salmon, a piece of smoked eel, a fillet of smoked trout and a few smoked oysters on a plate to serve with the sauce.

> 150 ml (¼ pt) whipping
>   cream
> 4 tablespoons cold apple
>   purée
> 1 teaspoon finely grated
>   zest of lemon
> 1 tablespoon Provençal
>   capers
> salt

Whisk the cream until stiff. Fold in the apple purée and lemon zest. Rinse the capers in warm water, drain well and chop finely. Add to the cream with a little salt.

Chill the sauce for at least two hours before serving.

FISH

We sat under the acacia, very still in the heat, cloudy glasses of pastis beside us. It was noon; only the cicadas in the long grass and the bees above disturbed the silence. Eventually I stirred. I'll get some lunch, I mumbled, and moved off into the kitchen.

On a long dish in the pantry lay a dozen or so fresh, silver-glinting sardines, bought in the morning's market. Looking at them I decided they needed to be cooked outside, over flames.

For safety's sake we used the paved floor of a demolished outbuilding as a base and on it built a low circular wall of stones from the collapsed vine terraces around the garden. We filled the centre with dry vine prunings and on top wedged a metal grid from the kitchen oven. Then I brought out the freshly rinsed fish and wrapped each one in vine leaves. We lit the prunings and they burned brightly giving an intense heat, perfuming the air with a woody, winy fragrance. As the flames died down I placed the fish on the grid. Turned once, they are cooked in 4–5 minutes. And, if eaten straight away, as you unwrap each fish, the vine leaves peel away the skin to reveal moist flesh, tasting lemony from the leaves and smoky from the fire. With a *baguette* broken in two and a bottle of spicy Syrah wine from the Côtes d'Ardèche, it was a lunch to dream about on a wet February day in England.

That morning the market had two fish stalls and another selling salt cod only. I counted twenty-three different fish, leaving aside the crayfish, lobsters, mussels, oysters, clams, cockles, tiny smooth-shelled *clovisses*, sea-urchins, curious-looking *violets* and grey-speckled squid. To us, the choice was stupendous; to the French housewives, busy buying *daurade* or *merlan, rouget, St Pierre* or a selection of small fish labelled 'for soup', it was perfectly normal. Everything was so fresh, there was no smell of fish as the sun rose higher – there was simply a smell of the sea. We bought sardines and a huge slice of dull red tunny fish. Since these fish are sometimes now available in Britain I was anxious to try recipes that I could also, in time, cook at home.

A few days earlier in Ste Eulalie in Haute Ardèche, I had walked down to the bridge over the Loire and watched the trout leap out of the water to catch any fly reckless enough to dip too close to the surface. It was a perfect, lazy, midsummer afternoon. A little further downstream small children were playing in the river, damming the trickling streams that run down between each meadow, in the same way that my own children once played beside the Dordogne. Upstream two men were fishing, sitting in the sun on the smooth cream rocks. Later I saw them carry their catch home where, no doubt, these trout would be quickly cleaned and tossed into foaming butter to be served simply, just a scattering of finely chopped parsley added to the buttery pan with a splash of wine or lemon juice, and spooned over fish that could not have been fresher.

This freshness is taken to a high degree in the market at Ganges where the sound of rushing water attracts one's attention. Walking across I find a van with a huge tank of bubbling, constantly changing water at the back, in which fat trout swim and dart. The customer selects his fish, the stallholder weighs it live, stuns it and it is yours. If you run home you could cook and serve it within minutes should you so wish. Doubtless some do. Eaten like this, fish is a totally different experience; it has never seen the inside of a waxed box or a plastic bag, or been buried for months in a deep freeze. These days some of us have become unaccustomed to seeing beautiful, whole, fresh fish. A friend who runs a cooking school recently told me that at the start of her fish day she held up various freshly caught fish; some people gasped, covered their eyes and chose not to look. What has happened to us? It is not just our food that has become processed – we have too.

Fresh fish is best cooked gently and quickly. It's more like cooking an egg; you are setting the flesh, not treating it as if it were meat. Fish is cooked once the flesh is opaque and is just coming free of the bone. Served in solitary splendour with just the oil or butter it was cooked in spooned over it, fish has a delicacy no other food can match. Equally though, fish can be the greatest challenge to one's culinary skill, responding wonderfully to a complex yet light sauce or eaten cold in a jelly made from the reduced *fumet*.

When you consider that in Britain our encircling cold seas are full of some of the most delicious fish in the world, far superior in many cases to those of the Mediterranean, it is a tragedy to see that we have forgotten how to appreciate this noble wild food. Instead we sleep while huge refrigerated lorries full of this silvery harvest race through the night on their way to markets in Paris and Brussels,

where our fish will grace expensive menus and, perhaps even more galling, we as tourists will pay for it. Use it or lose it applies to our food as well as to our hearts.

SOUPE DE POISSONS

FISH SOUP

How beautifully the spectrum of French fish soups reflects the changing degrees of latitude and the intensity of the light. Starting with Normandy, whose soup is palely gleaming, creamy with flashes of peach-shaded mussels, one then travels south to the freshwater *matelotes* of the Loire and onwards to lively, robustly flavoured soups, red-gold with tomato and saffron and eaten with *rouille*, the magnificent fiery-tasting, rust-coloured sauce of the Midi.

This recipe comes from Vézénobres, north of Nîmes, the city of the great nineteenth-century chef, Charles Durand. When making this soup in France it's a good idea to tell the stallholder – he often sells a mixture of small fish specially for soup and he'll make a selection for you. In England, use heads and bones of a variety of white fish like cod and haddock but try to include some conger eel to give body.

2–3 tablespoons olive oil
1 onion, chopped
1–2 cloves of garlic
680 g (1½ lb) fish
225 g (8 oz) tomatoes,
    peeled and chopped
bouquet garni
1 wineglass red wine
salt, a few peppercorns
½ teaspoon strands of
    saffron

Rouille
1 *piment* or red chilli
    pepper
2–3 cloves of garlic
70–85 g (2½–3 oz) white
    bread, crustless
6–8 tablespoons olive oil
1 teaspoon tomato paste
    (optional)

To serve
half a *baguette* or French
    stick
Gruyère cheese, finely
    grated

Heat the oil in a large saucepan and soften the onion and garlic in it. Add the fish and quickly turn it over in the oil. Add the tomatoes, bouquet garni, 1 litre (1¾ pt) water, the red wine, some salt and the peppercorns, and bring to the boil. Cover the pan, turn down the heat and allow the soup to simmer for 30–40 minutes.

Strain the soup through a sieve, pressing the fish gently to extract the full flavour. Return the liquid to the pan, add the saffron and simmer for 20 minutes to take the colour and flavour from the spice. Taste and adjust the seasoning of the soup.

To make the *rouille*: halve and de-seed the red chilli (if using a dried pepper soak in warm water for a few minutes to soften), and chop finely. Pound the chilli pepper to a paste with the garlic. Soak the bread in cold water, squeeze dry and gradually work into the chilli paste with the olive oil, beating well all the time as for mayonnaise. Add the tomato paste to heighten the colour if you wish. Spoon the *rouille* into a pottery bowl.

Slice and toast the bread. Serve the soup in hot bowls and hand the *rouille*, toasted croûtons and grated Gruyère cheese separately. Each person floats a croûton or two – covered with *rouille* or cheese or both – in the soup, stirring to incorporate the flavours. Serves 4.

HUÎTRES AU SEL ROSE

OYSTERS WITH ROSY SALT

Especially in coastal France, but also surprisingly far inland, oysters and most other shellfish are far easier to buy than here. We have neglected our own shellfish industry most disgracefully, with the result that the French and other Europeans rush our superb lobsters, crabs, oysters and mussels to their own northern regions.

In the south of France there is usually an inspiring array of fish (in the market of Arles I counted six varieties of oyster) of all kinds, many unrecognizable to the newcomer. But armed with Alan Davidson's invaluable *Mediterranean Seafood* you may step into these uncharted waters with confidence. While tracking down a variety of clam known as 'Warty Venus', I tried some *violets* on the advice of this guide; a *violet* is an extraordinary fungoid-looking creature whose yellow insides are eaten raw. I can't say that I shall rush to buy them again but I am still confident that Sir Arnold Bax's advice – try anything once except folk-dancing and incest – holds good for gastronomes.

6–12 oysters per person	1 dessertspoon sweet
lemon juice	paprika
1 tablespoon fine ground	1 coffeespoon cayenne
sea salt	pepper

Open the oysters and discard the top shell, arrange the lower shells on a bed of cracked ice. Sprinkle with lemon juice.

Mix the salt, paprika and cayenne pepper together and let each person season their oysters just before eating them.

This rosy salt is Raymond Oliver's. He recommends it for sprinkling on thinly sliced truffle or peewits' eggs. I've never knowingly eaten the egg of a peewit but have found rosy salt is good on quails' eggs.

L'ANCHOÏADE

The slim tins of anchovy fillets, packed in oil, will make a fine *anchoïade* but if you are able to track down (which is easier in France) a small jar or glass of whole anchovies, skinned and preserved in vinegar the flavour of this versatile Provençal sauce will be superb.

Anchoïade, thinned with rather more olive oil than usual and a dash of wine vinegar, makes a good dressing for *crudités*. A bowl of the sauce surrounded by neat piles of raw vegetables – fingers of crisp celery, some slim rosy radishes, tiny batons of cucumber or curving strips of Florentine fennel and green and red peppers – is a lovely hors d'oeuvre.

Or try an exciting contrast of temperatures by pouring the chilled dressing over hot, boiled, new potatoes. The same combination, allowed to cool before adding some black olives, quartered hard-boiled eggs, a few rinsed capers and a handful of parsley, finely chopped, makes a very good lunch.

55 g (2 oz) anchovies,
  preserved in vinegar or
  oil
1–2 cloves of garlic,
  crushed

2–3 tablespoons olive oil
milled pepper
8–12 slices French bread
juice of half a lemon

Drain the anchovies and, if necessary, remove the backbones. Chop the fish roughly and pound in a mortar or purée in a blender with the garlic until smooth. Gradually add the olive oil and mix to a paste. Season with pepper.

Spread the *anchoïade* on the slices of bread and toast under a very hot grill until the bread is changing colour at the edges and the anchovy mixture is piping hot. Squeeze a little lemon juice over each slice and serve straight away to accompany a robust red wine.

DAURADE À LA DUGLÈRE

SEA-BREAM À LA DUGLÈRE

In England buy sea-bream; in France a finer variety of the same family called *daurade* will probably be available. The recipe also works well with sole, turbot, brill or John Dory.

4 fillets of sea-bream
salt, milled pepper
juice of half a lemon
55 g (2 oz) butter
1 shallot, finely chopped
225 g (8 oz) tomatoes,
  peeled and chopped
1 tablespoon chopped
  parsley

1 wineglass dry white wine
150 ml (¼ pt) *crème fraîche*
  or soured cream
a little extra chopped
  parsley

Rinse the fish in cold water and dry on kitchen paper. Place on a plate, season with salt and pepper and sprinkle with lemon juice.

Melt the butter in a wide pan and soften the shallot in it. Then add the tomatoes and parsley. Place the fish on top and pour in the wine. Cover with a buttered paper and cook on the hob or in a moderate oven (Mark 4, 180°C, 350°F) for 7–9 minutes until the fish is cooked.

Transfer the fish to a hot serving dish. Sieve the sauce, pushing the vegetables through, and reduce over high heat until thick and syrupy. Stir in the cream and bring back to heat.

Spoon the sauce over the fish and sprinkle with chopped parsley. Serves 4.

TRUITE À LA MODE D'ARCENS

ARCENS-STYLE TROUT

One appropriately wet day in Arcens, in a small restaurant half a kilometre downstream from the water-bottling plant, a fine trout cooked in an Ardèche Syrah was a most welcome dish.

4 trout, river or farm
55 g (2 oz) butter
1 shallot, finely chopped
225 g (8 oz) button
   mushrooms
salt, milled pepper

1 wineglass Ardèche red
   wine, preferably Syrah
150 ml (¼ pt) *crème fraîche*
   or soured cream
finely chopped parsley

Clean the trout, rinse in cold water and dry on kitchen paper.

Melt half the butter and cook the shallot and chopped mushroom stalks until soft. Add the trout to the pan and cook for 2 minutes on each side. Season the fish lightly with pepper and salt. Pour in the wine and bring to the boil.

Cover the fish with a buttered paper and cook on the hob or in a moderate oven (Mark 4, 180°C, 350°F) for 10–15 minutes, or until the flesh comes free of the bone. Transfer the fish to a serving plate and strain the wine into a cup.

Cook the sliced mushrooms in the remainder of the butter and spoon over the fish. Pour the wine back into the pan and cook fast until reduced by half. Stir in the cream and, when hot, taste to check the seasoning. Spoon the sauce over the fish and sprinkle with chopped parsley. Serve straight away with plain boiled potatoes. Serves 4.

SARTAGNADO DE PETITS POISSONS

PAN-FRIED SMALL FISH

Sartagnado or *poêlée* or *crespeou* is the Provençal name for a dish of small fish dipped in flour and shallow-fried so close together that they form a kind of Mediterranean fish cake. Often in markets in Provence you will see a mound of small fish: anchovies, baby sardines, grey shrimps and tiny cuttlefish, sometimes labelled *sartagnado*, sold for making this dish.

450 g (1 lb) small fish (see above)	salt, milled pepper
2–3 tablespoons flour	1 tablespoon white wine vinegar
olive oil	

Wash the fish under cold running water, drain well and dry on kitchen paper.

Spread the flour in a shallow dish or a plastic bag. Dip in each fish and remove when coated with flour.

Heat the oil in a wide pan and add the fish all at once, pressing them together slightly with the blade of a knife or a fish slice. Shake the pan now and again to prevent their sticking to the base. If necessary run the blade underneath the fish, which should cake together.

Fry for 7–8 minutes over a high heat and then turn over and fry the other side until golden.

Turn the *sartagnado* out on to a hot serving dish and season with salt and pepper. Add the vinegar to the pan and when hot sprinkle over the fish. Serve straight away. Serves 4.

BRANDADE DE MORUE

CREAM OF SALT COD

My memory of Nîmes seems to be stored in my limbs, heavy and sated with the sun, as I sit in the Jardins de Luxembourg gazing at a butterfly that flits over the floating stage of one of the loveliest theatres in Europe. Every afternoon Nîmois with time to spare come to these gardens built on the site of the Roman baths. Groups of middle-aged ladies sit in the shade; they crochet or embroider and discuss the goings-on of other middle-aged ladies not yet ready for these activities. Children play slowly and men, young and old, sit motionless in the overpowering heat. My torpor is increased by the unforgettably delicious lunch of *brandade de morue*. It was served in the cool, mirrored almost empty dining-room at Le Cheval Blanc overlooking the arena; somewhere in the background a Duke Ellington tape played quietly. I ate slowly and resolved to return some day, for the jazz festival and the *morue*.

A few days later I recreated this famous dish in the kitchen at Le Presbytère. It was, perhaps, even more delicious, creamy and fat with an amazing blend of the flavours of fish and olive oil, a dish of the south. Mme Marquet is astounded that I have attempted it in the sparsely equipped kitchen: 'You need an electric mixer to make a *brandade*, borrow mine,' she remarked. I grinned and showed her the recipe I'd used from *Le Cuisinier Durand*, by the famous nineteenth-century chef of Nîmes, and she laughed at my enjoyment and smiled benignly, perhaps pondering this strange Englishwoman who wanted to cook in the style of her grandmother.

450 g (1 lb) *morue* or salt cod – choose a thick fillet, not too dry
150 –300 ml (¼–½ pt) fruity olive oil
150–300 ml (¼–½ pt) milk
1 lemon

1–2 cloves garlic, crushed (optional)
triangles of bread, lightly toasted
a little butter
finely chopped parsley

Soak the *morue* in cold water overnight; change the water several times if the fish is very salty. Drain and cover with cold water in a pan. Slowly bring almost to the boil. Add a glass of cold water and remove from the heat. Cover and leave for 15–20 minutes. Lift out the fish and carefully remove all the skin and every trace of bone. Flake the fish and return it to a heavy-based pan.

Gently bring the oil and milk up to blood heat in small separate pans, and keep both warm, on heat-spreading mats if necessary.

Beat the fish with the lemon juice over very low heat using a wooden spoon and add, alternately, a dash of oil and a dash of milk, beating well after each addition. At a certain point the mixture will thicken and turn into a buttery mass as when making mayonnaise. To avoid separation take care not to overheat.

How much oil and milk you add is a matter of judgement – at a certain point, somehow, one knows that adding more of either will not improve the taste or consistency. The *brandade* should be creamy in texture and have a gentle balance of flavour between the fish and the olive oil. If you care to, add a little garlic. In the past truffles and ground anchovies and even orange sauce were added to the *brandade*, but that, to my mind, would impair the beautiful simplicity of the dish. Bought *brandade de morue* often contains mashed potato, hence its dismal grey tone. Home-made *brandade* glows pale yellow due to the olive oil.

Butter the corners of the toasted bread and dip each corner in the parsley. Turn the *brandade* on to a warm serving dish and surround with the green-cornered triangles. Serves 3–4.

Don't reckon to be energetic afterwards – this dish is very rich.

Should you have any *brandade de morue* left over divide it between some small oven dishes, place one or two poached eggs on top, warm through in the oven and spoon a little *hollandaise* sauce on top to make *oeufs bénédictine*. *Brandade de morue* is also excellent as the filling in small puff-pastry turnovers or *chaussons*, served hot.

POISSON D'AVRIL À MOI

MY APRIL FOOL FISH

The king of Mediterranean fish, the *loup de mer* or sea-bass, is most often prepared over a bed of flaming fennel stalks and eaten hot. This fish is, however, also very fine served cold, rather as we would serve cold salmon trout in the summer, with a *sauce verte*. But one spring, not long after seeing the film *French Connection*, in which on the fish quay at Marseilles, amongst the shimmering live fish, traditional paper fish are pinned on the unsuspecting, I decided to prepare my own April Fool fish as here. On this day all over France fish are to be seen, made from pastry, bread dough and genoise sponge-cake – and, of course, there are plenty of real ones too.

1¼ kg (2¾ lb) *loup de mer* or sea-bass
olive oil or sunflower oil
2 tablespoons *duxelles* (see p. 79) or the finely diced stalks of the mushrooms softened in oil
1 small wineglass dry white wine
approx 340 g (12 oz) cultivated mushrooms, of even size
flat parsley
lemon juice

Usually the fishmonger will run his knife down the fish to de-scale it for you straight after cleaning it. Otherwise simply scrape the blade of a knife along the fish from tail to the head to remove the scales on both sides. Rinse the fish under cold water inside and out, and dry well on kitchen paper.

Place the fish on a large sheet of double-thickness foil, lightly oiled, resting on a baking sheet. Season the fish inside and on top, and spoon the *duxelles* or mushroom stalks into the body cavity. Pour over the white wine and fold up the foil to enclose the fish, squeezing the edges together to make a parcel.

Bake in the centre of a moderate oven (Mark 5, 190°C, 375°F) for 20–25 minutes. The fish is cooked when the flesh is opaque – take care not to overcook it.

Remove from the oven, allow the fish to cool for 10–15 minutes, and transfer to a large serving-dish. Make a neat cut through the skin in a curved line behind the head. Then gently pull off the skin on the body, in sections if easier, removing the gills but leaving the tail intact.

Wipe the mushrooms with a damp cloth and remove the stalks – unless you have used them in the stuffing. (Use them in soup.) Slice the mushrooms thinly and evenly, and cook in olive oil until softened and most of the liquid has been driven off.

Make a collar of parsley leaves just behind the head of the fish. Arrange the sliced mushrooms just slightly overlapping, with the curved side towards the head, either covering the body of the fish or decorating it in bands. Brush the fish all over with a little oil mixed with lemon juice and leave in a cold place until ready to serve. Serves 4–6.

PALOURDES FARCIES

STUFFED CLAMS

All kinds of clams are popular in France from the *praire* and *coque* to the tiny, smooth-shelled *clovisse*. The simple *moules marinière* treatment is excellent for them all, particularly the *clovisse* which would be fiddly to prepare any other way. But larger varieties like the *palourde* can be eaten raw and are very good stuffed. Try either a snail butter or this mixture of shallots, cream and cheese.

40–50 *palourdes* or clams
2 shallots, very finely chopped
200 ml (7 fl oz) *crème fraîche*
2 tablespoons finely chopped parsley

1 tablespoon dry white wine or lemon juice
salt, milled pepper
2–3 tablespoons Gruyère cheese, finely grated

Use an oyster knife or a strong, short-bladed vegetable knife to prise open the shells, inserting the knife near the hinge and swivelling the blade across to free the clam from the shell. Discard any liquid and the upper shell.

Arrange the clams on crumpled foil to keep them steady in one large or several smaller gratin dishes. Mix the shallots with the cream, parsley and wine, and season lightly with salt and pepper.

Spoon cream into each clam shell and sprinkle a little Gruyère cheese on top. Bake the stuffed clams in a hot oven (Mark 6, 200°C, 400°F) for 6–8 minutes until the cream is bubbling. Serve straight away. Serves 3–4.

Moules au Beurre d'Amande

MUSSELS WITH ALMOND BUTTER

Possibly the worst crime committed against a mussel is to overcook it; they should be meltingly tender. Here the almond butter provides all the sauce they need.

450 g (1 lb) mussels	**70 g (2½ oz) whole**
½ wineglass dry white wine	**blanched almonds**
2 slices onion	**70 g (2½ oz) butter, softened**
a few stalks of parsley	**a squeeze of lemon juice**
a bay leaf	**1 tablespoon finely chopped parsley**
	salt

Scrub the mussels under cold running water, knock off any small limpets and remove the beard of threads. Discard any mussels that do not close as you clean them and any that are unnaturally heavy – they may contain mud or sand. Drain the mussels in a colander.

Pour the wine and ½ wineglass water into your largest pan, and add the onion, parsley stalks and bay leaf. Bring to the boil and simmer for 2 minutes.

Add the mussels and cover. Shake the pan over the heat for 1 minute; then remove from the heat and leave, covered, for 5 minutes, to allow the mussels to open in the steam.

Meanwhile toast the almonds under a high grill until just turning colour, and chop them fairly finely in a processor or blender. Tip two thirds of them into a bowl; grind the remainder to a fine powder and add to the rest. Work in the softened butter and mix with the lemon juice and parsley until soft and spreadable.

Discard one of the shells from each opened mussel and spread a little almond butter over the cooked mussel in the other shell. Arrange the mussels in one large or four small oven dishes.

Place in a moderately hot oven (Mark 6, 200°C, 400°F) for 4–5 minutes until the butter is melting and the mussels are really hot. Serve straight away with French bread. Serves 2–4.

BROCHETTES DE MOULES

MUSSELS ON SKEWERS

Toulon is famous for its large mussels which, at times, are available further inland. I have also tried the recipe with our northern, small sweet mussels and it is still good, if not so spectacular.

40–50 Toulon mussels	3–4 tablespoons olive oil
275 ml (½ pt) water or dry white wine	fennel seed
1 shallot, finely chopped	2–4 tablespoons dry breadcrumbs
3–4 slices *lard fumé* or smoked streaky bacon	1 lemon, cut in wedges

Scrub and beard the mussels, and discard any that remain open while you do this. Pour the water or wine into a large pan, add the shallot and the mussels and bring to the boil. Cover and remove from the heat. Leave to stand for 5–8 minutes.

Extract the mussels from the opened shells. Cut the *lard fumé* into small neat pieces or, if using rashers of bacon, cut into strips and make small rolls. Thread the mussels, evenly spaced, with pieces of bacon, on to skewers. Dribble or brush with olive oil, sprinkle with the fennel seed and then coat lightly with dry breadcrumbs.

Place under a very hot grill and cook, turning once, for 5–6 minutes. Serve straight away with a wedge of lemon to squeeze over. Serves 4.

SOLE À LA CRÈME DE PAMPLEMOUSSE

SOLE WITH GRAPEFRUIT CREAM

It sounded an interesting combination, we knew the chef was good and so, it turned out, was the dish, with its creamy yet refreshing alliance of flavours.

4 fillets of Dover or lemon sole	1 large grapefruit
55 g (2 oz) butter	150 ml (¼ pt) *crème fraîche* or double cream
salt, milled pepper	

Dry the fish on kitchen paper. Melt half the butter in a pan and when hot, gently turn the fish over in it for 2–3 minutes but don't let it brown at all. Season the fish lightly with salt and pepper and transfer to a moderate oven (Mark 4, 180°C, 350°F) for a few minutes to finish cooking while you make the sauce.

Peel the grapefruit and cut into eight neat segments free of skin or pith. Squeeze the juice from the remainder of the fruit.

Melt the remaining butter in a small pan and sauté the grapefruit segments lightly on both sides. Use a slotted spoon to lift out the fruit and place two segments on each fillet of fish.

Pour the juice into the buttery pan, bring to the boil and reduce by one third. Stir in the cream and simmer for 2 minutes. Season lightly and spoon over the fish. Serves 2 as a main course or 4 as a fish course.

TERRINE DE TRUITES

TROUT TERRINE

Somehow there never seem to be enough cold fish dishes, so this very good terrine is worth knowing about. It makes an admirable lunch on a hot day or a first course to a formal meal. Local river trout, once known as *perdrix des eaux douces*, are used in the Ardèche; here rainbow trout may be more easily available.

4 medium-sized trout
150 ml (¼ pt) plus 4
  tablespoons dry white
  wine
bouquet garni
salt, milled pepper
3 eggs, beaten
100 g (3½ oz) button
  mushrooms, finely diced
150 ml (¼ pt) *crème fraîche*
  or whipping cream
grated nutmeg
finely chopped chervil or
  parsley

Pastry
300 g (10½ oz) plain flour
a pinch of salt
100 g (3½ oz) butter,
  softened
1 large egg

Clean the fish, rinse in cold water and dry on kitchen paper. Pour 150 ml (¼ pt) wine and 150 ml (¼ pt) water into a pan large enough to hold the fish in a single layer. Add the bouquet garni and some salt and pepper and the fish. Bring the liquid slowly to the boil, cover and simmer for 3 minutes. Remove from the heat and allow to cool for 30 minutes.

Meanwhile make the pastry: sift the flour and salt on to a marble slab or into a wide shallow bowl. Make a well in the centre and mix in the butter and egg, using your fingertips, until well combined.

Remove all the flesh from the fish and flake into a bowl. Stir in almost all the beaten egg (reserve a little to glaze the pastry), the mushrooms, 4 tablespoons wine, the cream and a generous seasoning of nutmeg, the chervil and some salt and pepper. Mix the ingredients together gently, keeping a sharp eye open for any errant fish bones.

On a floured board roll out three quarters of the pastry and line a well-buttered 1 litre (2 pt) capacity terrine. Spoon the fish filling into the terrine and cover with the remaining pastry, joining the edges firmly together. Make leaves with any pastry trimmings and decorate the top of the terrine. Cut three steam vents and brush the top with the reserved egg.

Bake in a moderately hot oven (Mark 4, 180°C, 350°F) for 50–60 minutes until the pastry is crisp. Cover the lid with greaseproof paper if it is browning too quickly. Remove from the oven, allow to cool in the terrine and cut into slices when cold. Serve with a *sauce verte* or a lemony mayonnaise. Serves 6–8.

THON À LA PROVENÇALE

PROVENÇAL TUNA FISH

Long before *thon*, tunny fish or tuna, got into a tin the Sicilians used to preserve fine fillets in small barrels of olive oil which they exported to Nice and other Provençal ports. Today fresh tuna is widely available in the south of France and now and again I have discovered some in London. Fresh tuna tastes far superior to the tinned kind, with a more delicate flavour, and, if not overcooked, a less woolly texture. The flavour of this dish depends on the quality of the bouquet garni, which is easier to obtain in France, where bunches of fresh herbs are often available on market stalls. But it's more fun when possible to make your own by tying a piece of leek with a few stalks of parsley, some thyme, a bay leaf and a short stalk of celery or leaves of celeriac.

This is a filling dish and, on account of the meatiness of the flesh and the absence of bones, it is popular with children. Incidentally a very similar recipe appears in nineteenth-century books as *thon chartreuse* and includes a glass of the liqueur; later the recipe appears under the same name but without the distinguishing alcohol.

450 g (1 lb) fresh tuna, cut across in one slice
2–3 tablespoons olive oil
2 medium-sized onions, mild-flavoured and finely chopped
2 tomatoes, peeled and chopped

1 clove garlic, flattened but whole
bouquet garni (see above)
1 wineglass dry white or rosé wine
salt, a few peppercorns

Rinse the tuna fish in cold water and dry on kitchen paper. Heat the oil in a pan just large enough to contain the fish and sear the tuna on both sides. Remove and leave on a plate while you prepare the sauce.

Add the onions to the pan and cook, stirring, for 4 minutes until soft but not coloured. Add the tomatoes, garlic, bouquet garni, wine, a little salt and a few peppercorns. Cook over a high heat for 10–15 minutes until reduced and thickened.

Draw half of the mixture to one side, place the tuna on a layer of vegetables and spoon over those from the side of the pan. Cover the pan and lower the heat so that the fish cooks gently for 8–10 minutes or until the flesh is just coming free of the centre bone.

Transfer the tuna to a hot serving dish and remove the skin and bone. Discard the bouquet garni and the garlic, and reduce the sauce over high heat. Either spoon the sauce over the fish as it is or press through a sieve first. Sometimes I prefer the contrast in texture by not sieving the sauce but it depends on the rest of the meal to some extent and one's energy or *batterie de cuisine*. If you prefer to serve the fish cold, then the smoother sauce is better, as it will set, if chilled, into a light jelly. Serves 3–4.

MAQUEREAUX FARCIS

STUFFED MACKEREL

Fresh herbs are essential for this stuffing but they can vary with the time of year.

4 mackerel	fresh herbs – tarragon,
salt, milled pepper	chervil, mint, parsley,
lemon juice	chives, all finely
2 handfuls fresh spinach	chopped
2 tablespoons olive oil	

Clean the fish, open up and remove the backbone and check that any other stray bones are discarded. Season the fish with salt and pepper and sprinkle with lemon juice. Set aside while you make the stuffing.

Cook the spinach in boiling salted water just until it collapses. Drain well, chop finely and press well in a sieve or colander to remove as much moisture as possible.

Return the spinach to the pan with half the olive oil and stir over moderate heat until the spinach has absorbed the oil. Stir in the chopped herbs, add a sprinkling of salt and remove from the heat.

Divide the herb stuffing between the fish and fold each fish back into shape. Place the mackerel, sprinkled with the remainder of the oil, in a lightly oiled baking dish or wrap in oiled foil for cooking on a barbecue.

Bake in a moderate oven (Mark 4, 180°C, 350°F) for 20–30 minutes until cooked. Serve hot or cold. Serves 4.

SARDINES AUX FEUILLES DE VIGNE

SARDINES BARBECUED IN VINE LEAVES

You can usually depend on finding fresh sardines in markets during summer in the south of France. Luckily it is now far easier to buy them here too; they may be Portuguese – check whether they have been frozen. But given a supply of fresh vine leaves, pale green and tender (even those from a decorative wall vine work well) this is an unforgettably delicious way of cooking sardines or any other small oily fish. The flesh takes on a smoky, lemony flavour from the leaves and the fire. As you peel off the leaf the fish is neatly skinned and ready to eat.

about 24 sardines
salt
about 50 vine leaves

Rinse the sardines in cold water and dry them well on kitchen paper. Leave them whole and sprinkle with salt if you wish.

Wrap each fish in a leaf or two depending on size and place on a plate until the fire is ready for cooking. The best fire is made from vine prunings but the twigs of any fruit wood will give a delicious result.

Place a cooking grid over the hot embers of the fire and arrange the fish on top. Cook for 3–5 minutes turning them once. Serve straight away with bread and wine. Serves 2–3.

BOURRIDE

Bourride is far simpler to prepare than its more famous relative *bouillabaise* and, for me, its simplicity makes it more appealing. Marius Morard in his *Manuel complet de la cuisinière provençale* (1886) declares the true name to be *aïoli-bourride*, drawing attention to the composition of the dish. (He also claims that the invention of *aïoli* should be attributed to Virgil.) If possible, have three or four kinds of white sea fish for *bourride*: bass, turbot, brill, monkfish, gurnard, sea-bream or conger eel.

1–1½ kg (2–3 lb) fish on the bone	salt, milled pepper
1 wineglass dry white wine	4–5 egg yolks
white part of a leek, sliced	2–3 cloves of garlic, crushed
a bay leaf	275 ml (½ pt) olive oil
a head of fennel seed	1 stick of celery
a strip of orange peel	slices of toasted French bread
a few sprigs of thyme	finely chopped parsley
parsley stalks	

Fillet the fish, remove the skin and cut the flesh into chunks and thick slices.

Make a *court-bouillon* by simmering the heads and bones of the fish with a little over 1 litre (about 2 pt) water, the wine, leek, herbs and orange peel for 10–15 minutes.

Meanwhile prepare the *aïoli* with 2 of the egg yolks, garlic and olive oil (see p. 29). Strain the *court-bouillon* into a pan, add the celery and season lightly. Poach the fish, starting with the thicker, denser pieces but do not overcook. Transfer the drained, cooked fish to a hot serving dish.

In another pan, whisk half the *aïoli* with the egg yolks and 275 ml (½ pt) of the fish stock until it just thickens.

Arrange 2–3 slices of toast in each dish, place some fish on top and pour over the yellow sauce. Sprinkle with a little chopped parsley and serve with plain boiled potatoes and the remainder of the *aïoli*. Serves 4.

SALADE DE SCIPIONS

CUTTLEFISH SALAD

Scipion is the Provençal name for very small cuttlefish, no longer than the first joint on your finger. *Scipions* are also delicious, tossed in flour and deep fried, served hot with aoïli.

450 g (1 lb) *scipions*
1 wineglass dry white wine
a slice of onion
a clove of garlic, bruised
bouquet garni
a few peppercorns
salt

Vinaigrette
6–8 tablespoons olive oil
1–2 tablespoons white wine vinegar
salt, milled pepper

Salad
1 carrot, peeled
1 small turnip, peeled
1 stick celery
half a head of *endive frisée*

Wash the *scipions* in cold running water and, if necessary, open the tentacle end of each fish and squeeze out the small pea-sized lump of gristle in the centre. Leave the fish in a colander to drain.

In a pan, bring the wine and a wineglass of water to the boil with the onion, garlic, bouquet garni, peppercorns and salt and simmer for 4–5 minutes. Add the *scipions* and cook gently for 15–30 minutes depending on their size until the white part of each fish is cooked but still tender. Drain the fish well and turn them into a bowl.

Whisk the oil, vinegar and some salt and pepper together to make the vinaigrette. Pour just enough of the vinaigrette over the fish to coat them lightly. Cover the bowl and chill until ready to serve the salad.

Cut the carrot, turnip and celery into short, slim batons and steam or blanch for 2–3 minutes to soften very slightly. Drain and toss in a little vinaigrette.

When ready to serve, wash and dry the endive and if necessary break into smaller pieces and dress with a thin layer of vinaigrette. Arrange the endive on a large dish to make a background for the rest of the salad. Scatter the sticks of carrot, turnip and celery over and arrange the fish in the centre. Serves 3–4.

MUSHROOMS AND FUNGI

Grandmère Moulin introduced me to wild mushrooming. As I walked down the hill towards the village, past the farmhouse thatched with short-stemmed broom bushes, I noticed a grey-haired figure bent double in a meadow bordering the road. I drew near and she came across to talk. In answer to my query she held open her apron to show me a cushion of delicate purple flowers – the heads of hundreds of violets. 'I pick some each day, to dry, for the fair. And also,' reaching into her pocket, 'for my lunch, some *mousserons*.'

I had already seen a basket of these tiny wild mushrooms being dried in the sun by another villager in Ste Eulalie but, until Mme Moulin offered me one to eat raw, I was quite unprepared for their amazing flavour. With its pale, creamy-beige cap no bigger than a thumbnail, it was a surprise to discover that the *mousseron* can taste so good. They have a strong meaty flavour that makes them highly prized in these upland regions of the Ardèche, where they are gathered in spring and autumn.

But you have to look hard, as I found the next day when I spent an hour or two searching for them with no luck. However, on the third day the *mousserons* were back, nestling amongst the grass which you brush aside with your hand in order to discover these miniature but delicious umbrella-shaped fungi.

Apart from the spectacular *oronge*, *Amanita caesara* (its name indicating its favour with the Romans), unprepossessing looks are everything in the world of edible fungi. A fresh truffle looks like a stone – in fact I've seen some meteorites which look almost identical until you pick them up or sniff them. But unless you are in France during the autumn or have a rare and secret source in Britain, your truffles may have to come in a tin, and even tinned truffles are not cheap. Now and again, though, I buy one (even the peelings are tinned but, although they are less expensive, they are also far less pungent) to slice and place under the skin of a chicken or turkey, or to add to a pâté or to flavour an omelette.

Should you find yourself with a fresh truffle, it's a good idea to adopt the country custom of placing it amongst some eggs overnight. The eggs will absorb the smoky, mushroomy flavour of the truffle and only a few slivers need be added to the omelette.

But if your truffle is a high quality tinned specimen, you may like to make the most of it by mixing Fredy Girardet's vinaigrette that makes good use of the truffle juice. Simply warm together two tablespoons of the truffle liquid with the same quantity of mild white wine vinegar and one tablespoon each of peanut (*arachide*) and walnut (*noix*) oil and a little salt and pepper. He recommends serving this dressing over warm, freshly cooked asparagus – with a little thinly sliced truffle, of course.

Fungi seem to have an affinity with eggs. An Ardéchois omelette contains a handful of hot buttery croûtons and whatever wild mushrooms are available. *Cèpes* or *bolets* (boletus), *girolles* or *chanterelles*, or the diminutive *mousseron vrai* (*Tricholoma georgii* or St George's mushroom) or the *mousseron faux* (*Marasmius oreades*, Scotsman's bonnet or fairy ring mushroom) are all highly delicious edible fungi. To extend their season I find drying the best method of preservation. Pick only sound specimens, but do so advisedly. Roger Phillips's vividly illustrated book *Mushrooms* makes a wise companion on mushroom forays. And there are several good French guides, each photograph enlivened with an accompanying sketch of a skull or hospital bed to dissuade you from being too adventurous, but also with knives and forks to encourage you towards the kitchen. But the best advice comes from local people, who are usually only too happy to help. And it is worth remembering that unidentifiable fungi can always be named by a pharmacist in France. In fact, during the summer they often display named varieties in their shop windows.

To dry mushrooms at home, wipe them with a clean dry cloth and cut the stalk across cleanly. Use a darning needle and some strong thread to string the mushrooms together through their centres and make a garland. In farmhouses this is hung over the fireplace where in two to three days the mushrooms are usually dry enough to unthread and store in a dark, lidded jar until required. Small fungi like *mousserons* are best spread on clean paper in a box and placed outside every day in fine weather until they feel bone dry.

When you want to use dried mushrooms in cooking, simply soak them in a little warm water for a few minutes until softened, then add to the dish. The soaking water can be used to enrich a vegetable stock.

Wild mushrooms are also available in brine or in oil as well as dried. Jars of *cèpes* (*Boletus*) mixed with *grisettes* (*coucoumelles grises* or *Amanita vaginata*) are worth bringing back from France. Even cultivated mushrooms, known in France as *champignons de Paris* (button mushrooms) and *champignons de couche* are delicious preserved in oil – use the best you can afford and tuck in a few bay leaves. The mushrooms make a fine addition to any pasta dish and the oil is superb for salads. French country women also used to preserve mushrooms in salt and in vinegar for use during the winter months. But however enjoyable a morning ramble looking for wild mushrooms may be, for most of us it is a rare event, savoured all the more for that. Fortunately, and especially in France, there are those who regularly rise with the lark to collect wild mushrooms and edible fungi to sell. Whenever you see these on sale in a market, pounce straight away. The stallholder will be pleased to tell you how he recommends preparing the fungi. But usually the simplest method is the best. Cook the cleaned fungi in melted butter, season lightly and serve.

RISOTTO AU RIZ DE CAMARGUE AUX CHAMPIGNONS DES BOIS

CAMARGUE RICE RISOTTO WITH WILD MUSHROOMS

In the markets of the south I look for Camargue rice. These days there are more stalls selling grains, pulses and spices and a variety of rice, and the local Camargue rice is now produced in considerable quantities. Yet Waverley Root, writing in 1958, saw rice-growing as an interim stage in the process of turning the wild Camargue into conventional high-yielding agricultural land. Mercifully this has not come to pass; the hectares under rice have increased, but large tracts of the Camargue remain undisturbed as a protected wildlife reserve with a unique sense of space and peace.

55 g (2 oz) butter	300–400 ml (about ½–¾ pt)
1 red onion, chopped	chicken stock
1 clove of garlic, chopped	fresh, dried or tinned wild
(optional)	mushrooms, the amount
225 g (8 oz) Camargue	according to your supply
polished rice or Italian	salt, milled pepper
arborio rice	Parmesan or Pecorino
1 wineglass dry white wine	cheese, freshly grated

Fresh or tinned wild mushrooms are best sliced and cooked in extra butter. Dried mushrooms should be covered with warm water and left to soften while the rice cooks.

Melt the butter in a heavy-based pan and cook the onion and the garlic over moderate heat until soft. Stir in the rice and when translucent add the wine. Cook, stirring, until all the liquid is absorbed. Continue to add stock, a ladleful at a time, always waiting until the rice has absorbed it all before adding more. Different types of rice vary in how much liquid they will absorb.

When the rice is almost cooked add the wild mushrooms, season with salt and pepper and continue to cook until the rice has lost any hardness in the centre of the grain.

Add a splash of wine and turn the risotto into a hot serving dish.

Serve with freshly grated Parmesan or Pecorino cheese. Serves 2–4.

BESSIGNE À LA FAÇON DE JEANNETTE

JEANNETTE'S SAUTÉED PUFFBALL

Puffballs seem to come and go in one's life. For the last decade in our Devon garden, each autumn, within a few feet of the compost heap, several specimens of *Lycoperdum giganteum*, the giant puffball, have appeared mysteriously, almost overnight. Some of my friends in the Ardèche say that puffballs, known as *la bessigne* or *la vesse de loup géante*, are now less common than a generation ago. But when they do appear, they are seized upon and have even been fought over in the past. The clever trick here is the initial blanching which shrinks the fungi and intensifies the flavour.

1 giant puffball (or a thick slice)	**butter**
salt	**garlic, finely chopped**
fat from a roasting chicken or bacon dripping	**chopped parsley**

Cut the puffball into slices, remove the skin and cut into large dice. Blanch in boiling salted water for 5–10 minutes until shrunk. Drain well.

Heat the fat with the butter and toss in the blanched puffball. Sauté until lightly browned. Add the garlic and parsley and stir until cooked.

Serve straight away; it is particularly good with roast chicken.

CÈPES FARCIS

STUFFED CÈPES

For two hundred years or more, a steady trickle of young Auvergnats have made their way to Paris to train as restaurant chefs. A few years ago about twenty founded an association: l'Amicale des Cuisiniers et Pâtissiers Auvergnats de Paris. Their book *Cuisine d'Auvergne* was written to record and honour the good country cooking of their family homes. Some of the dishes show signs of being altered to suit Parisian clients, in the way that Jane Grigson has called *'la cuisine pastorale'*. Others reflect their rustic origins more faithfully. This recipe is one such – I have been served *cèpes* in this fashion in the high plateau region of the Ardèche where it touches the Auvergne.

In the Auvergne the *bolet à pied rouge* (*Erythropus*) is common; in Britain field mushrooms replace them quite well.

225 g (8 oz) fresh *cèpes* or field mushrooms
55 g (2 oz) *lard gras* or streaky bacon, finely diced
1 clove garlic, crushed
1 tablespoon finely chopped parsley
1 tablespoon finely chopped chervil

55 g (2 oz) white bread soaked in cold water and squeezed out
1 egg
salt, milled pepper
nut or olive oil
1 onion, finely chopped

Cut the stalks of the *cèpes* level with the caps. Chop the stalks and mix with the bacon, garlic, parsley, chervil, bread and egg to make the stuffing. Season with salt and pepper and spoon on to the gill side of each *cèpe* or mushroom, pressing it down to make a little mound on each.

Brush an oven dish with the oil and spread the chopped onion over the base. Place the stuffed *cèpes* on top and sprinkle with a little more oil. Cover with a lid or a sheet of foil and cook in a slow oven (Mark 3, 160°C, 325°F) for 45–60 minutes, depending on size.

Remove the lid 10 minutes before the end of the cooking time to allow the stuffing to brown a little. Serves 3–4.

OMELETTE ARDÉCHOISE

OMELETTE WITH CÈPES AND CROÛTONS

In Haute Ardèche butter alone moistens the omelette pan whereas further south where the influence of the Midi is felt, olive oil and a little garlic enrich the flavours of this omelette, which contains the subtle, smoky-tasting *cèpe* contrasted with cubes of crisp croûtons.

French bread, sliced	salt, milled pepper
30 g (1 oz) butter	a handful of fresh *cèpes* or
a little olive oil	the dried equivalent,
1 clove of garlic, chopped	soaked in warm water for
4 eggs	a few minutes

Toast the bread until golden brown and cut into dice.

Melt some butter in an omelette pan and add some oil and garlic, if you wish. Toss the croûtons in the butter and fry, turning them over until they are crisp and they have absorbed the butter. Transfer the croûtons to a hot plate and keep hot. Wipe the pan with kitchen paper.

Lightly beat the eggs and season with salt and pepper. Cut the *cèpes* into pieces and, if desired, sauté briefly in a knob of butter. Add to the croûtons.

Heat a little more butter in the pan and when it ceases to bubble pour in the egg mixture. When the omelette is half set but still runny (*baveuse*) on top, scatter the *cèpes* and the croûtons into the pan. Cook a little more, fold over the omelette and slide on to a hot plate. Rub a little butter over the top and serve. Serves 2.

ENDIVE BELGE ÉTUVÉE AUX CHAMPIGNONS

BRAISED CHICORY WITH MUSHROOMS

Chicory, its white leaves folded into each other, is just as good cooked in butter and served hot as it is raw, in a salad with oranges and walnuts. Here I've cooked the blanched chicory with a mushroom sauce.

2 heads of chicory	½ teaspoon sweet paprika
30 g (1 oz) butter	¼ teaspoon ground
1 tablespoon olive oil	cinnamon
1 thin slice of *lard fumé* or	2–3 tablespoons dry white
streaky bacon, diced	wine
115 g (4 oz) cultivated	salt, milled pepper
mushrooms, sliced	a little *crème fraîche* or
1 tomato, peeled and	plain yoghurt (optional)
chopped	finely chopped parsley

Trim the base of the stalk from the chicory and cut each head in half lengthways. Heat the butter with the oil and lightly brown the chicory all over. Transfer to an oven dish and keep hot.

Add the *lard fumé* or bacon to the pan and cook, stirring, for 2 minutes. Stir in the mushrooms and tomato and cook for 3 minutes. Then add the paprika, ground cinnamon, the wine and some salt and pepper. Spoon over the chicory, cover with foil and bake in a moderate oven (Mark 4, 180°C, 350°F) for 20–25 minutes. Alternatively return the chicory to the pan and cook in the sauce, covered, on the hob.

If you wish, spoon the cream or yoghurt on top. Sprinkle with the chopped parsley and serve. Serves 4.

FEUILLÉTÉ DE PIGEON AUX CÈPES

BREAST OF PIGEON WITH CÈPES AND PUFF PASTRY

The pastry can be made and baked ahead if preferred. The contrasts of flavours and textures in this dish make it particularly pleasing.

85 g (3 oz) prepared puff pastry	2 slices of *lard fumé* or smoked streaky bacon
egg yolk	1 shallot, finely chopped
the breasts from two woodpigeons (make stock with the carcasses)	1 wineglass red wine
	1 wineglass stock
salt, milled pepper	*cèpes*, fresh, tinned or dried and softened in warm water
45 g (1½ oz) butter	

On a floured board roll out the pastry to make an oblong measuring 20 × 12 cm (8 × 5 in). Trim the edges straight and cut into four rectangles. Brush the pastry with the egg yolk and decorate the centre of each rectangle with a few leaves and berries made from the trimmings. Transfer to a wetted baking tray and chill for 15 minutes.

Bake in the centre of a moderately hot oven (Mark 6, 200°C, 400°F) for 10–15 minutes until well risen and golden brown. Transfer the pastry to a wire rack and reheat when ready to serve.

Slice the breasts of woodpigeon thinly and season lightly. Heat two thirds of the butter and cook the bacon and shallot until starting to colour. Add the woodpigeon and sauté for only 2–3 minutes if they are cut thinly; finally add the *cèpes* and when cooked transfer the contents of the pan to a hot dish. Cover and keep hot. Pour the wine and the stock into the pan and bring to the boil, scraping to incorporate all the pan juices. Reduce over high heat by about half, remove from the heat and add the remaining butter. When melted pour the sauce over the meat.

Slice each piece of puff pastry in two layers. Place one layer on a plate, arrange some of the woodpigeon and *cèpes* on top. Cover with the pastry lid and spoon a little sauce around. Serve straight away. Serves 4.

CÈPES À LA CRÈME

CÈPES COOKED WITH CREAM

Cèpes, field mushrooms or larger cultivated mushrooms are all really delicious cooked this way. Serve as a separate course or with chicken or veal.

225 g (8 oz) freshly picked *cèpes* or mushrooms	**salt, milled pepper**
55 g (2 oz) butter	**a little finely chopped parsley**
1 shallot, finely chopped	
150 ml (¼ pt) *crème fraîche*, or double cream and a squeeze of lemon juice	

Wipe the *cèpes* or mushrooms with a damp cloth to remove specks and cut the stalks level with the caps. Leave whole or slice if huge.

Melt the butter, stir in the *cèpes* and shallot and cook, over moderate heat, shaking or stirring from time to time for 3–4 minutes.

Set 3 tablespoons of the cream aside and stir the remainder into the mushrooms. Cook gently for 10–15 minutes until the liquid has evaporated and the mushrooms are coated in a shiny sauce.

Add the reserved cream and season lightly with salt and pepper. Serve with a very light dusting of chopped parsley. Serves 2–3.

Should your cultivated mushrooms lack flavour, a dash of madeira can't do any harm to the dish. I also recommend serving *Cèpes à la crème* in hot bread *croustades* or very thin pastry cases.

There are two ways of making a *croustade*. Either use a round cookie cutter to cut a circle from a slice of bread and gently press the circle into a well-buttered tart or patty tin; or cut a 5 cm (2 in) thick slice from a loaf of bread, and cut away the crusts to leave a 7.5 cm (3 in) square of bread. Use a small serrated knife to remove the centre of each square, leaving a 1 cm (½ in) wall and base in the shape of a box.

Brush each *croustade* with melted butter and bake in a moderately hot oven (Mark 6, 200°C, 400°F) for 15–20 minutes until golden brown.

CRÈME DE CHAMPIGNONS

CREAM OF MUSHROOM SOUP

85 g (3 oz) butter	2 tablespoons flour
1 onion, chopped	150 ml (¼ pt) creamy milk
2 cloves of garlic, chopped	150 ml (¼ pt) *crème fraîche*
340 g (12 oz) mushrooms	salt, milled pepper
570 ml (1 pt) chicken stock	

Melt two thirds of the butter and sweat the onion and the garlic in it. Wipe the mushrooms with a damp cloth and slice. Add to the pan and stir until coated with butter. Cook over moderate heat until the mushrooms have collapsed and given up their liquid. Pour in the stock, cover and simmer for 10–15 minutes.

Purée the contents of the pan in a blender or processor but leave a slight texture to the soup. Melt the remaining butter in the pan and stir in the flour for 1–2 minutes. Gradually add the milk, stirring all the time, then add the purée. Simmer for 5 minutes.

Whisk in the *crème fraîche* and season to taste. Serve in hot bowls; 4–6 servings.

POMMES DE TERRE AUX CHAMPIGNONS À LA CAROL TILBURY

CAROL TILBURY'S POTATOES WITH MUSHROOMS

Some years ago a francophile friend prepared this dish and served it to us in a small cottage near the Rollright Stones in Oxfordshire. It was so delicious that I am amazed that it has taken me so long to get around to cooking it myself.

450 g (1 lb) waxy potatoes
  (e.g. Desirée)
salt
1 shallot, finely chopped
1 sliver of garlic, crushed
55 g (2 oz) butter

115 g (4 oz) cultivated
  button mushrooms
2 teaspoons flour
150 ml (¼ pt) single cream
salt, milled pepper
freshly grated nutmeg

Peel the potatoes and cut into pieces about the size of a walnut. Cook in salted water until *just* tender. Drain and keep hot in the pan under a folded cloth.

Cook the shallot and the garlic in the butter for a few minutes, add the mushrooms and cook, stirring, until they have softened and almost all their liquid has evaporated.

Stir in the flour for 1–2 minutes and then the cream. Season to taste with the salt, pepper and nutmeg. Turn the potatoes into a hot oven dish and pour over the mushrooms. Cover and reheat thoroughly in a hot oven for 10 minutes. Serves 3–4.

TARTE AUX CHAMPIGNONS

MUSHROOM TART

Pâte brisée
115 g (4 oz) flour
55 g (2 oz) butter, slightly
  softened
1 egg yolk
2 tablespoons ice-cold
  water
¼ teaspoon salt

Filling
55 g (2 oz) butter
2 cloves of garlic, finely
  chopped
340 g (12 oz) mushrooms,
  sliced
grated nutmeg
salt, milled pepper
1 egg
1 egg yolk
about 250 ml (about ½ pt)
  crème fraîche

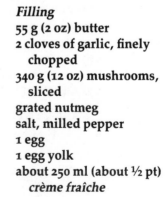

Sift the flour into a heap on a cold work surface or into a wide shallow bowl. Make a well in the centre and add the butter, egg yolk and water mixed with the salt.

Work the ingredients together with your fingertips, gradually drawing the flour into the centre until the mixture forms small lumps. Take these and push away from you on the work surface, using the heel of your hand to spread the dough, and then scrape it together with a knife blade or pastry scraper until the dough forms into a ball.

If the pastry is still cold (otherwise chill it for 30 minutes), roll it out and line a 23 cm (9 in) tart tin; prick the base all over and chill in the refrigerator for 15 minutes.

Bake in the centre of a moderately hot oven (Mark 6, 200°C, 400°F) for 10–15 minutes until set and lightly coloured. Lower the oven to Mark 4 (180°C, 350°F).

Melt the butter in a wide pan, stir in the garlic and after a minute or so the mushrooms. Coat with butter and cook over moderate heat until almost all the liquid has evaporated. Season with nutmeg, salt and pepper. Spoon the mixture into the pastry case.

Lightly beat the egg, egg yolk and cream (the amount will depend on the depth of the pastry case) together and pour over the mushrooms.

Bake in the centre of the oven for 20–30 minutes until set. Serves 6.

DUXELLES

This versatile mushroom seasoning is thought to have been devised by La Varenne, master cook to the Marquis d'Uxelles and author of the first modern cookery book in France, *Le Cuisinier françois*, which appeared in 1651. A pot of *duxelles* will store in the refrigerator for a few days, or for longer, ideally in cubes, in the freezer. Add to sauces, stuffings (especially for fish), soups and pies.

225 g (8 oz) mushrooms
2 tablespoons butter
1 tablespoon olive oil
1 shallot, finely chopped
1 slim clove of garlic,
   chopped (optional)

salt, milled pepper
a little finely chopped
   parsley

Wipe the mushrooms with a damp cloth and chop finely. Heat the butter with the oil and stir in the shallot and garlic. When softened add the mushrooms and cook, stirring, until they have given up their liquid. Reduce the heat slightly and cook until almost all the liquid has evaporated.

I prefer to store the mixture at this stage so that I can season as I wish, say with nutmeg or mint when I come to use it. But if you wish, season now with salt and pepper and mix in the parsley.

Spoon into a lidded container and store in the refrigerator for up to 1 week or in the freezer for 1–2 months.

BROUILLADE AUX TRUFFES

SCRAMBLED EGGS WITH TRUFFLES

Truffle peelings are fine here, especially if you have stored the truffle and the eggs together beforehand. One of the best ways to make scrambled eggs meltingly soft is to use more yolks than whites and to cook them really gently so that the liquid egg sets but does not toughen.

**5 eggs
2 egg yolks
truffle peelings, chopped
salt, milled pepper
55 g (2 oz) butter**

Beat the eggs lightly with the yolks and stir in the truffle. Set aside, covered, in a cool place for about an hour if you wish to extract the maximum flavour. Season lightly with salt and pepper.

Melt the butter in a heavy-based pan and add the eggs. Cook gently over low to moderate heat, stirring now and again until the mixture sets. Serve straight away with bread or fingers of toast. Serves 2–3.

SALADE DE CHAMPIGNONS ET DE CONCOMBRE

MUSHROOM AND CUCUMBER SALAD

To illustrate how delicious mushrooms are raw I devised this salad. Dill is not widely used in France but my French friends are taking to it.

1 cucumber	225 g (8 oz) cultivated
2 tablespoons olive oil	mushrooms, small caps
1½ tablespoons fresh dill	or buttons
fronds, finely chopped or	150 ml (¼ pt) *crème fraîche*
use freeze-dried dill	1 lime, finely grated rind
salt, milled pepper	and juice

To give a more interesting appearance to the salad, remove the peel from half the cucumber, halve the whole cucumber, remove the seeds and cut into short slender batons. Steam, lightly salted for 3–4 minutes until cooked but not mushy. Refresh under cold water and drain well on a cloth. Toss with half the oil, most of the dill and a little salt and pepper and arrange around the rim of a serving dish.

Wipe the mushrooms with a damp cloth; trim the stalks and slice the mushrooms.

Mix the *crème fraîche* with the remaining oil and sufficient of the grated rind and juice of the lime to give a balance of flavours. Season lightly and toss the mushrooms in the dressing. Spoon into the centre of the serving dish and sprinkle with the remaining dill.

Serve straight away or chill for no longer than 1 hour. Serves 4.

CHAMPIGNONS À LA CASTIGLIONE

CASTIGLIONE MUSHROOMS

Mushrooms prepared this way and served with small pieces of bone marrow are a classic garnish for beef dishes. Times have changed, the garnish has become the main event. Minus the bone marrow,

Castiglione mushrooms make a handsome vegetable course or hors d'oeuvre. I presume that a chef to Count Baldasar Castiglione, the fifteenth-century Italian writer, was originally responsible for this dish. Those were the days when the dish bore the name of the person who employed the chef. Self-employed designer chefs have changed all that.

8 large flat mushrooms	1 wineglass dry white wine
1 large aubergine	100 g (3½ oz) cooked ham,
salt	diced
a knob of butter	chopped parsley
225 g (8 oz) polished	*quatre-épices* (see p. 89)
Camargue rice or Italian	a little seasoned flour
risotto rice	breadcrumbs
olive oil	
1 shallot, chopped	
300 ml (about ½ pt) good	
ham or chicken stock	

Wipe the mushrooms and cut off the stalks, chop the stalks finely. Place the mushrooms gill side up in a baking dish and prepare the filling.

Cut the aubergine into eight slices, salt and leave to drain in a colander.

Melt the butter in a pan, add a splash of oil and cook the shallot until soft. Stir in the rice and cook, stirring, for a few minutes until transparent. Gradually add the stock, the mushroom stalks and the wine in three or four batches, allowing the rice to absorb the liquid fully each time before adding more. Cook until the rice is tender.

Add the ham and parsley and season with a little *quatre-épices*, and remove from the heat.

Rinse the aubergine in cold water; drain and dry on a cloth. Dip each slice in seasoned flour and fry briefly in olive oil. Drain on kitchen paper.

Divide the rice mixture between the mushrooms, making a neat pile on each. Flatten slightly and place a slice of aubergine on top and sprinkle with breadcrumbs.

Add a little extra wine to the baking dish and cover with a buttered paper or foil. The mushrooms can now be set aside for an hour or so if preferred.

Bake in the centre of a moderate oven (Mark 5, 190°C, 375°F) for 25–35 minutes. Serves 4.

CHAMPIGNONS AUX FEUILLES DE VIGNE

MUSHROOMS COOKED IN VINE LEAVES

The original of this dish is Elizabeth David's *cèpes à la genoise*. I have slightly adapted her version to use small field mushrooms or the cultivated kind that have opened into medium-sized caps and so have more flavour. The vine leaves should be thin and tender and large enough to enclose the mushrooms.

12–18 vine leaves
12–18 mushrooms
4 tablespoons olive oil
1 or 2 cloves of garlic, crushed

salt, milled pepper
45 g (1½ oz) dry breadcrumbs

Blanch the vine leaves in boiling salted water for 1–2 minutes. Refresh in cold water and spread out on a clean teacloth while you prepare the mushrooms.

Cut the stalks level with the caps. Chop the stalks finely and mix with most of the olive oil, garlic, some salt and pepper, and sufficient breadcrumbs to make a paste.

Divide the mixture between the mushrooms, spreading it over the gill side, and wrap each in a vine leaf. Arrange them in an oven dish and dribble the remaining olive oil on top.

Cover the dish and cook in a slow oven (Mark 3, 160°C, 325°F) for about 30 minutes. Serve hot or cold. Serves 3–4.

CONSERVE DE CHAMPIGNONS À L'HUILE

MUSHROOMS PRESERVED IN OIL

In the tradition of good country living there is much preserving in the Ardèche. Here is a more delicious way of storing September's mushrooms than freezing or drying them. If you have some small unopened field mushrooms they are excellent – otherwise use cultivated button mushrooms. Add the preserved mushrooms to winter salads or serve them as part of an hors d'oeuvre; they are also good in hot vegetable dishes.

**450 g (1 lb) small firm
  mushrooms
olive oil
bay leaves**

Wipe the mushrooms with a cloth but do not peel them if they are sound. Remove a sliver from the base of each stalk but leave the stalks in place.

Heat a little oil in a wide pan and gently cook the mushrooms, in batches if necessary, for 10–15 minutes until they have shrunk and given up their liquid but are still soft and only lightly coloured.

Drain the mushrooms on kitchen paper and allow to cool completely. Then pack into a lidded jar. Tuck in a bay leaf or two and cover with olive oil. Screw the top down tightly.

Keep the jar in a very cool, dark place or the refrigerator. Keep for 2–3 weeks before using.

THE PIG

The autumn day on which the pig is killed, *la tuade*, is always an event. The butchering is a great deal of work for one person, and two will have their hands full. In Germany one year it took four of us nearly all day; in England my husband and I worked solidly for a day and a half. And in France you involve as many people as possible, because the sooner the pig is disposed of the sooner the jollity can begin. Everybody is invited back later in the week or on the following Sunday for the *repas de fête*: the slaughterer and his wife, one's family and friends all arrive for an evening of eating, singing and dancing late into the night.

This is part of a European cultural tradition. Flora Thompson writes of the same event in an Oxfordshire village in the nineteenth century. 'It was time to rejoice, and rejoice they did, with beer flowing freely and the first delicious dish of pig's fry sizzling in the pan.'

The particular nature of the pig dictates the order in which the meat must be butchered and prepared, so the procedure is little different in a farmhouse in the Auvergne from one in the Lake District. But the way the French utilize every scrap of pig (only the squeak is uneaten) to prepare delicious food with such finesse is, to us with a different tradition, nothing short of a marvel.

As soon as the pig is killed the first task is to drain the blood. Then the *boudin noir*, blood sausage or black pudding is made. Any fibrin is cleared from the blood by hand and then pork fat or cream, breadcrumbs, thyme, basil and spices are added and mixed well. The best *boudin* I've eaten was delicately spiced with nutmeg and it went specially well with the fried apples which are the traditional accompaniment.

The mixture is fed into the washed but not scraped intestines (*les tripes*), using a funnel (*un entonnoir*), and the *boudin* is then poached in water that is kept just below boiling point for 3–4 hours. This sausage is very rich but a few slices, gently sautéed in butter and served with a squeeze of lemon juice and a purée of apples, can make a very good first course or, in larger amounts, a hearty meal.

While the main carcass of the meat is allowed to hang for some hours to tenderize, the first meal of the pig, the *repas de cochon* or the *tuffenant*, is prepared. Potatoes are fried in some of the pork fat and, as in Britain, *les tripes* or chitterlings are added to the pan. This meal is still popular in Devon with chitterlings from the butcher.

Soon after this, *le présent* or gift of some pork fat or some *boudin* is taken to nearby friends. 'Those who begrudge the pig will themselves be killed,' they still say in the country, and it's taken seriously.

The remaining intestines are scraped free of fat with the blade of a knife, cleaned with a goose feather and washed. They are needed for the sausages.

The pork is now butchered into joints in the French manner, dividing the carcass according to the different muscles, leaving the minimum of fat attached. Where the method of cooking means that extra fat is needed a thin layer of fat is tied on – barding – or a ribbon of fat may be woven in, which is known as larding. But both these methods are mainly used on meat with low fat, like beef or veal. It is important to bear in mind the different French style of butchering when cooking French dishes outside France. Some supermarket chains and high-class butchers are now supplying cuts of meat prepared to continental standards and it is a welcome development.

In the past a remarkably small proportion of the pork was eaten fresh. Farmers' freezers have changed that today, but in France it is still the case that far more meat is reserved for the *saloir* or salting trough or is put into brine (*saumure*), than is usual on most British farms. Belly pork is salted for eight days to become *petit salé*. Some pork fat is salted for fifteen days to become *lard*, and the hams (*jambons*) for one month. Meat for smoking, like the hams, is placed in sacks and hung in the chimney to one side of a lowish fire, for up to one month.

The offal and remaining meat is transformed by the art of *charcuterie* into some of the finest pork dishes in the world. Jane Grigson's classic work, *Charcuterie and French Pork Cookery*, is essential reading for anyone interested in this form of French cuisine.

Fresh sausages (*saucisses*) are made by mixing chopped meat and fat with the seasoning favoured in the region. The mixture is fed into the casing of the small intestine.

Sausages for drying and keeping (*saucissons*) are made from a more finely chopped mixture of pork and fat plus a little saltpetre to give the meat a rosy colour. In Arles beef is added to make a very close-textured and well-flavoured *saucisson*. The seasoning of these fine sausages varies according to the region of France. And the local *saucisson sec* is known by its own name; the *rosette* of Lyon, although the same sausage made in the Ardèche often tastes better, or as the *jesu* of the Languedoc or the *brides* of Provence. It is always a good idea to ask which is the local *saucisson sec* at the charcuterie; in the market the farmers' wives come in from the country to sell their home-made charcuterie, sometimes accompanied by a colour photograph of the pigs or ducks that are the source of their wares. It is usual to make four large *saucissons* from each pig and one very large type known in the country as *la fin de la monde*.

What is left of the pig is made into *confits* and *fricandeaux* – *pâtés*, *terrines* and meats preserved in fat. Here the local and household specialities are made with great pride. Cooks hug their recipes to themselves and will pass them on only to their daughters, along with the reputation for making the best *caillettes* or *saucisson de couenne* in the district.

In some of the following recipes I have specified *quatre-épices* – a valuable mixture of spices widely available in France and a frequent ingredient of pork cookery. Sometimes the cinnamon is replaced by ground ginger, and one part of the black pepper can be ground allspice or Jamaican pepper.

Quatre-épices:	7 parts ground black pepper
	1 part ground nutmeg
	1 part ground cloves
	1 part ground cinnamon

Mix the spices together well and store in a small screw-top jar.

In rural France the recipes and traditional practices for pork cookery and charcuterie are often memorized, or some may be jotted down in a small notebook, but they are characterized by their largely unchanging nature. A few years ago in a village in the Ardèche, a group of children collected and recorded *Recettes de cochonailles* or 'Recipes for Pork Cookery' which, the introduction said, 'had been passed on by tradition, orally or hidden in small time-worn notebooks'. It seems to me that with such a sense of the past, a country's culinary heritage is in safe, albeit young, hands.

CIVET DE PORCELET

PORK STEWED WITH RED WINE

A civet is a rich stew whose sauce is sometimes thickened with the blood of the animal, as in *civet de lièvre* (hare). And, strictly speaking, *porcelet* is sucking pig. Having said that, this is a fine pork stew made with shoulder or loin and cooked with red wine. A simple excellent dish from St Maximin.

1 kg (2¼ lb) shoulder or loin of pork, boned	85 g (3 oz) *petit salé* or salted belly pork
1 clove of garlic, finely chopped	1 large onion, chopped
1 sprig of thyme	275 ml (½ pt) red wine
a few leaves of sage	*beurre manié* (1 teaspoon each of butter and flour blended together)
a bay leaf	
grated nutmeg	rabbit or pork blood (if available)
3 juniper berries, crushed	
4 tablespoons olive oil	

Cut the meat into 2.5 cm (1 in) pieces. Place in a bowl with the garlic, thyme, sage and bay leaf. Add the nutmeg, juniper berries and olive oil and mix well. Cover the bowl tightly and chill overnight in the refrigerator.

Next day sauté the *petit salé* or salt pork in a pan until the fat runs. Add the onion and cook, stirring, until lightly browned. Transfer to a hot lidded casserole. Lightly brown the meat in the pan in batches if necessary and spoon into the casserole.

Deglaze the pan with the red wine and thicken with the *beurre manié* added in small pieces. Pour over the meat, season lightly and add the herbs from the marinade. Cover and cook in a moderate oven (Mark 4, 180°C, 350°F) for 1–1½ hours or until tender. Or simmer the dish very gently on the hob.

If you wish, the sauce can now be thickened with the blood, but do not let it boil; however, the dish is still good even without it. Serves 5–6.

BOMBINE

ARDÉCHOIS PORK WITH POTATOES

La bombine is a good hearty dish that varies, in the way of true country food, according to circumstances. In times of plenty, meat is added; otherwise the vegetables alone suffice, although they are sometimes given the flavour of meat by cooking the dish with pork fat. Jean-Paul Barras's version, from which he banishes pepper, includes black olives and dried *cèpes*. This indicates that his *bombine* comes from southern Ardèche where the Midi laps at its toes. In other parts of the region a cook will swear that the dish should be prepared only with pork fat and certainly no olives.

4 pork cutlets, boned	salt
olive oil or dripping	8–12 dried *cèpes*
1 large onion, finely	about ¾ kg (1½–2 lb)
chopped	potatoes, peeled and
4 bay leaves	thinly sliced
a few sprigs of thyme	115 g black olives
stock or water	

In France the pork will have little fat on it. In Britain it is usually necessary to trim it off – the dish would otherwise be too greasy. Lightly brown the meat in olive oil or pork dripping in a flameproof casserole. Transfer the meat to a plate and soften the onion in the casserole. Replace the meat on top of the onion and add the bay leaves and thyme. Pour in sufficient stock or water to almost cover the meat. Season with salt and bring to the boil. Soften the *cèpes* in a little water.

Arrange the sliced potatoes on top of the pork adding the *cèpes* between the layers with a little salt.

Cover the casserole and cook over low heat or in a moderate oven (Mark 4, 180°C, 350°F) for about 1 hour. Add the olives and cook for another 15–20 minutes. Serves 4.

CASSOULET

A great deal has been written about this famous country dish. And while I should like to pay respect to Prosper Montagné's two versions in Larousse and those of Elizabeth David in *French Country Cooking* and *French Provincial Cooking*, I offer two further versions. The first is an authentic *cassoulet* from Castelnaudry. It is the only French recipe given to me in English. It was copied and translated from the Daquet's family manuscript book by my friends and their relatives Josette and Stan Ramsden and I am most grateful to them. I quote it verbatim.

CASSOULET DAQUET

Skin a duck or goose, trim all the fat off and melt it with the skin. Pepper and salt the bird, cut in portions and cook in its own fat for one hour. It can be put in a sealed jar, in the fat it has cooked in and kept in a cold place. This is *confit d'oie*.

Traditionally, the cassoulet is made with goose or duck but pork could be used.

Soak overnight small white beans (haricots); cook in water that comes about 5 cm (2 in) above the beans, with pork skin, pig's trotter, an *andouille* (sausage made with pig's intestine, tripe, etc . . .).

Fry the bird portions to take the fat off, add a *persillade* (parsley ground with garlic), tomatoes, and mix with the beans.

Put in a *cassole* (big basin-type ovenproof dish with a lip, which gives its name to the dish), add a sausage on top and cook in the oven for 1½ hours.

This was the traditional Sunday meal and it was cooked in the baker's oven. The poorer people used to replace the meat by a roll made of bread soaked in milk, eggs, seasoning and wrapped in a cabbage leaf. This was called the *farci*. It was cooked in the oven with just the beans to make a Poor Man's Cassoulet.

The second *cassoulet* is an Englishman's version of the dish. It comes from a friend in Devon, Nicholas Dimbleby, who lives a few fields away in Clyst Hydon. In his own words, 'We lived like paupers for nine months in Riberac.' Again I quote verbatim.

CASSOULET DIMBLEBY

Nine months surviving on 250 francs a week (eight years ago) in a run-down *gîte* in the south-west Charente subjected my family and me to the best and worst that French country life can offer. Memories of the best remain: Riberac market, home-grown onions, banks of wild orchids, the guttural greeting of the post van, and still with us today, the heartwarming *cassoulet*.

The culinary ethics of a farmer's wife were demonstrated unforgettably when I witnessed the slaughter and dressing of a chicken. Not one part was wasted – the undigested grain was removed from the crop and, via the kitchen window, was fed back to her cousins in the yard. Such scrupulous housekeeping provides the thrifty with a cheap but nourishing basis for many meals.

Though not for the squeamish, flayed goose neck and severed eel head became regular items in the bulging baskets that returned from the Friday market. These 'throwaways' were the basis for much of our favourite food. Speed, economy and compromise dominated my cooking for a family of six.

This is my own hybrid version of the classic French *cassoulet* but I treat the dish as a basis for a variety of forms. Here is one. Having a goose neck is a luxury, but it makes a wonderfully strong glutinous base. I often make the dish around Christmas when we've had a goose and there is goose stock available. Otherwise I use turkey or chicken stock. When times are hard I use strips of pork belly or mince instead of *cassoulet* sausage. These are now more widely available.* Buy a lot when you find them – they freeze well.

450 g (1 lb) dried haricot or red kidney beans
1 tablespoon olive oil or sunflower
225 g (8 oz) smoked streaky bacon, diced
2 onions, sliced
2 large carrots, each cut in four
400 g (14 oz) fresh or tinned tomatoes, peeled
2–3 cloves of garlic, flattened with a knife
1 goose neck
6 *cassoulet* or garlic sausages
bouquet garni of bay leaf, rosemary and thyme
1 litre (1¾ pt) goose or other poultry stock
parsley, finely chopped

Soak the beans overnight in plenty of water; then boil for 15 minutes. Discard the water.

Heat the oil in a cast-iron casserole, add the bacon and cook until the fat runs. Now add the onions and cook until soft.

Add the carrots, tomatoes, garlic, goose neck and sausages. Place the bouquet garni on top and cover with the beans. Pour over sufficient stock to cover and bring to the boil.

* From Fenns of Piccadilly, Berwick Street, London, and from Nigel Schofield, Bangers, 1 Eppletons Farm, Copplestone, Crediton, Devon EX17 5LE (Copplestone 485).

Place a tight-fitting lid on the casserole and cook in a slow oven (Mark 2, 150°C, 300°F) for 3–4 hours or cook overnight in the bottom oven of the Aga.

Serve the dish sprinkled with parsley.

Note: this stew, like so many others, tastes better on reheating; beware however that the beans do not stick to the bottom. I have cooked this dish in a pressure-cooker for 1½ hours. But add more water for the cooking and then reduce the liquid, with the lid removed, over high heat on the top of the stove.

Variation: Moroccan style
Use minced lamb instead of sausage and add a heaped teaspoon of cumin and the peel of a lemon. Also gently fry the lamb with the onion. Remove the lemon peel before serving.

DAUBE PROVENÇALE DE PORCELET

PROVENÇAL DAUBE OF PORK

The excellent flavour of this dish depends on 1–2 days marinating of the meat. 'There are no short cuts in good cooking,' said the chef Michel Chareton, who gave me the recipe in a small hotel-restaurant in Carcès mainly used by the locals.

1 kg (2¼ lb) loin of pork, in one piece	1 orange
	710 ml (1¼ pt) red wine
1 head of garlic	4 tablespoons olive oil
2 carrots	100 g (3½ oz) *petit salé* or
1 onion	salt pork, diced
1 shallot	1 tablespoon flour
green part of a leek	1 teaspoon peppercorns
a stalk of celery	1 wineglass Vieux Marc de
a few stalks of parsley	Provence or brandy
2 bay leaves	salt, milled pepper
2–3 sprigs of fresh thyme	

Place the meat in a deep bowl. Slightly crush each clove of garlic with the blade of a knife. Dice the carrots, onion, shallots, leek and celery to make a mirepoix. Tip the vegetables into the bowl and add the parsley, bay leaves, thyme and finely grated zest of the orange. Add the wine and garlic and cover the bowl tightly. Leave in a cold place or the refrigerator for 1–2 days.

Take the meat from the marinade, remove the bone and cut the meat into 3 cm (1 in) cubes. Brown the bone in a pan, cover with water and simmer for 1 hour to make some stock. Take out the bone and reduce the stock over high heat to make 200 ml (a generous ¼ pint).

Strain the marinade and bring the liquid to the boil; skim off the froth and set the liquid aside.

Sauté the meat, in batches if necessary, in olive oil until nicely browned. Transfer the meat to a hot lidded casserole and sauté the *petit salé* or salt pork with the vegetable mirepoix until the fat runs. Sprinkle the flour into the pan, cook, stirring until it colours pale brown. Add the *marc* and set light to it, and gradually stir in the wine and reduced stock until the sauce thickens. Pour over the meat and deglaze the pan with the juice of the orange.

Cover the casserole and cook in a moderate oven (Mark 4, 180°C, 350°F) for 1–1½ hours until the meat is tender and the sauce is dark and flavourful. If it is too thin reduce it over high heat.

Serve the *daube* with noodles or boiled potatoes. Serves 5–6.

This is hardly the kind of recipe to tackle if time or tempers are short. But for people who find cooking a relaxing weekend activity it does make a fine dish on Saturday or Sunday evening.

CAILLETTES

Caillettes are an Ardéchois speciality. They are made from chopped pork mixed either with spinach, lettuce and herbs or puréed potatoes, and resemble English faggots which are also cooked under a veil of caul.

This recipe is probably of more interest to those readers who acquire their pork in whole or half carcass and are therefore anxious to dispose in some palatable way of those curious looking items that arrive from the slaughterhouse alongside the more recognizable joints of meat. And looking at the amount of spinach it takes, I reckon you need to grow that too: a recipe for the self-sufficient.

3 kg (6½ lb) small Swiss chard leaves or spinach	3 tablespoons salt
	milled pepper
300 g (10½ oz) lights	4 cloves of garlic, crushed
300 g (10½ oz) pig's liver	a bunch of parsley, finely
½ pig's heart	chopped
300 g (10½ oz) hard pork fat	1 pig's caul

Wash the Swiss chard or spinach in plenty of cold water, and cook in boiling salted water until tender. Drain and rinse in cold water, drain well, tip into a cloth and press out as much moisture as possible. Chop finely.

Mince all the pork on medium setting, and then mince again. Turn the meat into a bowl with the salt, pepper, garlic, parsley and spinach. Mix together well to combine everything really thoroughly.

Take small handfuls weighing about 140 g (5 oz) and form the *caillettes* into the shape of a ball. Place them in a roasting tin and cover with the pig's caul stretched out thinly.

Cook in a moderate oven (Mark 5, 190°C, 375°F) for 1–1½ hours. Remove from the oven and allow to cool. Then cut the *caillettes* apart and serve hot with potatoes; or serve cold with a salad.

JAMBON DE CAMPAGNE AU FOIN

HOME-CURED HAM BAKED WITH HAY

Brillat-Savarin may have been the philosopher in the kitchen but at times we all have to be philosophical about our cooking. A dish that you've exhausted yourself over is a flop, yet on another occasion something you threw together while keeping the ship afloat is a triumph. So it was with a ham that I prepared by taking a series of short cuts – it turned out to be the most delicious for years. Instead of spending time devising my own cure I relied on a double quantity of Jane Grigson's *saumure anglaise*. Then my plans to smoke the ham in true country fashion were foiled. So I cooked it in water first and then baked it with hay, which gives the meat an exquisite flavour. And doing it this way gives you one ham with two different flavours.

5–6 kg (about 12 lb) leg of pork	2 bay leaves
680 g (1½ lb) sea salt	6 sprigs of thyme
680 g (1½ lb) brown sugar	2 teaspoons peppercorns
115 g (4 oz) saltpetre	8 cloves
2 teaspoons juniper berries	1 cloved onion
2 small end pieces of nutmeg	2 carrots, sliced
	2 bay leaves
	an armful of hay

John, my butcher in Devon, readily agreed to half-bone and salt a leg of pork for 24 hours. He argues that today's pork needs this treatment to draw out surplus water. If you rear your own pigs as in the past we have, and certainly if you run your pigs on grass like Gloucester Old Spots, you'll find that there is no need for pre-salting. But if you are buying your meat it's probably best to take the advice of your butcher. If salted, wash off the surplus and set the meat aside.

Measure 6 litres (10 pt) rain or spring water, and put it into a pan with the salt, sugar and saltpetre; bring very slowly to the boil, stirring occasionally. Skim off any froth as it appears and then remove the pan from the heat.

Tie the juniper berries, nutmeg, bay leaves, thyme, peppercorns and cloves in a small square of muslin and add to the hot brine. Leave the cure to cool completely.

Place the pork in a scalded crock or plastic container and pour the cure over the meat. If necessary place a large stone or weight, wrapped in a plastic bag, on top of the meat to keep it below the surface of the brine. After 2 days extract the bag of spices and discard.

I find in cold weather that 10–14 days is about the best length of time to brine – less, of course, in hot weather.

Remove the meat and soak in cold water for 6–10 hours. Place in a preserving pan or large saucepan and cover with cold water. Slowly bring to the boil and taste the water – if it is very salty, pour off and replace with fresh water. Add a cloved onion and the carrots and bay leaves and bring to the boil. Turn down the heat and keep the temperature just below simmering for 3–3½ hours. If you prefer to cook the ham right through at this stage it will need longer cooking but a meat thermometer put into the thickest part of the meat will indicate when the meat is cooked.

Remove the pan from the heat and allow to cool for about 1 hour. Then lift out the ham and remove the skin. Leave the meat to cool overnight. Then carve off about one third to half the meat.

Spread a large sheet of heavy-duty foil in a roasting pan and place half the hay on it. Place the ham on top and cover with another layer of hay. Fold up the foil to enclose the meat completely and bake in a moderate oven (Mark 4, 180°C, 350°F) for about 1 hour. Remove from the oven – do not unwrap it – and leave to cool. When the ham is cold, unwrap it and discard the hay, taking care to remove every strand. Leave the ham in a cold place for 6–8 hours before carving. The flavour is superb and, for serving at Easter, is preferable to that of smoked ham.

Serve both flavours of ham on large platters.

FOIE DE PORC FARCI

STUFFED PIG'S LIVER

If you can get your butcher to sell you a pig's liver whole, before he slices it up, then you may like to try this Périgord recipe for a hearty and definitely cold weather dish, slightly adapted from La Mazille.

1 pig's liver
30 g (1 oz) *lard fumé* or smoked streaky bacon, diced
2 shallots, finely chopped
1 clove of garlic, finely chopped
2 tablespoons fresh breadcrumbs
2 eggs, beaten
salt, milled pepper
finely grated zest of a lemon
a piece of pork skin if available
1 onion, sliced
a few tablespoons tomato juice

With a sharp knife cut a pocket in the pig's liver large enough to take the stuffing.

Sauté the *lard fumé* in a pan, add the shallots and garlic and, when softened, remove from the heat. Stir in the breadcrumbs, the eggs and some salt and pepper. My addition to the recipe is some finely grated zest of lemon but you may prefer to leave it out.

Pack the stuffing into the pig's liver and close up the opening, securing the edges with small needle skewers if necessary.

If you have it, line a casserole with the piece of pork skin, fat side up. Place the pig's liver on top and cover with the onion. Pour over the tomato juice and cover with a lid or a piece of foil. Cook in a moderate oven (Mark 4, 180°C, 350°F) for 30 minutes or until cooked. Serve cut into slices with puréed potatoes. Serves 3–4.

SAUCISSON EN BRIOCHE

BRIOCHE STUFFED WITH SAUSAGE

Judging from charcuterie windows this very superior kind of sausage roll is not normally made at home. But if you've already devoted some time to preparing a brioche dough or, as I do, simply enjoy yeast cooking, you may like to bake a garlic sausage this way. I use an 840 ml (1½ pt) loaf tin and the ideal sausage for this is 4–5 cm (1½–2 in) across and about 2.5 cm (1 inch) shorter than the tin.

15 g (½ oz) fresh yeast *or* 2
   teaspoons dried yeast
½ teaspoon caster sugar
225 g (8 oz) strong white
   bread flour
2 large eggs

½ teaspoon salt
85 g (3 oz) butter, melted
340 g (12 oz) garlic sausage
1 beaten egg
a little extra flour

Cream the fresh yeast with the sugar in a warm mixing bowl and blend in 2 tablespoons warm water. If using dried yeast simply stir the yeast and the sugar into the water. Set aside in a warm place for 5–10 minutes until the mixture is frothy.

Add the flour to one side of the bowl and pour the eggs beaten with the salt into the centre of the bowl. Pour the melted butter to the other side of the bowl. Use a wooden spoon to mix everything together. Then beat with the spoon for 5–10 minutes, stretching the dough as much as possible, until it becomes elastic and less sticky. Alternatively mix the dough in a processor for 1 minute.

Cover the bowl with a plastic bag and leave at room temperature for 1–2 hours until the dough has doubled in bulk. Gently knock down the dough and place in a plastic bag. Chill in the refrigerator for about 1 hour.

Skin the sausage, brush with egg and roll in flour. On a floured surface roll out the dough to make a rectangle just large enough to wrap round the sausage. Press the joins together and cut away any surplus dough, place the sausage roll, join side down, in the well-greased tin.

Brush the top with beaten egg and decorate with leaves cut from the dough trimmings. Leave the tin in a warm place for about 30 minutes until the dough is puffy.

Bake in a moderately hot oven (Mark 6, 200°C, 400°F) for 25–30 minutes, until the brioche crust is golden brown and is starting to shrink away from the sides of the tin.

Turn out on to a wire rack to cool or serve hot, cut in slices. Serves 6.

BROCHETTES DE MERGUEZ

MERGUEZ SAUSAGES ON SKEWERS

Of course, a *merguez* sausage* is very good threaded on to a skewer, grilled over charcoal, and served as it is. But I prefer to add some mushrooms, ideally those preserved in oil (see p. 84) and some red and green peppers; these vegetables contrast well with the spicy sausages seasoned with *harissa* (the fiery north African tomato paste) to make excellent outdoor food.

1 large red pepper	salt, milled pepper
1 large green pepper	450 g (1 lb) *merguez*
18–24 button mushrooms	sausages
2–3 tablespoons olive oil	
finely chopped chives or spring onions	

Halve and de-seed the peppers and cut into neat pieces large enough to thread on to skewers. Mix the peppers in a dish with the mushrooms and spoon over the olive oil mixed with the chives or spring onions and a little salt and pepper. Toss the vegetables lightly until completely coated.

When ready to cook, thread skewers with alternating pieces of green and red peppers, mushrooms and *merguez* sausages, bending each sausage round so that you thread it twice with a piece of pepper in between.

Place the skewers under a hot grill or over a barbecue and cook,

* From Fenns of Piccadilly and Nigel Schofield (addresses on p. 93); *harissa* can also be obtained from Fenns of Piccadilly.

turning now and again until the fat runs from the sausages and they are completely cooked. Serve with French bread. Serves 3–4.

FROMAGE DE TÊTE

BRAWN

This recipe for brawn, also known, in a direct translation, as head cheese, comes from a booklet of old family recipes written by the mothers and grandmothers of Valvignères for a group of young people in the village who were keen to preserve them. With great enterprise, they photocopied the collection and sold them at the annual village festival.

First salt the pig's head, or half-head, for 2–3 days. You may be able to persuade your butcher to do this for you. But otherwise make a good layer of salt in a large bowl and bed the pig's head into it, rub salt into the cut surfaces and sprinkle a good layer of salt over the head. Leave in a cool place for 2–3 days but pour off the liquid each day.

Wash off the salt and soak the head in cold water for 8–12 hours. Place in a large pan (I usually use a preserving pan) and pour in water to cover. Add 3 glasses of white wine, some cloves of garlic, parsley, carrots, onions, leeks, a few cloves and peppercorns and very little salt, if any. It's best to add salt later.

Bring the water to the boil very slowly, turn down the heat and allow the pig's head to simmer very gently, for 4–8 hours until the meat falls easily from the bone. Add extra water during the cooking, if necessary.

Take out the head and on several large plates take all the meat from the bones and chop it neatly but not too small. Spoon the meat into one large or several smaller bowls or jars.

Strain the stock and taste. Reduce ½–1 litre (1–2 pints) with a glass of white wine, checking the taste now and again until you have about the right amount to pour over the meat. (If the stock that's over tastes good enough, store in the freezer for cooking dried peas or beans.)

Leave the containers of brawn in a cool place until set, turn out and slice. Serve as a hors d'oeuvre or place the sliced brawn on a serving dish, pour over a vinaigrette mixed with plenty of fresh herbs and serve as one of the cold dishes at a family lunch or buffet meal.

VERMICELLES SAUTÉES

VERMICELLI WITH PORK AND PRAWNS

The influence of a past or present empire on the cuisine of a country is fascinating to observe. During the last twenty years some eastern foods, bowls of *tabbouleh* or a pile of neatly folded *nems* made from thin rice pancakes, have started to appear in charcuterie windows alongside the traditional French pork dishes. And Vietnamese restaurants are becoming as common in France as Indian ones here. The Vietnamese restaurant we know best is an unexpected find, deep in the Ardèche countryside. This recipe was given to me in a village in the Var by a Vietnamese girl whose family had arrived as refugees some years ago. It is quickly prepared and delicious, ideal for holiday cooking.

250 g (9 oz) angel's hair vermicelli or rice sticks
2 or 3 boneless pork shoulder steaks
salt, milled pepper
2 tablespoons light-coloured soy sauce
1 medium-sized leek
1 carrot
115 g (4 oz) button mushrooms
250 g (9 oz) peeled, cooked prawns
sunflower oil

Cover the vermicelli with boiling water, leave to soften and then drain well.

Cut the pork into narrow strips. Toss the meat in a bowl with some salt, pepper and the soy sauce. Mix well and leave for 15 minutes.

Cut the leek and carrot into fine matchsticks and quarter the mushrooms. Heat a tablespoon or so of the oil in a pan or wok and add the meat. Stir-fry for 4 minutes. Add the leek, carrot and mushrooms and stir-fry for another 2–3 minutes.

Transfer the meat and vegetables to a hot serving dish. Add a little more oil to the pan and add the vermicelli. Stir-fry until transparent and taste to check the vermicelli is cooked. Return the meat and vegetables to the pan and when hot add the prawns. Stir everything together and serve straight away. Serves 4.

PÂTÉ DE FOIE DE PORC

PORK LIVER PÂTÉ

Nowadays, unless it is needed for a large party, I prefer to cook a pâté in several small jars. Some I seal with fat – these will keep well in a very cold room or the refrigerator for a week or so. But if I have some small preserving jars free, I use them to store some of the pâté; sealed with a rubber ring and a glass top, it will keep for several months in a cold place. This is a basic recipe – I vary the spices or seasonings each time I make it; sometimes I add a little rosemary or thyme or perhaps some finely shredded leaves of celery, which lightens the flavour of pork liver.

750 g (1 lb 11 oz) belly pork
255 g (9 oz) pork fat
450 g (1 lb) pig's liver
1 shallot, finely chopped
a slim clove of garlic, finely
  chopped
½ wineglass dry white
  wine

2 tablespoons brandy
1–2 tablespoons salt
2 teaspoons *quatre-épices*
  (see p. 89)
2 eggs, beaten

Cut the belly pork into pieces, removing any bones or pieces of gristle. Mince the belly pork with the pork fat and the liver on a medium or fine setting. Mix together well in a large bowl with the shallot, garlic, wine, brandy, salt and spices. Cover and leave overnight in a cold place.

Next day mix in the eggs and, if you wish to check the flavour, test-fry a teaspoonful and adjust the seasoning as necessary.

Spoon the mixture into a 1 litre (2 pt) ceramic or cast-iron terrine. Or fill several heat-proof glass storage jars, leaving 2.5 cm (1 in) space under the glass lids (fitted with new rubber rings).

Cook in a bain-marie in a moderate oven (Mark 4, 180°C, 350°F) for about 2 hours for the terrine or about 1 hour for the jars. The pâté is cooked when a needle comes out of the centre clean. Remove and leave to cool. When lukewarm place a weight on top of the terrine to compress the mixture and make it easier to slice.

Jars of pâté without lids can be covered with a layer of melted pork fat or greaseproof paper if the pâté is to be served within 4 days. Store in the refrigerator. Makes about 1½ kg (3 lb) of pâté.

SAUCISSES DE CAMPAGNE

COUNTRY-STYLE SAUSAGES

I've made English-style sausages, without skins, for some time. And now I've tried this French kind, with a coarser cut and more highly seasoned filling. They taste very good and make excellent outdoor eating.

1 kg (2¼ lb) lean shoulder of pork, boned	½ teaspoon *quatre-épices* (see p. 89)
½ kg (18 oz) belly pork	4 tablespoons red wine
2 tablespoons salt	1 clove of garlic, crushed
½ teaspoon crushed peppercorns	a pinch of saltpetre
	2 m (7 ft) sausage casings

Cut up the meat and mince it coarsely into a bowl. Add the salt, peppercorns, *quatre-épices*, wine, garlic and saltpetre. Mix together well, using your hands so that the seasonings penetrate the meat. If you wish, fry a teaspoon of the mixture to check on the seasoning and adjust if necessary.

Wash the sausage casing in warm water. Knot one end and, using a sausage-filling funnel (*un entonnoir*) and a baton, fill the casing – or use a sausage-filling machine. Do not pack the meat in too tightly. Tie the end and, every 15 cm (6 in), twist the casing to make the sausages. Use a fine needle to prick the string of sausages in several places for any air to escape and hang them in a very cold place for 2–4 days depending on the time of year. Makes 1½ kg (about 3 lb) sausages.

In the Ardèche the sausages are fried in a pan over high heat with a little lard and some unpeeled cloves of garlic for 5 minutes. Pour in a glass of wine or water and cover the pan. Lower the heat and simmer for 10 minutes until cooked. Serve with potatoes.

SAINDOUX

LARD

Lard is simple to make at home where it is easy to improve its flavour further, if you wish, by adding some Provençal herbs. Rosemary or thyme give an extra dimension to this pure pork fat, which is the main cooking medium of upland central France, notably the Auvergne.

Cut about 1 kg (2 lb) of hard white pork fat into even-sized pieces. Place in a pan with a wineglass of cold water and gradually bring to the boil, stirring now and again.

Add a sprig or two of rosemary or thyme, or a little *herbes de Provence* (see p. 19) and cook over moderate heat until the fat is totally liquid.

Cool slightly and then strain through a muslin-lined metal sieve into mugs or bowls. Leave to set, and then cover and store in a very cold place or the refrigerator until needed for cooking.

In the south of France the small crisp pieces of skin and harder fat are used to make a *fougasse* (see p. 109).

SAUCISSON SEC DE CAMPAGNE

A matured *saucisson sec* is one of the most delicious examples of French charcuterie. Farmers' wives still produce these salami-type sausages in country districts. A friend who makes them several times a year stores the sausages in wood ash until they are ready to eat. When a small notice appears on the corner of the farmhouse telling you they are for sale, I dash across to buy one straight away. They travel well for picnics, but are also good served thinly sliced as an hors d'oeuvre with olives.

1 kg (2¼ lb) lean shoulder of pork	1 teaspoon *quatre-épices*
340 g (12 oz) hard back fat	½ teaspoon caster sugar
1 clove of garlic, crushed	1 teaspoon saltpetre
4 tablespoons salt	about ½ m (20 in) large
1 teaspoon black peppercorns	intestine

Mince the meat, dice the fat finely and mix with the meat, garlic, salt, peppercorns, *quatre-épices*, saltpetre and sugar. Use your hands or a wooden spoon to mix everything together well for 4–5 minutes so that the spices flavour the meat.

Test-fry a teaspoonful if you wish to check the taste; this sausage should be highly seasoned.

Attach one end of the intestine to a tap and rinse out well with warm water. Tie one end with string and fill the casing with the pork mixture, using a wide funnel and a rammer, packing the meat in tightly. If you find any air pockets, prick the casing with a fine needle to release the air.

Tie both ends of each sausage with string. Hang the sausage in a dry place, with a constant temperature of 25°C (60°F), for 4 to 5 days. Move the sausages to a cool, dry place for 1–2 months. Then, if you wish, store the sausages in wood ash for a few days; finally brush off the dust and hang the sausages in a cool, airy place until you wish to eat them. Cut in very thin slices for serving.

ROGNONS EN CHEMISE

KIDNEYS ROASTED IN THEIR OWN FAT

This must be the simplest way ever to cook a kidney. And the result is highly delicious. Both pig's and lamb's kidneys can be roasted this way. The most difficult part is buying the kidneys still in their covering of fat – you need two or three for each person. Place the kidneys on a trivet in a roasting pan and cook in a moderately hot oven (Mark 6, 200°C, 400°F) for 15–20 minutes until the fat has melted (pour it off and keep it for roasting potatoes on another occasion) and the kidney is just cooked and is still tender.

Serve the roast kidneys with apple sauce and creamed potatoes mixed with chopped chives.

GRATTONS OU GRATTERONS

These are the French equivalent of scratchings, small pieces of pork skin cooked until crisp and golden. We like them, served hot from the oven, sprinkled with a few crushed dried *herbes de Provence*

(see p. 19) to go with beer, cider or a country wine after an autumn morning of gardening or hill-walking.

Cut the skin from a piece of belly pork or a joint of loin of pork. It can be from any piece of the pig. Leave a layer of fat under the skin about 2 cm (¾ in) thick.

Use a very sharp knife to cut the pork skin into 6 cm (2½ in) squares. Make a few gashes across the fat side to help the fat melt more quickly.

Take a cast-iron casserole or pan and, when quite hot, add the pork skin, fat side down; shake the pan now and again to ensure that the pork has not stuck to the base.

Transfer the pan to a slow oven (Mark 2, 150°C, 300°F) for 3–4 hours. Or cook on the hob, set at low to medium, over a heat-spreading mat, for 2–3 hours or until the *grattons* are golden and crisp, like the best crackling, and the fat has totally melted.

Pour off the liquid fat and reserve for cooking potatoes; lift out the *grattons*, sprinkle with salt and serve. In country districts they are served with a plate of puréed potatoes.

FOUGASSE

If you bake your own bread you may like to make these crisp, flat loaves from the south of France. A *fougasse* is seasoned with crushed *grattons* (see above) and is made in a distinctive shape, either like a hand with short fingers or the dough is slashed to make a kind of trellis; it bakes to a golden brown and children, especially, love breaking off the pieces from these oddly shaped loaves to crunch as a snack.

> **450 g (1 lb) white bread**
> **dough, ready for baking**
> **85 g (3 oz) *grattons***
> **1–2 tablespoons olive oil**

Place the bread dough on a floured board and flatten slightly.

Crush the *grattons* – either tip them into a plastic bag and pound into small pieces with a rolling-pin or chop until small in a processor or blender.

Spread the *grattons* over the dough, fold over and knead for 3–4 minutes until well distributed. Divide the dough in half and roll out each piece to an oval shape about 1 cm (½ in) thick.

Take the first oval and make about six cuts around the outside radiating from one end to make short stubby fingers. Place on a floured baking sheet.

Roll out the second piece of dough until longer. Make 5 or 6 parallel cuts in the short direction right through the dough so that the loaf resembles a ladder. Stretch slightly to separate the rung-like strips of dough and place on a floured baking sheet. Brush both loaves with olive oil.

Leave in a warm place for about 30 minutes until the dough is puffy. Bake in a very hot oven (Mark 8, 230°C, 450°F) for 10 minutes; lower the heat to Mark 6 (200°C, 400°F) for 20 minutes, when the bread should be golden and crisp. Remove from the oven, brush with olive oil and cool on a wire tray.

THE OLIVE

Nothing in the south seems older than the olive. Neither the smooth symmetry of the arena of Nîmes, nor the fretted outline of the Pont du Gard, nor even the rocks themselves, bleached white by the sun. Olive trees have grown here since before the Romans came. It's thought that the Phocaean Greeks introduced the olive to Provence around 650 BC. To northern eyes, accustomed to a sappy verdure, the olive tree appears almost dead; its dull grey-green sabre leaves rustle like old paper even when new, and its twisted and contorted limbs seem beyond life. But in fact, the lifespan of an olive tree is immense – most live from three to six hundred years, and a few span ten centuries.

Olive trees have an almost hypnotic effect on me; I cannot remain unaware of them. Whether I see one or a hundred, my attention is held. It's an odd yet peaceful feeling. And while for me this experience is a personal and private celebration of a venerable tree and its life-giving fruit, the people of the south are gloriously public about it.

On the first Saturday in July, in Nyons, ten men dressed in white, their green waistcoats trimmed with red, raise trumpets to their mouths and a fanfare echoes across the square to announce the start of the olive festival. These are the *Chevaliers des Olives*, an association founded by the mayor a generation or so ago to protect and propagate the appreciation of the olive.

Nyons, itself, sheltered from the *mistral* wind by the low hills of Les Baronnies, is home to the most delicious olive in France. Small, oval and black, its dry yet buttery flavour has an intensity and almost wine-like taste unequalled anywhere. And, of course, the oil produced from these olives is superb. No matter that the oil has collected prizes and accolades for a century, your tongue and your palate will tell you that this is a classic among olive oils. It's not just a liquid that you slurp over salads or mix with lemon juice or wine vinegar; it is also a food with a flavour and consistency to be valued in its own right. One of my grandfathers swallowed a teaspoonful every day of his life when olive oil was kept in the medicine cupboard. Thank heavens that today, in Britain, this generous liquid has made its way on to supermarket shelves and into grocers' shops. And although you can still buy olive oil at the chemist's, it is now on the food counter.

It is an old country custom that olives should be picked with a waxing moon. The first olives are picked green and unripe in September; these are known as *olives d'été* or *olives amères*, because they will still have a slightly bitter flavour when eaten the following summer. The bitterness is not leached out as is necessary with other green olives. They are simply put into a 10 per cent solution of brine with some Provençal herbs and are cured for 6–8 months before serving.

In October the main crop of green olives is picked. They are soaked in an alkaline solution, sometimes made by mixing wood ash with water to remove some of the bitterness, and are then pickled in brine for a month or so. A few olives are picked when they are turning purple and on their way to acquiring the brown-black colour of the fully ripe fruit. Ripe olives need only to be soaked in cold water for twenty-four hours before brining.

There are a few varieties of olive which remain green when fully ripe. The Verdales variety grown around the village of Beaumes de Venise is picked, when green, specially for pressing to produce one of the finest *vierge extra* olive oils in France.

The olive oil cooperative La Balméene has sixty-four members and they each bring their olive crop – sometimes only a few kilos but for others a trailer load – to the mill at the crossroads in Beaumes as soon as the olives are ripe enough to press. Here they are stored at room temperature for three to four days until very slightly fermented. After the dust of the countryside has been washed away the olives travel down a chute into the mill itself. Every stage of the operation is carried out at as low a temperature as possible in order to retain the fine bouquet and flavour of the oil. And because olive oil attacks iron, every piece of equipment at the mill must be stainless steel.

M. Joel, the manager of the mill, showed me how the olives are first crushed gently between two cylindrical rollers, *éclatteurs*. Then a flanged screw – as in a domestic mincer – pushes the crushed olives into the mill which is as wide as a bed and about seven metres long. The oil is crushed from the olives by a series of massive ballbearings, at first the size of a cannon ball and weighing seven kilos, then reducing in size through the four chambers of the mill, each separated by an increasingly fine stainless-steel mesh.

The cylindrical mill revolves fifty times a minute; as the mixture of olive pulp and oil moves into the *pressoir* the olive stones are extracted. These are shrewdly stored and burnt as fuel for the mill's heating system. The olive pulp is now extracted; in some areas of France it is converted into animal feed, in others it becomes fertilizer. The mixture of oil and water is filtered into a centrifuge where the oil rises to the top, to be siphoned off into storage tanks for bottling.

If you are living near by you may prefer to buy the oil in a large plastic container which sits easily in the back of the 2CV beside the similar plastic container of *vin de pays* from the *caves* up the road. In England, Yapp Brothers of Mere, Wiltshire, sell the Beaumes de Venise olive oil from La Balméene as well as another Provençal olive oil, from Paul and Pierre Bunan in Bandol.

In many villages in Provence the older, stone oil mills are still to be found. There is a particularly fine example which is easy to view in the Syndicat d'Initiative in Carcès – an attractive small town in Var. Here you can see the huge stone wheel which tracks round the circular trough, crushing the olives in its path. The design is remarkably like that of a stone cider mill still in use in our Devon village. A stone conduit led the oil and water mixture to a vat which was heated by a small fire lit underneath. The heat evaporated the water from the mixture and the oil – which was once also a source of heat and light in Provence – was run into wooden barrels. These then travelled back to the farms and cottages set amongst the olive groves.

The best olive oil is cold pressed and the finest oil is graded as *vierge extra*, or virgin extra, and it contains no more than 1 per cent oleic acid. But a *vierge* or virgin oil with a slightly higher acidity of up to 4 per cent is still a fine oil. Although oils are graded by their acidity, the really important test is performed by the palate. On occasions one prefers an oil with a pronounced bouquet, at other times the feel of the oil with its sensation of buttery fatness takes preference. All olive oil should be kept just below room temperature and out of sunlight, preferably in a dark cupboard.

To my mind, the finest salad in France is dressed with the olive oil from Provence. It is served in a bowl made from the wavy light and dark shaded wood of the tree itself, a tree which also gives us the symbol of peace – the olive branch.

TOURTE AUX OLIVES ET AUX ANCHOIS

OLIVE AND ANCHOVY TART

Pâte brisée
115 g (4 oz) flour
55 g (2 oz) butter, softened
1 egg yolk
¼ teaspoon salt
1–2 tablespoons ice-cold
   water.

Filling
115 g (4 oz) green olives
5 anchovy fillets
1 tablespoon capers
1 slim clove of garlic
2 tablespoons olive oil
1 large egg
2–3 tablespoons boiled rice
1 teaspoon finely grated
   zest of lemon
1 tablespoon parsley, finely
   chopped

Make the pastry in the usual way (see p. 78). Roll out thinly and line a 20–23 cm (8–9 in) tart tin or six 10 cm (4 in) tartlet tins. Prick the base of the pastry all over and chill the cases in the refrigerator for 15–30 minutes.

Bake in a moderately hot oven (Mark 6, 200°C, 400°F) for 10–15 minutes until lightly coloured.

Stone the olives and set aside one third; chop the remainder finely and mix with the rinsed and finely chopped anchovies, the capers and the garlic. Pound the mixture together, or mix in a processor, until finely chopped. Stir in half the olive oil, the egg, rice, lemon zest and the parsley.

Spoon into the pastry case or cases and spread level. Scatter the remaining olives, roughly chopped, on top and dribble over the rest of the oil.

Bake in a moderately hot oven for 10–15 minutes until set. Serve hot or cold. Serves 6.

OLIVES À L'ESCABÈCHE

ESCABECHE-STYLE OLIVES

Fried fish more commonly receives the attention of this hot spicy Arab seasoning, but nowadays Moroccan olives are prepared this way too.

225 g (8 oz) green olives	**½ teaspoon coriander seed,**
½ lemon, thinly sliced	**bruised**
1 clove of garlic, sliced	**2 teaspoons tomato paste**
½ usual size red chilli or 2	
of the miniature size	

If the olives are in brine, drain well and tip them into a bowl. Quarter the slices of lemon and add to the bowl with the garlic, chopped chilli pepper, coriander seed and tomato paste.

Mix everything together and spoon into a jar. Cover and keep in a very cold place or the refrigerator, turning the jar every day, for 3 days before serving.

OLIVES VERTES D'ABEL BROC

ABEL BROC'S GREEN OLIVES

M. Abel Broc lives next door to the Marquets. In early October when his olives are still green he picks some for home preserving, and the rest are left to ripen on the trees to be crushed for oil.

12 kg (26 lb) green olives	**Brine**
1 litre (1¾ pt) sodium	**80 g (scant 3 oz) salt per**
hydroxide	**litre of water**

Wash the dust from the olives and remove their stalks. Prick each olive with a hatpin if you have time.

Mix 9 litres (2 gallons) cold water with the sodium carbonate, stir until dissolved and then add the olives. Leave in the solution for 8 hours and then pour off the liquid. Cover with clean cold water and leave for 4–5 days, changing the water every night and morning. Then drain the olives.

Pack into jars or a barrel. Dissolve the salt in the water. Make up more brine as you see how much you need and pour over the olives, making sure they are covered.

If you wish, tuck a few herbs into the brine: fennel, rosemary or a bay leaf. Store the olives in a cold place for at least a month before eating.

OLIVES NOIRES EN HUILE

BLACK OLIVES IN OIL

Fully ripened brown-black olives have a mild earthy flavour with no trace of the astringency we value in green olives. Black olives are simpler to prepare.

1½ kg (3–3½ lb) black olives	4–6 cloves of garlic, chopped
450 g (1 lb) salt	1 litre (1¾ pt) olive oil
1 tablespoon black peppercorns	

Wash and drain the olives if dusty. Mix the olives with the salt and tip into a jar or crock. Leave in a cold place for a week.

Pour off the brine and taste an olive; if too salty, rinse the olives in cold water and drain well.

Pack the olives into jars or one larger container. Add the peppercorns and garlic and pour over the olive oil, making sure all the olives are covered. Seal and leave the container in a cold place. Use a pierced olive spoon to take out olives as required. Use the oil in salad dressings.

The best way to store bought olives, black or green, is under oil. Simply empty the olives into a jar. Add any dry herbs, a clove of garlic or some peppercorns or a sliced lemon and cover with olive oil.

OLIVES VIOLETTES

PURPLE OLIVES

Purple olives are picked when they have passed from the green stage and are half-way to being fully ripe. They are frequently prepared with lemon or with bitter oranges.

> 1½ kg (3–3½ lb) purple
>   olives
> 3–4 lemons
> 340 g (12 oz) salt

Wash the olives and drain well. Make a slit in the side of each olive; if the olives are specially large make a slit on each side.

Tip the olives into a crock or preserving jar and cover with cold water. Cover with a close-fitting lid and leave in a cold place for 5 weeks, changing the water after 3½ weeks.

Slice the lemons and mix with the salt.

Drain and rinse the olives. Replace in the crock or preserving jar, layering with the salted lemon mixture, making sure to have a lemon layer on top.

Next day, if necessary, add a little cold water so that the liquid covers the olives. Cover and leave for 7 days. The olives should then be ready to eat.

OLIVES À LA PICHOLINE

PICHOLINE-STYLE OLIVES

Picholine is the name given to a variety of olive, large and long and always picked green. Although grown in parts of Languedoc, Drôme and the Ardèche, the method of preparing them is also used with fleshy green olives from elsewhere in the south.

> 5 kg (11 lb) fleshy green   5 kg (11 lb) wood ash
>   olives   cold water

Brine
1 kg (2¼ lb) salt
bay leaves
a few flat heads of fennel
   seeds

a strip of orange peel
1 tablespoon coriander
   seed, lightly crushed

Turn the olives, free of stems or leaves, into a large bowl or bucket. Mix in the wood ash and sufficient water to make a thick paste.

Leave the olives in this *lessive*, stirring them once or twice a day, for 10–12 days, or until under pressure of your fingernail the flesh comes away easily from the stone.

Rinse the olives thoroughly in plenty of cold water which is changed every day for 9 days.

Make the brine in a large pan by dissolving the salt in 10 litres (a generous 2 gallons) water and bring to the boil with the bay leaf, fennel, orange rind and coriander seed. Simmer for 10 minutes and allow to cool.

Cover the drained olives with the cold brine and store, covered, stirring every day, for at least one week before eating.

Caneton aux Olives

DUCK WITH OLIVES

A classic dish in French cooking. The slightly bitter green olives act as a beautiful foil to the rich-tasting duck.

2–2½ kg (4–5 lb) duckling
salt, milled pepper
1 slice *lard fumé* or smoked
   streaky bacon, diced
1 shallot, finely chopped
1 tablespoon olive oil
3–4 tablespoons *vieux*
   marc or whisky

100 g (3½ oz) fresh, white
   breadcrumbs
about 24 green olives
finely grated zest of ½
   orange
a small knob of butter
¼ teaspoon flour
stock made with the giblets

If necessary dry the duckling with kitchen paper and then sprinkle lightly with salt.

Cook the diced bacon and chopped shallot in the olive oil until soft, add half the *marc* and tip the contents of the pan into a bowl. Mix in the breadcrumbs, some salt and milled pepper, the chopped flesh of half the olives and the zest of orange. If the mixture is too dry, add a little hot water to bind. Spoon the stuffing into the duck.

Melt the butter and brown the duck all over. Transfer to a trivet in a roasting tin and roast the duck in a moderately hot oven (Mark 6, 200°C, 400°F) for 1–1¼ hours or until cooked to your wishes. Pour off excess fat during the cooking.

Transfer the duck to a hot serving plate and keep warm until ready to serve.

Pour off all excess fat from the roasting tin and stir the flour into the juices. Flame with the remaining *marc* and add the rest of the olives and sufficient stock to make a small quantity of sauce. Taste and adjust the seasoning.

Carve the duck and serve with the stuffing and sauce. Serves 4.

PAN BAGNA

This is the well-known sandwich of the south of France. Sad to say, but I feel that *pan bagna* never tastes quite as good anywhere else. But the sandwich is still worth making in Britain, in a hot summer. *Pan bagna* is ideal for a picnic and children love assembling and especially squashing one. In France a *flûte* makes a better *pan bagna*, a *baguette* is too narrow. For a large number of people I use country bread, like *pain de seigle*, which is baked in a round or oval shape. These thicker loaves are best cut in three or four layers to make a three- or four-fold *pan bagna*.

Cut the *flûte* into two layers, rub a clove of garlic over both cut surfaces and dribble a good fruity olive oil over them.

Now build the filling on one half of the loaf: make a layer of sliced tomato and strew a few torn leaves of basil on top, then perhaps some very thinly sliced salami or *saucisson sec*, but remember to take off the skin first, some anchovy fillets always go well and a few stoned black olives for a true taste of the Midi. Then add whatever items you feel would improve the sandwich, bearing in mind what you have already included.

Place the other half of the loaf on top and wrap the sandwich in foil and then in a clean teacloth. Place the *pan bagna* on the kitchen table or at the bottom of a cool box or picnic basket. Arrange some books, stones or other moderately heavy weights on top and leave for up to 1 hour, until the filling is pressed into the bread and the flavours of each have blended together. For serving, cut the *pan bagna* into sections. Serves 2–4.

BEURRE DE MONTPELLIER

MONTPELLIER BUTTER

A non-butter butter which depends on egg yolks and olive oil to thicken the purée of herbs. I find the flavour of Montpellier butter improves if made about 8 hours ahead. Serve it on hot or cold fish and eggs.

115 g (4 oz) mixed fresh herbs and leaves comprising equal quantities of the following: tarragon, chives, parsley, chervil, watercress, and a few leaves of sorrel and spinach
1 slim shallot, very finely chopped
5 anchovy fillets, rinsed and chopped

1 tablespoon capers
2 small pickled gherkins, finely chopped
1 slim clove of garlic
3 egg yolks, hard-boiled
1 egg yolk, raw
55–85 ml (2–3 fl oz) olive oil
lemon juice
salt
cayenne pepper

Remove the stems from the herbs and shred the larger leaves. Stir the shallot into a pan of salted boiling water and add the herbs. Blanch for 1 minute, drain well in a sieve, pressing out as much water as possible, and turn the mixture on to a plate to cool.

Chop the herbs finely in a processor, blender or *moulinette* and mix to a purée with the anchovy fillets, capers, gherkins, garlic, cooked egg yolks and raw egg yolk.

When the mixture is almost uniformly green, beat in sufficient olive oil to make a thickish sauce. Sharpen the taste slightly with lemon juice and season with salt and cayenne pepper. For a very smooth, uniform Montpellier butter the mixture could now be sieved but I prefer the delicately flecked look. Spoon the butter into a dish, cover and chill for a few hours before serving.

FAISAN AUX OLIVES

PHEASANT WITH OLIVES

a brace of young pheasants	1 clove of garlic, chopped
a walnut-sized knob of butter	a bay leaf
	about 18 black olives
1 tablespoon olive oil	1 wineglass red wine
salt, milled pepper	1–2 tablespoons whisky or brandy
2 slim leeks, shredded	
1 carrot, sliced	about 12 green olives

Take a cast-iron casserole large enough to hold both pheasants. Melt the butter with the oil and brown the birds all over; lift them out on to a plate and season all over with salt and pepper.

Soften the leeks, carrot and garlic in the remaining oil. Add a bay leaf, half the black olives, stoned, and the wine. Place the pheasants on top, breast side down, and cover with a lid.

Cook in a moderate oven (Mark 5, 190°C, 375°F) for 1–1½ hours until the pheasants are cooked.

Move the pheasants on to a hot serving dish. Halve or joint them now, if more convenient. Scoop any surplus fat from the sauce; set the casserole over high heat and flame with the whisky or brandy. Mash the vegetables in the sauce to a purée (sieve if necessary) and add all the remaining olives. Heat the sauce through; if too thick, thin with a little stock. Then spoon over the pheasant. Serves 4–6.

Happily, there is always more of France to discover. Only a year or so ago we found ourselves in Haute Provence, an upland region of great beauty. I remember travelling from Forcalquier, near the silver-domed national observatory, along a road that swoops down to Manosque and the valley of the river Durance. It crossed the most northerly end of the Lubéron hills where vast rocks embedded in mossy banks bordered the narrow route. Pink and blue alpine flowers and stubby broom bushes in yellow and white emblazoned the path for mile after mile. It was like some huge rock garden, landscaped and arranged by a benevolent landowner for everyone's pleasure. Now and again a narrow track disappeared into the hills on either side of the road. Sometimes a signboard told us that a game farm lay at the end of the track. Here quail and pheasant, guinea-fowl and partridge live in pastoral splendour, but behind bars. Farm-reared game is sold locally, but each year more and more of it travels to Lyons, Paris, Nice and even London. This has happened partly because the French enjoy the relentless pursuit of *la chasse*; on Sundays, in season, thousands of guns are allowed to let fly at almost anything that moves. Only on private and protected estates are you likely to see what, thankfully, is almost a daily sight in spring near my Devon home – a cock pheasant strutting proudly through a field of young wheat. But there is also a trend in France towards eating game, which I predict will travel over or under the Channel towards us. This is an excellent development.

For a start, well-reared game and poultry tastes superb. Each breed has a unique flavour, which anyone who enjoys good food appreciates. And, compared with quadrupeds, the meat on game or poultry is weight for weight cheaper to produce. Although a farm-reared quail may have slightly less of a gamy flavour than a wild specimen, this matters less than the fact that by producing these tiny but delicious birds in greater numbers, many more people can use them to add interest and variety to their menus.

I find game a most exciting ingredient. There is, of course, a treasury of game recipes from the past. But in range of flavour and texture, and in the variety of shape and size, I find game makes an inspiring starting point for new recipes. I have included some in this chapter. My style of game cooking is lighter than most traditional recipes: fillet of hare with home-made raspberry vinegar, or quail wrapped in a layer of Florentine fennel to keep it moist and succulent, or woodpigeon braised on a bed of brown rice.

Along with game it is always good, in France, to be able to enjoy chicken again. The golden-fleshed *poulet de Bresse* sit with their blue certificates of authenticity in most butchers' windows. These birds come in all sizes but the neat young *poussin* rarely weighs more than 300 g (10 oz) and its tender flesh has great delicacy. The standard *poulet*, sometimes labelled *de grain*, weighs from ¾–2 kg (1½–4½ lb); it is a spring chicken suitable for roasting, poaching or braising. A *poularde* is a fat hen weighing more than 2 kg (4½ lb) and is usually roasted. A *chapon* is a castrated cock – we know it as a capon – which may be cooked in the same manner as a *poulet*.

Game and cheese are surely the two great partners of wine. Game, of course, is often cooked with wine, particularly in a marinade. And, one realizes, when cooking in France, that the local wine is usually preferable. Not only does the wine made in the nearby *caves* or by your neighbourhood *vigneron* taste better in the place where it is made; it makes the best companion to the food of the region.

It has been encouraging to discover during the last two decades how much small local wines have improved. Access to EEC funds for a group of enterprising vine growers can result in a battery of gleaming stainless steel tanks, temperature-controlled fermenting vats and the panoply of equipment now advised by the Department of Oenology at the University of Bordeaux. Even so, there are still plenty of one-man operations which I always enjoy visiting.

It is also worth keeping a lookout for posters announcing one of the small local wine fairs which punctuate the summer most agreeably in many towns and villages.

The wine fair we enjoyed most recently coincided with the town's celebrations for Bastille Day. The local *vignerons* and representatives from the *caves* of the surrounding villages displayed their wares on tables set up in the dappled shade from the plane trees. Carrying our commemorative wine glasses we made a pilgrimage to each table. Sometimes we knew the *vigneron* or we met friends who were ahead of us in this tasting marathon. There was much merriment along with the knowledgeable discussion of *cépage*, or the vine type, the location and the weather conditions which had played their part in producing each wine.

The *vignerons* feel encouraged to promote their wares in a lively fashion. One had persuaded the local baker to produce a true *pain fantaisie* by mixing the dough with half red wine and half water. The resulting pink bread was eaten with much laughter by the merry company.

Half-way through the afternoon a procession of bewigged aristocrats made their way through the fair preceded by a tumbril accompanied by a stately pope, a blood-stained executioner straight from his cardboard guillotine and the man dressed as Marat who continued to harangue the bourgeoisie as we carried on sampling the wine with as much disdain for water as any tippling Marie Antoinette might display. Only the stall from the town's twin in Alsace was quiet – it was providing milk. But later, during the prize-giving, it was doing well with those about to drive home.

At least once during the summer the local cooperative *cave* holds an open day rather as the town fire-station does in Britain. Tables are set up outside and from early morning until late at night one may sample every wine produced by the *cave*, with a view to persuading you to buy rather more to take home. Between the tastings it is interesting to wander into the wine-making halls to see what is sensibly regarded in the country as an agricultural product with very special qualities. Mercifully there is none of the socially distancing wine snobbery that one comes across this side of the Channel. Here, wine drinking is regarded as a natural and enjoyable part of life, like singing or making love. This is true connoisseurship – in the art of living.

CAILLES AU FENOUIL

QUAILS IN FLORENTINE FENNEL

Due to increased farming here and in France quail is now cheaper. Although the quail is a small-boned bird the meat is surprisingly filling; usually one per person is adequate in a meal with several courses. This is a delightful summer dish which I devised in France but has now been cooked with great success many times here.

2 quails	finely chopped parsley
a large head of Florentine fennel	a squeeze of lemon juice
	salt, milled pepper
55 g (2 oz) butter	1–2 tablespoons Pernod
a few fronds of fennel shoots from the stalk	4 tablespoons *crème fraîche* or whipping cream

Wipe the quails with a damp cloth and set aside.

Detach two of the largest shell-shaped pieces of fennel, carefully detaching them without splitting them. Blanch the fennel in salted boiling water for 1–2 minutes, and then drain.

Soften half the butter and mix with the fennel fronds, finely chopped, the parsley and a squeeze of lemon juice. Melt the remainder of the butter in a flameproof casserole and slightly brown the quail all over. Lift out the birds and place a teaspoon of the savoury butter inside each; spread a little more over the breast of each bird. Reserve a little butter to finish the sauce with later.

Tuck each quail neatly into a shell of fennel so that the fennel looks like what a friend called angel's wings. Season each bird lightly with salt and pepper and place in the casserole. Sprinkle a little Pernod over the quail and cover with a butter paper and a lid. Cook in a moderate oven (Mark 5, 190°C, 375°F) for 30–40 minutes until the meat is cooked.

Transfer the quail and fennel to a hot serving dish, cover with the butter paper and keep hot. Add 1 tablespoon of Pernod to the juices in the casserole and simmer for 1–2 minutes. Stir in the cream and when hot, add the remainder of the herb butter. Taste and add a fraction more Pernod or seasoning if necessary, but the sauce should only hint at the aniseed flavour of the wine, just as an echo of the fennel.

Spoon the sauce over the quail and serve. Serves 2.

PERDREAU AU LAIT

PARTRIDGE COOKED IN MILK

Partridge has been cooked in milk for a very long time. In England, it appeared on the bill of fare at St James's Palace for 21 January 1740. Has the method died out here? In rural France it continues. This is a dish with a delicate but excellent flavour; the sauce simply complements this fine-fleshed bird.

1 partridge	150 ml (¼ pt) very creamy
a few sprigs of thyme or	milk
serpolet	a squeeze of lemon juice
30 g (1 oz) butter	a small knob of butter
1 onion, finely chopped	½ teaspoon flour
salt, milled pepper	

Wipe the partridge with a damp cloth and tuck the thyme or *serpolet* into the body cavity.

Melt the butter in a small flame-proof casserole and lightly brown the partridge all over. Remove the bird and soften the onion in the butter.

Place the partridge on top of the onion and season lightly with salt and pepper. Cover and cook in a moderate oven (Mark 4, 180°C, 350°F) for 30 minutes.

Pour the milk over the partridge, add a dash of lemon juice, cover the casserole and cook for a further 20–30 minutes or until the partridge is cooked.

Transfer the bird to a hot serving dish. Blend the butter with the flour and add to the cooking liquid in small lumps, stirring over moderate heat until thickened. Spoon over the partridge and serve. Serves 2.

PINTADEAU AUX FIGUES

GUINEA-FOWL WITH FIGS

I made this dish one July with a local Drômois guinea-fowl and garden figs. This is really only feasible if you have a glut of figs – rare in England but highly likely in the Midi. Chicken or joints of turkey can replace the guinea-fowl.

> about 2 kg (about 4 lb) guinea-fowl
> 85 g (3 oz) butter
> salt, milled pepper
>
> 900 g (2 lb) figs, washed and halved
> 425 ml (¾ pt) dry white wine

In a casserole, lightly brown the guinea-fowl in two thirds of the butter and season with salt and pepper.

Tuck half the figs around the bird and pour over the wine and 425 ml (¾ pt) water. Cover and cook over moderate heat for about 1 hour or until the guinea-fowl is cooked.

Transfer the bird to a hot serving dish and purée the sauce. Check the seasoning and spoon around the bird.

Sauté the remaining figs in the rest of the butter and garnish the dish with them. Serves 4.

TERRINE DE LIÈVRE
AU MADÈRE

HARE TERRINE WITH MADEIRA

One spring I decided to retrace, as far as possible, the route that Robert Louis Stevenson took in his *Travels with a Donkey in the Cevennes* in 1878. In a remote hamlet I was asked, '*Êtes-vous un Stevenson?*' – I gather that most summers parties of walkers retrace his steps. In Monastier there is even Le Bar Stevenson. During the journey I stayed at an inn at La Pradelles, a slightly tumbledown (I prefer rural France not too tidied-up) but friendly place where my room gave a spectacular view across the Gevaudan, snowy white in places with wild narcissus. *Le patron* served me a meal full of local specialities including a hare terrine with madeira from the charcuterie in the main square.

1 kg (2¼ lb) hare (Sainsbury's and Waitrose conveniently sell hare in portions)	a few sprigs of thyme
	a strip of orange peel
	2 wineglasses red wine
	1 wineglass madeira – verdelho or medium dry
450 g (1 lb) belly pork	1–2 teaspoons salt
450 g (1 lb) smoked streaky bacon, sliced	½ teaspoon milled pepper
1 large onion, chopped	¼–½ teaspoon ground mace
2 fat cloves of garlic, chopped	¼ teaspoon finely powdered dried thyme
2 bay leaves	

If not cut in portions, cut the hare to fit a lidded casserole. Add the belly pork, cut into cubes, and half the bacon, cut in strips. Mix the onion and garlic in with the meat; place the bay leaves, thyme and strip of orange peel on top and pour in the red wine. Cover and cook in a slow oven (Mark 3, 160°C, 325°F) for 45–60 minutes – the hare meat should come easily from the bone and most of the pork fat will have melted.

Discard all the herbs and orange peel and mince or chop in a processor (but not too finely) the boned meat and seasonings; strain the cooking liquor into a pan and, if necessary, reduce to 150 ml (¼ pint).

Mix the meat in a large bowl with the madeira, salt, pepper, ground mace, and ground thyme. If possible, cover and chill overnight.

Next day line a 1 litre (2 pint) terrine with the remainder of the bacon, reserving 2 or 3 slices for the top of the terrine. Spoon in the hare mixture and smooth level. Place the remaining bacon on top and pour over the reduced cooking liquid. Cover with a double layer of greaseproof paper and the lid.

Cook in a bain-marie in a slow oven (Mark 3, 160°C, 325°F) for 1–1¼ hours. Remove from the oven and replace the lid with a piece of wood (I keep a piece cut to fit the terrine specially for this – it's as well to write TERRINE on it in felt-tip pen otherwise I find some-body takes it to light the fire) wrapped in foil on top. Stand some scale weights on top and leave the terrine to cool in the bain-marie. When cool, chill; then briefly dip the terrine in very hot water to turn it out. This terrine will cut into 18–20 slices.

LAPIN EN PAPILLOTE

PARCELLED RABBIT

Both rabbit and joints of chicken are excellent cooked this way for serving hot or cold at a picnic, or the parcels may be prepared ahead and cooked over a barbecue.

4 joints of rabbit	**salt, milled pepper**
1–2 slices of *lard fumé* or	**marjoram and parsley,**
smoked streaky bacon,	**finely chopped**
in slivers	**olive oil**
1 clove of garlic, in slivers	**dry white wine or cider**

Rinse the rabbit in cold water and then dry well on kitchen paper (for chicken remove the skin).

Make a series of parallel cuts across the meat and slip into them the small pieces of bacon and garlic rolled in some salt and pepper and the finely chopped herbs.

Place each piece of meat on a square of lightly oiled foil and dribble a little wine or cider over the top. Fold up the foil and secure the edges together firmly by folding them over.

Place the parcels on a baking sheet or dish and cook in a moderate oven (Mark 4, 180°C, 350°F) for 30–40 minutes until tender. For cooking over a barbecue or outdoor fire use either heavy-duty foil or a double layer. Serves 4.

CANARD SAUVAGE AU GENIÈVRE

WILD DUCK WITH JUNIPER BERRIES

450–900 g (1–2 lb) wild
duck or mallard
a carrot, a small onion, a
stick of celery
15–18 juniper berries
salt

1 wineglass chicken stock
or water
½ wineglass gin
45 g (1½ oz) butter
watercress to garnish
(optional)

Wipe the duck with a damp cloth. If you have the giblets place them in a roasting pan with the chopped vegetables. Crush half of the juniper berries and place in the cavity of the duck; sprinkle salt over the skin.

Place the duck on the bed of vegetables and roast in a moderately hot oven (Mark 6, 200°C, 400°F) for 45 minutes. Pour off any surplus fat and turn the duck over so that it is breast side down. Roast for 10 minutes and then, if the duck is sufficiently cooked, transfer to a hot serving dish and keep hot.

Pour off the fat from the roasting tin and add the remaining juniper berries and the stock or water to the pan; boil fast for 4 minutes and strain the liquid into a jug, discarding the vegetables and giblets.

Pour the gin into the pan and set light to it. Return the strained pan juices and simmer for 2 minutes, stirring all the time. Remove from the heat and add the butter, in small pieces; shake until melted.

Carve the duck and serve with the sauce; garnish with watercress if you wish. Serves 2–4.

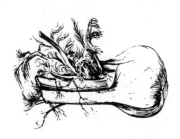

Poulet au Lard Fumé et à la Laitue

CHICKEN WITH SMOKED BACON AND LETTUCE

The mild smoky flavour of *lard fumé* enhances chicken considerably, but if not available replace with Italian *coppa* or a very lightly smoked English bacon.

2 chicken portions	1 shallot, chopped
85 g (3 oz) *lard fumé* or	salt
mild smoked streaky	1 wineglass *rosé* wine
bacon	2 large leaves of lettuce
30 g (1 oz) butter	

Skin the chicken and remove any fat from the meat. Finely dice the *lard fumé* or bacon and sauté in a pan until the fat runs. Add one third of the butter and sear the chicken all over. Remove the chicken and stir in the shallot for 3–4 minutes. Place the chicken back in the pan and season lightly. Add the wine. Cover the pan tightly and cook over moderate heat for 25–40 minutes depending on the size of the chicken portions. Check the liquid now and again, and add a splash of water if necessary.

Shred the lettuce and cut across a few times.

Remove the chicken to a hot serving dish. Toss the lettuce into the pan and stir over high heat until softened and the liquid in the pan is reduced. Stir in the remainder of the butter and remove from the heat. Spoon the sauce with the lettuce and bacon over the chicken and serve. Serves 2.

Confit d'Oie, Confit de Canard

GOOSE OR DUCK PRESERVED IN FAT

Confit d'oie is one of those legendary preparations of French country cooking which has been made for centuries. Pieces of goose or duck preserved in fat still play a considerable role in much of the cooking of south-west France, most notably in *cassoulet*. As with several other foods that are still made as a matter of course in farmhouses, *confit d'oie* is expensive to buy, yet is simple and satisfying to make at home. I find the ideal time to preserve goose or duck in this way is during January when there is a supply of Christmas goose fat to hand. At other times pork fat can be used just as well.

half a goose or a duck	2 bay leaves, broken in
2 tablespoons coarse sea	small pieces
salt	6 cloves, crushed
1 teaspoon dried thyme,	680 g (1½ lb) goose, duck or
ground in a coffee mill	pork fat

Cut the goose or duck into 6 pieces, separating the legs and wings, and cut up the carcass. Arrange the pieces in a single layer on a large plate and sprinkle with the salt, ground thyme, bay leaves and cloves. Cover and leave in a cold place or a refrigerator for 8–24 hours.

Transfer the goose or duck to a hot cast-iron casserole and sauté, skin side down, for about 15 minutes until the fat runs. Turn the meat once or twice as it cooks.

Spoon the goose fat over the meat. Cover the casserole and cook in a slow oven (Mark 2, 150°C, 300°F) for 1½–2 hours or until the meat falls from the bone.

Cool slightly; then spoon a layer of the cooking fat into one or two stoneware pots. There are straight-sided brown glazed pots specially made for *confit d'oie*; they are available from David Mellor or Habitat in Britain. Chill the pot until the fat is set. Meanwhile take off the meat from the larger bones – if your pots are small it is best to take all the meat off the bones. Pack the meat into the pots and spoon fat over to cover completely. Allow to set, and then keep the pots chilled in a very cold place until needed.

Traditionally a cloth is placed on top of the fat just before it sets. A layer of salt is spread over it and a paper cover is tied in place.

Spoonfuls of *confit d'oie* are added to soups and casseroles and larger amounts are extracted by standing the pot in hot water until the fat melts sufficiently for the meat to be lifted out.

MOLTANI DE GUADELOUPE

CHICKEN MOLTANI FROM GUADELOUPE

Although she has lived in a delightful valley full of flowers and wild asparagus for many years, a friend from Guadeloupe still finds the Var winter cold compared with her family home in the Leeward Islands. To warm herself, her family and friends she makes this chicken and lentil dish. It uses French curry power, which differs from most of those on sale in Britain – on spice stalls look for a mixture labelled 'Colombo'; alternatively mix your own curry spices, but add more ground cumin and coriander and less ground chilli than is usual here.

680 g (1½ lb) boned chicken	salt
2–3 tablespoons sunflower oil	425 ml (¾ pt) chicken stock
1 medium onion, chopped	225 g (8 oz) red lentils
1–2 cloves of garlic, finely chopped	1 small onion, chopped
1–2 tablespoons French curry powder	1 dried red chilli, seeded and chopped

Cut the chicken into 2.5 cm (1 in) cubes and brown it lightly in the sunflower oil. Transfer the meat to a plate and soften the larger onion and the garlic in the remaining oil. Stir in the curry powder for a few minutes, add the meat and mix until coated with the spice. Pour in the stock and cover the pan. Cook slowly for about 1 hour or until the chicken is tender.

Meanwhile cook the washed lentils with the small onion and the chilli pepper in water to cover by the thickness of two fingers until soft and mushy.

Turn the cooked lentils into a hot serving dish and spoon the chicken and its cooking juices on top. Covered with a buttered paper the dish will keep hot quite well for half an hour.

My only addition to this dish is to scatter some chopped fresh coriander leaves over the top; salad rocket, which tastes like peanuts, also goes well with it. Serves 4–6.

CHEVREUIL AUX LENTILLES DU PUY

VENISON WITH LE PUY LENTILS

In and around Le Puy I looked for fields of lentils, but it was too early in the season. I had to be satisfied with the vivid description of the small, blue-flowered plants given me by the charmingly lively ladies in the Baiser de Nègre pâtisserie which was doing a roaring trade in elaborate *croquembouches* (a pyramid of choux pastries) this Whitsuntide morning. The lentils themselves, dull, dark green, have a pepperiness which I find goes well with robustly flavoured meat like ham, pork, venison and game.

1 kg (2½ lb) piece of haunch of venison	salt, milled pepper
⅓ bottle Côtes du Rhône red wine	55 g (2 oz) butter
	225 g (8 oz) *lentilles du Puy*, green lentils
4 tablespoons olive oil	finely grated rind and juice of an orange
1 shallot, finely chopped	
1 clove garlic, finely sliced	2 tablespoons redcurrant jelly
a few sprigs of thyme	
a bay leaf	a little *vieux marc* or port

Place the venison in a bowl or a better idea is to use a plastic bag in the bowl so that, when sealed, with most of the air excluded, the marinade comes into contact with all surfaces of the meat.

Mix the wine and oil with the shallot, garlic, thyme, bay leaf and some salt and pepper and pour over the meat. Cover the bowl or seal the plastic bag. Leave for 1–2 days in the refrigerator or for 8–10 hours at room temperature, turning the meat over now and again.

Take the meat from the marinade and brown all over in half the butter in a cast-iron casserole. Add the marinade and bring to the boil. Place a buttered paper over the meat, cover with a tight-fitting lid and transfer to a moderate oven (Mark 4, 180°C, 350°F) and cook for 1 hour.

Meanwhile wash the lentils in cold water then cook in water to cover for 30–40 minutes, until tender. Rinse the lentils in clean hot water and drain well.

Lift the venison on to a plate and stir the lentils into the cooking juices. Replace the meat on top and cook in the oven for a further 30–40 minutes until the venison is tender and the lentils have absorbed the flavour of the cooking juices.

Transfer the meat to a carving board, stir the rind and juice of the orange and the redcurrant jelly into the lentils and cook over moderate heat for 2–3 minutes. Check for seasoning and spoon the lentils into a hot serving dish. There should still be some meat juices left to make a little sauce. Simmer with a dash of *marc* or port and, if necessary, a little water or stock. Remove from the heat, add the remaining butter in small pieces and shake until thickened. Serve the sauce with the carved venison, the lentils and ideally a sharp fruit jelly like crab apple or quince. Serves 5–6.

RILLETTES DE LAPIN

Pure pork rillettes have been a family favourite for years but nowadays I prefer the lighter, less rich version made with rabbit. Although not at all essential a slow-cooker or continuous burning stove really comes into its own when making this spreadable terrine.

900 g (2 lb) young rabbit	a sprig of rosemary
680 g (1½ lb) belly pork	salt, milled pepper
2 bay leaves	nutmeg
a few sprigs of thyme or serpolet	dried thyme

Rinse the rabbit in cold water; if you are lucky enough to have a wild rabbit, soak it in cold water for 1 hour, and then dry it on kitchen paper. Cut the rabbit into neat portions that will fit your pan or casserole.

Cut the rind from the pork (I keep it in the freezer for making *cassoulet* or slow-cooked meat dishes) and cut the belly pork into 2.5 cm (1 in) pieces.

Heat a heavy-based pan or casserole and add the pork (if necessary do this in several batches). Stir over moderate heat until the pork fat runs and the meat is slightly browned. Use a slotted spoon to transfer the pork to a slow-cooker or a plate while you brown the rabbit in the pork fat.

Mix the pork and the rabbit together in your cooking vessel. Add the bay leaves, thyme and rosemary. Cover tightly and cook in a very slow oven (Mark 1, 140°C, 275°F) for 4–5 hours or overnight in a continuous burning oven on low. Or use a slow cooker set to high for 1 hour and turned down to low for 5 hours. Cook the meat until the rabbit meat falls from the bone and all the pork fat is liquid.

Discard the herbs and all the bones. Spoon the meat into a sieve over a bowl so that the fat drips through. Chop the meat on a plate or board and mash with a fork to separate the fibres. Mix the meat into the fat.

Season with salt and pepper, grated nutmeg and powdered dried thyme. Spoon into pottery bowls or dishes – the best kind are stoneware with a band of brown glaze around the rim. Smooth the rillettes level, and serve straight away or cover with cling-film or a layer of pork fat and store in the fridge for 1–2 weeks or freeze.

As a variation I sometimes add a little garlic or a strip of orange peel to the meat while it cooks. Serve rillettes at room temperature with country bread and red wine.

MAGRETS DE CANARD AU COSTIÈRES DU GARD

DUCK BREASTS WITH RED WINE

I first cooked this dish in the Languedoc and used the local Costières du Gard, but any well-made local red wine works well. If you are cooking in France you are probably drinking the local wine and so it is appropriate to cook with it too.

4 duck breasts with skin	1 teaspoon tomato purée
100 g (3½ oz) butter	bouquet garni
1 carrot, sliced	2 juniper berries, crushed
1 onion, chopped	2 cloves
1 clove garlic, crushed	grated nutmeg
⅓ bottle Costières du Gard	salt, milled pepper

Trim the duck breasts until neatly shaped. Put the trimmings in a heavy-based pan with a knob of the butter and the carrots, onion and garlic. Stir over moderate heat until golden, and then add the wine, a wineglass full of water, the tomato purée, bouquet garni, juniper berries and cloves, and simmer, uncovered, until the liquid is reduced to about 150 ml (¼ pt). Strain through a nylon sieve, pressing lightly on the vegetables to extract all the flavour and just a little purée to thicken the sauce.

Meanwhile sauté the duck breasts in a heavy pan, skin side down, until the fat runs. Brown the meat on each side and then cook skin side down for 10–15 minutes.

Pour off surplus fat (keep all the duck fat produced by this dish for cooking potatoes on another occasion) and make a series of neat cuts into the skin only of the duck. Cook for 5 minutes to release any more duck fat. Then transfer the duck to a hot serving dish and pour off the rest of the duck fat.

Pour the wine sauce into the pan and stir well to incorporate all the pan juices. Season with grated nutmeg, salt and milled pepper. Add the remainder of the butter in small pieces and remove from the heat. Shake the pan to melt the butter into the sauce and spoon over the duck. Serves 4.

POULARDE AU RIZ SAUCE SUPRÊME

CHICKEN WITH RICE AND CREAM SAUCE

The cold, bumpy Channel crossing had left us feeling distinctly delicate. How gladly we sat down in a small, unpretentious restaurant in Normandy. This beautifully prepared dish arrived and it could not have been a more perfect restorer.

1½–2 kg (3–4 lb) roasting
  chicken
2 slices of unsmoked bacon
1 onion, studded with four
  cloves
2 carrots, sliced
a sliver of garlic (optional)
a bouquet of fresh herbs
salt, a few peppercorns

stock made from the giblets
285 g (10 oz) round-grain
  white rice
55 g (2 oz) butter
30 g (1 oz) flour
275 ml (½ pt) single cream
2 egg yolks
a squeeze of lemon juice
finely chopped parsley

Place the chicken in a flameproof casserole. Remove the rinds from the bacon and place inside the bird; wrap the slices over the breast meat.

Add the cloved onion, carrots, garlic, bouquet garni, some salt and the peppercorns. Pour in the stock and make up with cold water to just cover the legs of the chicken. Bring everything to the boil, turn down the heat and cover the pan. Poach the chicken very gently for 45 minutes.

Lift out the chicken and strain the stock into a jug. Place the rice in the casserole and cover with stock to come 3 cm (1 in) above. Place the chicken on top of the rice, replace the lid and cook gently for about 30 minutes until the rice is cooked. Remove the casserole from the heat but keep hot.

Meanwhile melt half the butter in a pan, stir in the flour for 1–2 minutes but do not let it colour. Whisk in about 275 ml (½ pt) of the reserved chicken stock and allow the sauce to cook until reduced by about one third to achieve a fine flavour.

When ready to serve, add the cream blended with the egg yolks; reheat and cook until thickened, but do not allow to boil. Add lemon juice according to taste, check the seasoning and stir in the parsley. Keep the sauce hot over hot water and just before serving beat in the remaining butter.

Place the whole chicken or, if more convenient, carve into joints first, in the centre of a hot serving dish. Spoon the rice on each side and spoon some sauce over the chicken; serve the remainder separately. Serves 4–5.

POULARDE DEMI-DEUIL
CHICKEN IN HALF MOURNING

In this classic chicken dish thin slices of truffle are slipped under the skin and over the breast meat of a really fine bird. Poached gently and served with a *sauce suprême* the chicken is a superb but possibly expensive treat. Nevertheless you may stumble upon (it has been known) or be given a fresh truffle and you'll then wish to know of a good way of cooking with it. In fact, for serving to more people, a small turkey can be prepared in the same manner. In the Ardèche the truffled bird was wrapped in a scalded cloth and buried in the ground overnight for the truffle to work its magic. In country regions a truffled chicken or turkey would usually be reserved for serving at Christmas. If you are anxious to try this dish with a tinned truffle, it will still be delicious but not at all in the same league.

2–2½ kg (4–5 lb) chicken, the best you can afford	bouquet garni
a fresh black truffle	salt, peppercorns
1 onion	30 g (1 oz) butter
the white part of a leek	20 g (¾ oz) flour
1 carrot	2 egg yolks
1 stick of celery	150 ml (¼ pt) double cream

The chicken should be truffled up to 24 hours ahead so that the perfume of the truffle can penetrate the meat.

A fresh truffle may be gritty if it comes from sandy soil. Use a brush to remove as much of the sand as possible and wash the rest away under a dribble of cold water. Then peel as thinly as possible. I tie the peelings in a square of muslin and add it to the poaching liquid.

Slice the truffle thinly. Lift the skin of the bird and slip in the black slices against the breast meat and pull the skin back down as snugly as possible. Halve the onion and put it in the cavity of the bird; then truss the bird. Roughly chop the vegetables and make a layer of half of them in a casserole just large enough to hold the bird so that it won't require too much liquid for cooking. Place the chicken on top and tuck the rest of the vegetables, the bouquet garni, some salt and peppercorns around it. Add hot water to almost cover the legs. Cover and bring to the boil. Lower the heat and just simmer (*frémir*) for 1¼–2 hours until a knife put into the leg releases only clear juices.

Lift the chicken clear of the stock and keep warm on a serving dish. Strain the liquor into a pan and reduce to 275 ml (½ pt) but taste now and again to ensure the flavour is not too salty.

Melt the butter and stir in the flour to make a roux. Gradually mix in the stock, stirring fast all the time. Mix the egg yolks with the cream and add a little hot sauce to them in the bowl; return the mixture to the pan and cook gently, stirring, until slightly thickened, but do not allow to boil. Check the seasoning and adjust if necessary. Carve the chicken and serve with the sauce. Serves 6–8.

LIÈVRE À LA CRÈME

HARE WITH SOURED CREAM

An Ardéchois recipe for an autumn hare, whose meat is often sufficiently tender to roast without marinating.

saddle of hare	4–5 slices of smoked
½ teaspoon juniper berries,	streaky bacon, cooked
crushed	until crisp
½ teaspoon crushed	salt
peppercorns	150 ml (¼ pt) soured cream
olive oil	or *crème fraîche*
1 large wineglass	
Ardéchois *vins de pays*	

Wipe the meat with a damp cloth and if you have not already done so, remove the thin bluish skin covering the meat. Press the juniper berries and peppercorns into the meat and place the bacon on top, tucking the ends underneath if necessary.

Place the hare in a lightly oiled roasting pan and cover with foil or butter paper. Roast the meat in a moderate oven (Mark 5, 190°C,

375°F) for 30–40 minutes. Pour the red wine over the meat and roast for 5–10 minutes – the hare should be cooked but still tender.

Transfer the hare to a hot serving dish and keep hot. Cut the crisp bacon into dice or narrow strips and set aside.

Simmer the wine and meat juices left in the roasting pan over moderate heat for a few minutes; add just a little water if the sauce is too reduced and season with salt. When ready to serve the hare, stir the soured cream into the pan and bring almost to the boil. Spoon the sauce over the hare, garnish with the bacon and serve. Serves 3–4.

POUSSIN CRAPAUDIN AU FOIE GRAS

SPATCHCOCK POUSSIN WITH FOIE GRAS

The week I acquired poultry shears virtually anything on legs was spatchcocked – poussins work especially well. Use the edges and fat from *foie gras*, not the prize centre, for the recipe.

2 poussins	**30 g (1 oz) butter**
salt, milled pepper	**a few drops of brandy,**
30 g (1 oz) *foie gras*	***marc* or lemon juice**

Use shears or strong scissors to cut up through the backbone of the poussins. I think this gives a more delicious result than cutting through the breast bone. Place each bird flat on a roasting or grilling pan and season with salt and pepper.

Place the birds under a hot grill for 20–25 minutes, turning them over once.

Meanwhile cream the *foie gras* with the butter and brandy, *marc* or lemon juice.

When the meat on the birds is almost cooked and only clear juices run from the leg, spread the *foie gras* over the skin side of the poussins. Grill for a further 5–7 minutes. Serve straight away with a green salad. Serves 2.

PERDREAU AUX RAISINS ET À LA SOCCA

PARTRIDGE WITH GRAPES AND SOCCA

Unfortunately I've never encountered any of the street-wise *gamins dégourdis* who once sold *la socca* in the narrow streets of the old town of Nice. This Niçoise speciality, said to have originated in Genoa, resembles polenta except that chick-pea flour replaces that made from maize.

The slightly sweet taste of the *socca* goes well with game and especially partridge. (Replace the *socca* with polenta in the recipe if you prefer.) The Vivarais is famed for its subtly flavoured red partridge, known as the rock partridge or *bartavelle*; Louis XIII had a keen appetite for them and they still fetch a high price in the Paris markets.

Unless you have a local supply you may like to know that Harrods sell red-legged partridge and the larger branches of Sainsbury's stock them on the game counter. Fortunately, like most game, partridge freeze well. One plump partridge can make a memorable meal for two.

Socca	2 slices of unsmoked
115 g (4 oz) chick-pea flour	streaky bacon
salt, milled pepper	55 g (2 oz) butter
olive oil	salt, milled pepper
butter	115 g (4 oz) white grapes,
	halved and seeded
1 plump partridge	1 wineglass dry white wine
1 tangerine or small dessert	
apple	

In a heavy-based pan, gradually mix the chick-pea flour with 150 ml (¼ pt) cold water until smooth. Stir over moderate heat, gradually adding 150–275 ml (¼–½ pt) hot water. Season with salt and pepper, lower the heat and cook, stirring all the time, until the mixture starts to come free of the pan and forms a ball.

Spread the mixture in a lightly oiled shallow pie dish or cake tin and spread level. Dribble olive oil over the top and grind some black pepper over the *socca*. Bake in a moderate oven (Mark 5, 190°C, 375°F) for 20–25 minutes until the outside is slightly crisp and the inside is still soft.

Cool in the tin then cut into fingers or triangles. When the partridge is almost cooked, lightly fry the pieces of *socca* in olive oil and butter. Drain on paper and keep hot.

Place the partridge in a small roasting pan; halve the tangerine or apple and tuck it into the body cavity, and add the rind from the bacon if you have it.

Spread the breast and legs of the partridge with butter and season with salt and pepper. Stretch the bacon, halved if necessary, over the bird. Roast in a moderately hot oven (Mark 6, 200°C, 400°F) for 30 minutes basting from time to time.

Split the bird in two through the breast bone, discard the fruit and place the halves on a hot serving dish; return to the oven, turned to low, until ready to serve.

Lightly sauté the grapes in the pan juices and butter in the roasting pan for a few minutes. Add the wine and simmer together. Spoon the grapes over or beside the partridge and add the remainder of the butter to the reduced sauce. Place the hot fingers of *socca* beside the partridge and serve with the sauce. Serves 2. Any *socca* over may be cut into small pieces, sautéd in oil and served to nibble with drinks.

FILET DE LIÈVRE AU VINAIGRE DE FRAMBOISE

HARE WITH RASPBERRY VINEGAR

I wanted to devise a lighter hare dish, yet one which still captures the rich gamy flavour of the meat. Cooking hare with raspberry vinegar seems to be a pleasing arranged marriage. Some people might garnish the dish with raspberries but to me that would be simply unnecessary and rather flashy. More important, the raspberries have already done their work in flavouring the vinegar and an addition would destroy the balance that one strives for in cooking. Because I have cooked from Julia Drysdale's *Classic Game*

Cookery with so much pleasure I include this recipe as a tribute to her.

2 pieces, about 500 g (about 1 lb) saddle of hare
a small onion, a carrot and ½ stick of celery
a bay leaf
2 tablespoons home-made raspberry vinegar (see p. 278)
2 tablespoons mild oil, sunflower or grapeseed
fingernail paring of garlic, crushed
30 g (1 oz) butter
2–3 tablespoons raspberry vinegar syrup
salt, pepper
finely chopped parsley

Use a short, sharp knife to cut the fillet from the backbone of the hare. Place the bones in a pan with the onion, carrot, celery and bay leaf, cover with water and simmer for 45 minutes to make a stock. Boil the strained stock fast until reduced to 2 tablespoons.

Cut the fillet into 1 cm (½ in) thick slices and bat out until thinner. Place the meat in a single layer in a shallow dish. Mix the raspberry vinegar with the oil and the garlic. Spoon over the meat, making sure that all the surfaces are coated. Cover and chill for 2–4 hours.

Melt half the butter in a pan and sauté the well-drained pieces of hare on both sides for 4–5 minutes. Transfer to a hot serving dish and add the marinating liquid to the pan. Bubble hard, then add the reduced stock and the raspberry vinegar syrup and simmer for 1 minute. Season with salt and pepper and taste. Add a little more syrup if necessary.

Remove the pan from the heat and add the remaining butter in small pieces; shake the pan until the butter has melted and then spoon the sauce over the hare and sprinkle with the parsley. Serve with buttered noodles. Serves 2–3.

BÉCASSE RÔTIE

ROAST WOODCOCK

Woodcock is usually regarded as the finest game bird. I think of it as the Roquefort of game, with its magnificently strong flavour. Charles Forot calls it royal game and adds that a roast woodcock, *'dans toute la cuisine, se répandra une odeur à réveiller un mort'*. This is because the intestines melt when cooked, heightening the flavour of the meat; they are then scraped out of the carcass and mixed into a purée which is spread on croûtons to be served with the bird. This dish needs a splendidly full-bodied wine to accompany it – I suggest a Cornas, Crozes-Hermitage or Châteauneuf du Pape.

15 g (½ oz) butter
1 woodcock
salt, milled pepper
1 slim shallot, finely
   chopped
a sprig of thyme
2 tablespoons dry white
   wine
a chicken liver, lightly
   cooked, or 1 tablespoon
   foie gras

1–2 teaspoons olive oil
½–1 teaspoon Dijon or
   white wine vinegar
a little Dijon or Bordelaise
   mustard
finely chopped parsley
a few drops of cognac
2 slices of bread, freshly
   toasted

Melt the butter in a small lidded casserole and turn the woodcock in it over moderate heat for 8–10 minutes until lightly browned. Turn the bird on its back and season with salt and pepper. Add the shallot, thyme and wine to the pan. Cover and cook in a moderate oven (Mark 4, 180°C, 350°F) for 50–70 minutes, or until the flesh on the leg is cooked and the intestines have turned to a dark liquid. Spoon off any surplus fat.

In a bowl or mortar, pound and mix the chicken liver or *foie gras* with the olive oil, vinegar, mustard, parsley and brandy.

Use poultry shears to halve the bird; scrape the dark purée from inside the bird into the cooking pan. Stir in the liver purée and heat gently.

Cut the toast to the same size as the woodcock. Spread each piece with the hot purée and place the woodcock on top. Serve straight away. Serves 2.

SAUCE MATELOTE

A simple, piquant wine sauce with mushrooms and baby onions goes well with grilled or roast chicken or veal.

12–18 small silverskin
  onions
225 g (8 oz) button
  mushrooms
55 g (2 oz) butter
2 teaspoons flour
150 ml (¼ pt) dry white
  wine

570 ml (1 pt) chicken stock
salt, milled pepper
grated nutmeg
2 egg yolks
lemon juice or wine
  vinegar

Peel the onions and wipe the mushrooms; if they are at all large quarter them.

Sauté the onions in the butter for 4 minutes, not allowing them to colour. Add the mushrooms and cook together until softened.

Sprinkle the flour into the pan and stir for 2 minutes. Gradually stir in the wine and the stock and cook the sauce, stirring, until thickened.

Season with salt, pepper and grated nutmeg to taste. Simmer the sauce very gently for 15–20 minutes. When ready to serve stir in the egg yolks and slightly sharpen to taste with lemon juice or wine vinegar. Pour into a bowl or sauceboat for serving.

I reckoned that if I stayed overnight somewhere cheaper, I'd be able to eat at Barattero. Those of us who have read and re-read Elizabeth David until the pages fall from their binding would all hope to eat at the Hôtel du Midi in Lamastre some day.

But as I drew up outside another hotel, something told me to drive on. And so I found myself, with the car parked in the Place Seignobos, walking in through the glass doors at Barattero. I explained that I was alone and should like the cheapest possible room because I had arrived to eat. A cheerful bespectacled young man carried my luggage upstairs to a room at the back of the hotel. And, after settling in, I arranged at what time I'd like to dine, and set off to investigate Lamastre.

I found medlar trees in bloom beside the river, while hens scratched and pecked under the bridge. I discovered the railway station from which, in the summer, the narrow-gauge railway follows one of the most breathtaking routes in France to arrive in Tournon. I bought some pale blue bowls for *café au lait*. And I sat in a café with sawdust on the floor, and drank coffee with a glass of *marc* and absorbed the feel of the place. And I felt at home in this unassuming country town in northern Ardèche.

At eight o'clock at Barattero I went down to dinner. A young, crisply efficient waiter conducted me to a table in the jade-green dining-room. I chose a menu and some wine. Sometimes the aroma of fresh, good cooking wafted across to me and then I was served, with the utmost decorum, a truly splendid meal.

First there was a salad of tiny leaves of lettuce, green but splashed here and there with red, and upon them nestled hot slivers of duck liver and some *chanterelles*. The dressing was made with walnut oil and the dish was light and fragrant with the freshness of spring.

Next came a vegetable mousse with a tomato and basil sauce – pale but with an astonishing depth of flavour. There was not a trace of leaf yet you felt that the basil plant must almost be on the table because the flavour was so unspoilt.

I sat a little further away from the table and slowly savoured this exceptional meal. Some pearly white turbot arrived, the flesh just set in a current of steam with the most delicately refined rosemary cream I've ever tasted. Beside the fish lay finger-sized courgettes.

A superb *filet mignon de boeuf sauce échalotte* arrived, with a

Crozes Hermitage from just across the Rhône. In my memory it is hard to separate the food from the wine, so harmonious were they. But I do remember thinking that, given such high-class ingredients, only a chef of some artistry could improve on them like this.

The cheeses were in fine condition and mainly local; the Saint Nectaire was especially good.

By the time the puddings arrived I sat alone in the dining-room. Very slowly I sampled every one. A tisane of lime flowers was all I could manage afterwards.

Roseate and replete, I made my way into the hall. The same young man who had carried my cases was waiting to hear my thoughts about the meal. This was Bernard Perrier. His wife sat at the table with their small daughter.

A sharp-eyed reader with a long memory might recall that in 1958 in an article in *Vogue*, Elizabeth David wrote about the *poulardes en vessie* at Barattero. In passing, she mentions Bernard Perrier, though not by name. She wrote,

Madame [Barattero] asserted that nothing was easier to cook than this dish – 'What do you mean, why can you not get a pig's bladder in England? You have pigs, do you not?' – and upheld her point by adding that the chef's eight-year-old son already knows how to prepare the *poulardes en vessie*.

By the time I met Bernard Perrier he was still preparing the dish that his father and, before him, Joseph Baraterro had cooked. Although, of course, the menus have changed at Barattero; Bernard Perrier explained to me that he had introduced the *chariot de desserts* and that he cooks in a lighter style more in tune with today's tastes. It is a style, though, as he is keen to point out, wholly in the tradition of his father, Élie, and in direct line from that of Joseph Barattero. He still prepares some of the classic dishes that have made the Hôtel du Midi famous: the *pain d'écrevisses sauce cardinal* and the *poularde en vessie*.

To discover in these days of globe-trotting, publicity-seeking kitchen superstars, that a dedicated and gifted chef cares to continue building a tradition of good food in an authentic family hotel is heartening indeed. The cult of the new which has penetrated so many areas of our lives often tramples on the past and pays it little attention, let alone gratitude. Yet the present and the future derive from the past and we forget that at our peril.

I drove south to see my friends the Marquets. I arrived as Mme

Marquet was preparing the evening meal – a *navarin* of lamb with spring vegetables from her garden. Her kitchen is simple, a wood-burning stove in the corner, a kitchen table and a sink, between them a dresser. Near the stove a row of hooks carry her *batterie de cuisine*: a few wooden spoons, several good knives, a *mouli-légumes*, a sieve, a balloon whisk and a palette knife. Under a cloth on the dresser is her latest acquisition – an electric mixer. But this is very recent and it does not yet play a major role in the kitchen. I cooked for years without it, she says, I still can.

I sat at her kitchen table and watched her cutting and shaping the vegetables so that they would all take the same time to cook. This way the tiny carrots and turnips will taste their best, not only enriching the flavours of the slowly cooked lamb but also adorning the dish. She worked fast and skilfully, evidently enjoying the task. We chatted about her husband and her family and we discussed what had happened in the village during the winter.

And as I sat there, I thought about Bernard Perrier, whom I'd watched that morning, cooking in his far larger kitchen in Lamastre, and Yvette Marquet working in front of me now. They were both dedicated to doing their best, both taking immense care, both being true to themselves and their talents. And I realized that they were both, in Norman Douglas's words, 'in harmony with what is permanent'. That, more than anything else, was what I liked and respected about them.

DAUBE PROVENÇALE DE BOEUF

BEEF AND WINE STEW FROM PROVENCE

This dish of beef slowly cooked with wine represents everything that I like about country food from the south of France. It is rich and aromatic and full of flavour. Serve it with the wine you've used in the cooking. This is a dish which transfers well to a northern kitchen; I recommend it for Sunday lunch.

1 kg (2¼ lb) topside of beef	115 g (4 oz) smoked streaky
275 ml (½ pt) Côtes du	bacon
Rhône red wine	1 onion, chopped
3 tablespoons olive oil	225 g (8 oz) tomatoes,
1–2 cloves of garlic,	peeled and chopped
crushed	a strip of orange peel
1 teaspoon dried *herbes de*	2 anchovy fillets, chopped
Provence	a handful of black olives
salt, pepper	

In Britain you may have to remove any strips of fat tied on to the beef.

In a bowl mix the wine with the olive oil, garlic, herbs and some salt and pepper. Add the meat to the marinade and turn it over in it. Nowadays I place the meat and the marinade in a plastic bag which I seal and place in the bowl. In this way the liquid makes better all-over contact with the meat. Leave in a cold place or the refrigerator for 1–2 days, turning the meat over now and again.

Cook the bacon with the onion in a cast-iron casserole until the fat runs. Add the beef and sear lightly all over.

Pour in the marinade with the tomatoes, orange peel and the anchovies and bring to the boil.

Cover the casserole with a tight-fitting lid and cook in a low oven (Mark 2, 160°C, 325°F) for 2–3 hours until beautifully tender. Add the olives 10 minutes before serving.

Carve the beef into slices and serve with the sauce and a dish of plain boiled rice or noodles. Serves 5–6.

CHOU FARCI À MME CHALENDAR
MME CHALENDAR'S STUFFED CABBAGE

While buying stoneware pots in Mme Chalendar's shop in Lamas-tre I mentioned that I was particularly interested in Ardéchois cooking. The effect was electric: in a flash Madame raced across the shop to call up the stairs to her daughter, Lily. A dark, pretty sixteen-year-old emerged, keen to tell me that she was starting to learn how to cook. In no time I was hustled into the kitchen behind the shop to sample Lily's latest dish, her *chou farci*, which tasted so good and was so simple to make that Madame insisted I was given the recipe. Between customers she dictated the recipe while Lily wrote and Lily's father, seated at a table in the kitchen interjected now and again 'Don't forget the garlic.'

about 750 g (a generous 1½ lb) white drumhead cabbage
450 g (1 lb) minced beef or veal
2 cloves of garlic, crushed
¼ teaspoon *quatre-épices* (see p. 89)

2 tablespoons parsley, chopped
2 tablespoons wine vinegar
150 ml (¼ pt) beef stock
salt
45 g (1½ oz) butter

Remove the stem and any damaged leaves from the cabbage, and cut into roughly 1 cm (½ in) squares. Blanch in salted, boiling water for 3 minutes, drain and refresh in cold water, and drain well.

Brown the minced meat and garlic in a pan without fat, stirring from time to time. Stir in the *quatre-épices*, parsley, vinegar, stock and salt. Bring to the boil and stir well to incorporate the pan juices.

Rub some of the butter inside an ovenproof dish. Either mix the meat with the cabbage or make three layers of cabbage separated by the meat mixture. Dot the top of the cabbage with the remainder of the butter. Cover the dish with a buttered paper and a lid.

Cook in the centre of a moderate oven (Mark 4, 180°C, 350°F) for 30 minutes. Serves 3–4 as a main course.

Navarin Printanier d'Agneau

SPRINGTIME NAVARIN OF LAMB

A classic country dish that uses spring lamb and new baby vegetables, ideally from the garden.

1½–2 kg (4 lb) shoulder of lamb, on the bone
30–55 g (1–2 oz) butter
1 tablespoon white sugar
275 ml (½ pt) stock or water
340 g (12 oz) tomatoes, peeled and chopped
1 clove of garlic, crushed
salt, pepper
1 tablespoon flour
bouquet garni: thyme, rosemary, bayleaf

about 500 g (1 lb) small new potatoes
about 500 g (1 lb) baby turnips
250 g (½ lb) baby onions
170 g (6 oz) young French beans
115 g (4 oz) shelled new peas

Cut the meat from the bone and discard all the skin and fat. Cut the meat into pieces of about 2–4 cm (1–2 in).

Melt the butter in a pan and sear the meat on all sides, in batches if necessary. Transfer the meat to a hot casserole. Add the sugar to the pan and allow it to brown and caramelize to give a good colour to the dish.

Pour the stock and the tomatoes into the pan and stir until all the sugar and the pan juices have dissolved. Add the garlic. Season the meat with salt and pepper and sprinkle the flour over. Then add the tomato flavoured stock. Bury the bouquet garni in the casserole. Cover and cook in a moderate oven (Mark 5, 190°C, 375°F) for 1 hour.

Meanwhile cook the potatoes, turnips and onions separately in salted water for 3 minutes. Drain the vegetables and add to the casserole, cook for 20 minutes.

Cook the beans and peas, drain and spoon over the meat. Spoon the sauce over the vegetables and serve. Serves 5–6.

BROUFFADE DES MARINIERS DU RHÔNE

BRAISED BEEF IN THE STYLE OF RHÔNE SAILORS

No one would want to visit Arles without, if possible, eating at Le Vaccarès, where Bernard Dumas not only serves the best food in town but composes his menus with respect to the location and history of this ancient city. He introduced me to *brouffade*, a dish which he says often appears incorrectly under the name *grillade*. But the true *brouffade*, once frequently prepared by the mariners of the Rhône (who still transport goods from Arles and Marseilles to Lyons, returning with other cargoes, many for export), is a dish of marinated beef. The characteristic of the dish is its intriguing combination of flavours – anchovies, capers and gherkins – which gives the beef an exciting and unusual taste.

680 g (1½ lb) topside of beef	2 tablespoons red wine vinegar
1 shallot, finely chopped	a few sprigs of thyme
2 cloves of garlic	2 bay leaves
6 fillets of anchovy, chopped	½ bottle Côtes du Rhône red wine
1½ tablespoons capers, chopped	salt, milled pepper
6 tablespoons olive oil	1–2 medium-sized gherkins, finely diced

Cut the beef into thin slices about 0.5 cm (¼ in) thick. In a mortar pound the shallot, garlic, anchovies and capers with 2 tablespoons of the oil and the wine vinegar to make a reasonably smooth purée.

Spread each slice of beef with the purée and arrange them in a shallow dish. Place the thyme and bay leaves on top and pour over half the wine. Cover the dish and leave in a cold place for 8 hours or overnight.

Heat 2 tablespoons of the oil in a pan and lightly brown the sliced beef. Add the liquid from the marinade and a little salt and pepper. Top up with extra wine if necessary so that the liquid almost covers the meat. Cover and cook in a slow oven (Mark 3, 160°C, 325°F) for 1½–2 hours until the beef is cooked. Transfer the meat to a hot serving dish. Pour the liquid into a pan and reduce by half over high heat. Add the gherkins. Spoon the remaining olive oil over the beef and pour the reduced sauce around it. Serve straight away with puréed potatoes or noodles. Serves 4–6.

SAUCE À PÂTE DE HUBERT LAURENT

HUBERT LAURENT'S SAUCE FOR PASTA

Hubert Laurent devotes his life to cooking and skiing. He is the chef at the small friendly hotel that his parents started a generation ago in the village of Ste Eulalie in the shadow of the Gerbier de Jonc.

The boom in skiing during the last decade has brought visitors back to these alpine villages of the Haute Ardèche, so the Hotel de la Poste is far busier in the winter than in the summer. Yet the early summer can be enchanting. Behind the hotel, in the meadow that slopes down to the burbling Loire, I counted twenty-four different wild flowers in bloom one June morning. And the bees from the blue, yellow and red painted hives on the far side of the meadow were foraging this paradise from dawn till dusk. The village is gloriously peaceful all summer until the second weekend in July when possibly the most ancient flower festival in Europe, la Foire de Violettes, is held. From all over the continent visitors come to buy the dried flowers. Pharmacists, scent and pot-pourri makers, herbalists and holiday-makers throng the long central street and surrounding meadows. Most people eat *en plein air* but those in the know eat at the Hôtel de la Poste which specializes in the good *cuisine bourgeoise* that Hubert learnt from his mother. His meat sauce for pasta is closely related to a *bolognaise* but I find the addition of *quatre-épices* transforms the flavour in a very Gallic and harmonious way.

15 g (½ oz) butter	225 g (8 oz) tomatoes,
large onion, very finely	peeled and de-seeded
chopped	bouquet garni of thyme,
100 g (3½ oz) lean beef,	bay leaf and parsley
very finely minced	salt, milled pepper
1 tablespoon flour	a good sprinkling of
1 litre (1¾ pt) chicken stock	*quatre-épices*
or water	(see p. 89)
3 cloves of garlic	

Melt the butter in a pan and cook the onion until golden and transparent. Add the beef and cook, stirring now and again, for 7–8 minutes. Stir in the flour and gradually add the stock, the garlic, tomatoes, bouquet garni, salt, pepper and the *quatre-épices* and bring to the boil.

Turn down the heat and allow to simmer gently for 30 minutes or until the sauce is reduced to 570 ml (1 pint). Serve with pasta. If you prefer a smoother sauce, purée briefly in a blender or processor before serving. Serves 3–4.

AGNEAU AUX PRUNES ET AU ROMARIN

LAMB WITH PLUMS AND ROSEMARY

The fruit that links the Ardèche kitchen I use and the one at home in Devon is the plum. In July Mme Marquet brings us a bowl of her red cherry plums every few days and here in our Devon village, which is named after a plum tree, we depend upon a large spreading tree planted fifty years ago in a field called Dippy Orchard. About the middle of August it produces far more plums than we can deal with. Neighbours and friends have baskets of large purple plums pressed into their hands and I devise endless ways of cooking with them. This dish is one of them.

4 lamb cutlets, trimmed
   free of fat
a little butter or oil
salt, milled pepper
1 wineglass red wine *des
   Côteaux de l'Ardèche*

a sprig of fresh rosemary
12 dark plums, quartered
small knob of butter
a few sprigs of rosemary
   for a garnish

Lightly brown the lamb cutlets in the butter or oil in a heavy cast-iron pan. Season the meat with salt and pepper and pour in the wine. Bring to the boil and place the rosemary over the meat. Cover with a buttered paper and a lid and cook in a moderate oven (Mark 5, 190°C, 375°F) for about 25 minutes.

Remove the lid and butter paper and discard the rosemary, which should have impregnated the meat with its flavour. Cover each cutlet with the quartered plums and place back in the oven for 10–15 minutes until everything is cooked.

Transfer the lamb and the plums to a hot serving dish and pour off any surplus fat. Add half a glass of water to the pan and scrape to incorporate all the pan juices. Simmer for a few minutes, add the knob of butter in small pieces and remove from the heat. Shake the pan to combine the sauce, then spoon a little around the meat, garnish with the fresh rosemary and serve with *pommes de terre fondantes* (see p. 185) or boiled new potatoes. Serves 4.

Noisettes d'Agneau aux Olives et au Fenouil

NOISETTES OF LAMB WITH OLIVES AND FENNEL

4–6 noisettes of lamb
2–3 tablespoons fruitiest
   olive oil
crushed green peppercorns
salt

4–6 fronds of fresh fennel
1 tablespoon Pernod
about 18 black Nyons
   olives

Pour the oil into a shallow dish, turn the noisettes over in the oil to coat them on all sides. Sprinkle with the crushed peppercorns. Cover the dish with cling-film and refrigerate for 6–8 hours or longer.

Heat a heavy-based frying pan until fairly hot. Sear the meat on all sides; then sprinkle it with salt.

Remove a few of the most tender shoots from the fennel and reserve to garnish the dish later. Place the rest of the fennel on top of the meat. Cover the pan and cook the meat, over moderate heat, for 20–25 minutes until tender.

Discard the cooked fennel. Transfer the lamb to a hot serving dish and add the finely chopped fennel shoots and the Pernod to the cooking juices. Bubble fast for 2–3 minutes, add the olives and check the seasoning. Spoon the sauce around the noisettes of lamb and serve with plain boiled potatoes. Serves 3–4.

GIGOT À LA MODE DE GASCOGNE

GASCONY-STYLE LAMB

This is a dish best prepared in the summer, as soon as possible after the garlic harvest. It is important that the Provençal garlic is fat, juicy and mild. But it is a beautiful way to cook what I regard as a British meat; Welsh or Dartmoor lamb is unrivalled in France. In some ways this would be my favourite dish to cook for French friends in the south. I've cooked the dish in England in July with garlic I've brought back from Uzès but now I plan to prepare it in France for my friends there.

I shall hurry south carrying a magnificent leg of Devon spring lamb maturing nicely in the cool box. As soon as I arrive I shall buy a plait of the new garlic and will set about preparing what will be a veritable feast. Later that evening everyone will arrive, the Marquets, the Doize sisters, M. Broc and his wife and my English friends Susan and Harry from a few miles away. There will be plenty of wine, some of Jean Marquet's and some from the *caves* in the next village and Harry will probably bring a bottle of his special Notre Dame des Neiges white wine. We will eat the splendid English lamb with French garlic. They will say that they are surprised at the high quality of the meat and we will congratulate them on the new season's garlic. There will be much laughter and plenty to talk about, lots of gossip to catch up on, a full report on the ravages of the winter and for me, another happy evening of eating and talking will be added to so many already in my memory.

1 good-sized leg of lamb, with the bone, in one piece	1 wineglass dry white wine
	1 wineglass stock or water
	a bouquet of thyme, bay
a little *lard fumé* or smoked streaky bacon, cut in slivers	leaf and parsley
	1 onion stuck with cloves
	30 cloves of garlic, peeled
1 clove of garlic, cut in slivers	2 tomatoes, peeled, seeded and finely diced
a knob of butter	
salt, milled pepper	

Make small slits all over the lamb and push the slivered bacon and garlic into them.

Melt the butter in a large cast-iron casserole and turn the lamb over in it until lightly coloured. Season with salt and pepper. Add the wine and stock to the casserole with the bouquet garni and the onion. Cover and cook very gently over low heat on the hob for 2–3 hours or cook in a slow oven (Mark 3, 160°C, 325°F) for 2–3 hours.

Half-way through the cooking time, bring 150 ml (¼ pt) water to boil in a pan, add the garlic, simmer for 1 minute and add the contents of the pan to the casserole, turning the meat over at the same time.

When the meat is cooked and beautifully tender transfer to a hot serving dish or carving plate. Skim off surplus fat from the casserole and discard the bouquet garni and onion. Press the remaining liquor and garlic through a sieve into a pan and add the tomatoes. Bring the sauce to the boil, check for seasoning and serve with the lamb. Serves 10–12.

RÔTI D'AGNEAU AU PISTOU

ROAST LAMB STUFFED WITH PISTOU

In this dish the stuffing for the lamb is mixed with the basil sauce, *pistou*, to give the meat a very good flavour.

1 kg (2¼ lb) half leg of lamb	30 g (1 oz) freshly grated Parmesan cheese
15 g (½ oz) basil leaves	2–3 slices French bread, crusts removed, and turned into breadcrumbs
3 cloves of garlic	
2–4 tablespoons olive oil	

Bone the lamb and open the meat out flat. Cut gashes into any thick parts so that the meat is mainly the same thickness.

Chop the basil, garlic and olive oil together in a processor or blender. Add the cheese and breadcrumbs, and mix with 2–3 tablespoons hot water to make a spreadable paste.

Spread the stuffing over the cut surface of the meat, making sure it reaches into the cuts in the meat. Roll up the meat neatly, re-forming the shape. Tie with string in two or three places to maintain its shape during cooking.

Roast the meat in a slow oven (Mark 3, 160°C, 325°F) for 1–1½ hours or until cooked to your taste. The dish tastes best when the lamb is still pink. Remove the meat from the oven and leave in a warm place for 15–20 minutes. Then carve across in thick slices.

Serve with boiled Camargue rice or another white, round-grained rice, cooked with bay leaves and butter. Serves 4–6.

A friend cooked this recipe in midwinter by mixing a 115 g (4 oz) jar of bought prepared *pesto* with some breadcrumbs to make a quick stuffing and it was almost as good.

BLANQUETTE DE CHEVREAU

KID MEAT WITH CREAM SAUCE

Occasionally what is labelled 'wild' goat meat from North Devon is on sale in Exeter. How wild is wild, I wondered, but bought some all the same; I cooked it in a Greek recipe and it tasted Greek enough. On the whole I prefer the taste and texture of kid meat which has long been popular in Provence. Does the growth of goat cheese-making in Britain mean that in time kid will become more widely available? Mme Marquet's advice is to cook kid as you would veal. Most veal and kid recipes are interchangeable, and both meats need to be well cooked to be satisfactory.

¾ kg (about 1½ lb)
   shoulder of kid, boned
salt
1 carrot
1 onion stuck with 6 cloves
white part of a leek
half a stick of celery
1 clove of garlic

bouquet garni
170 g (6 oz) button
   mushrooms
30 g (1 oz) butter
30 g (1 oz) flour
ground mace or nutmeg
2 egg yolks
150 ml (¼ pt) double cream

Cut the meat in 5 cm (2 in) cubes and soak in cold water for 1 hour. Drain and cover with fresh water. Add a little salt and bring the water to the boil. Skim off any froth and add the carrot, onion, leek, celery, garlic and bouquet garni. Cover, lower the heat and cook very slowly for 1–1½ hours or until the meat is tender.

Use a slotted spoon to lift out the meat and place in a hot serving dish. Strain the liquid and add the mushrooms. When they are cooked use a slotted spoon to lift them out and add to the meat. Reduce the liquid over high heat until it measures 425 ml (¾ pint) and pour it into a jug.

Melt the butter in the pan and stir in the flour for 1–2 minutes but do not let it colour. Gradually whisk in the stock and cook until thickened. Whisk the egg yolks with the cream and gradually pour into the sauce, whisking all the time, but do not let it boil. Season with mace or nutmeg, and add a dash of lemon juice to sharpen the flavour slightly.

Pour the sauce over the meat and mushrooms and serve with rice or noodles. Serves 4.

Near les Baux

ALOUETTES SANS TÊTES

SMALL VEAL 'BIRDS'

In this dish thin escalopes of veal are made to resemble birds by wrapping them around a mint and lemon stuffing and cooking them in a wine sauce.

8–10 escalopes of veal, Camembert size
salt, milled pepper
55 g (2 oz) fresh white breadcrumbs
100 g (3½ oz) *saucisson sec* or salami
2 tablespoons chopped mint and parsley
½ lemon, finely grated zest and juice

2 eggs, beaten
115 g (4 oz) butter, melted
1 shallot, chopped
1 stick of celery, chopped
1 carrot, sliced
150 ml (¼ pt) dry white wine
a bay leaf
stock or water
sprigs of flat parsley to garnish

Beat each escalope until very thin, season lightly with salt and pepper and set aside while you make the stuffing.

Mix together the breadcrumbs, *saucisson*, mint, parsley, lemon zest and juice, eggs, half the butter and some salt and pepper.

Divide the stuffing between the escalopes. Then fold over the sides and roll up each 'bird' neatly. Secure with cotton string but do not pull it too tight.

Pour the remainder of the melted butter into a flameproof casserole large enough to hold the parcels in a single layer. Gently sauté the shallot, celery and carrot for a few minutes. Use a slotted spoon to transfer to a plate. Add the veal birds and cook until lightly browned. Pour in the wine, add the bay leaf and the vegetables and sufficient stock to come level with the meat. Season very lightly.

Cover and cook over low heat or in a moderate oven (Mark 4, 180°C, 350°F) for 30–40 minutes or until the meat is tender. Transfer the 'birds' to a hot serving dish and snip off the string. Boil the liquid to reduce by half then strain over the meat. If you wish, garnish the meat with flat parsley. Serve with noodles, rice or potatoes. Serves 4.

CERVELLES D'AGNEAU AU BEURRE NOIR

LAMB'S BRAINS WITH BLACK BUTTER

Both lamb's and calf's brains are delicious cooked in this way. Calf's brains must be skinned half-way through the soaking in cold water.

2–3 lamb's brains	salt
1 onion spiked with cloves	finely chopped parsley
bouquet garni	45 g (1½ oz) butter
4 tablespoons white wine vinegar	

Some butchers sell brains soaked and ready to cook. But if the brains have not been soaked, put them in cold water for 2 hours, changing the water every half hour or so. Or leave the brains in a bowl in the sink under a trickling tap.

Meanwhile simmer the onion, bouquet garni, 2 tablespoons of the wine vinegar and the salt with 700 ml (1¼ pt) water for 20 minutes. Strain and return the stock to the pan. Add the brains and poach very gently for 10–15 minutes until cooked. Use a slotted spoon to lift out on to a cloth, making sure that the brains drain well. Place on a hot serving dish and sprinkle the parsley over them.

Melt the butter in a pan and cook until nut brown. Pour over the brains and add the remaining 2 tablespoons of the vinegar to the buttery pan. Swill round over the heat and pour over the brains. Serve straight away. Serves 2.

RÔTI DE VEAU AU ROMARIN

ROAST VEAL WITH ROSEMARY

It is encouraging that in Britain veal is becoming better value and more popular every year. The alliance of veal with rosemary is well established and is very good.

1½–2 kg (about 3–4 lb) piece of roasting veal	salt, milled pepper
1–2 cloves of garlic	85 g (3 oz) butter
a few young shoots of fresh rosemary	2 wineglasses dry white wine
	1 large tomato

Use a sharp-pointed knife to make 12–18 small incisions all over the meat. Tuck a sliver of garlic and a few spikes of rosemary into each. Season the meat and spread most of the butter over it.

Place the joint in a lightly buttered roasting tin and pour in half a glass of wine.

Roast the meat in a moderate oven (Mark 5, 190°C, 375°F) for 20–25 minutes per ½ kg (1 lb) or until cooked to your preference; roast veal should be well cooked. Baste the meat now and again during the cooking. Add the tomato to the pan towards the end of the cooking time.

Transfer the meat to a hot carving dish and keep warm for 15–20 minutes, to make it easier to carve. Pour off the surplus fat from the roasting pan and add the wine. Bring to the boil and simmer for 5 minutes while stirring to incorporate the pan juices and crush the tomato into the gravy. Strain the gravy into a small pan, check the seasoning and keep hot. When ready to serve, carve the meat and whisk a knob of butter into the gravy. Serves 6–8.

COUSCOUS À LA MARGA

COUSCOUS FROM THE MAGREB

Couscous, the national dish of north Africa, is now widely eaten in the south of France. This spiced meat and vegetable stew makes a good dish for a large party of people and goes well served late in the evening when the weather is very hot.

This slightly adapted recipe comes from Prosper Montagné's *Le Grand Livre de la cuisine*, but for a version to feed fewer people you could not do better than use Claudia Roden's in *A Book of Middle Eastern Food*.

I have eaten many versions of *couscous* but one of the best was served by a Brazilian couturier who was running a pension in the

Rhône valley while waiting for a lawsuit in Paris to be completed. Alas, Carlos no longer serves us his *couscous royale* in his pink dining-room in between darting back into the television room, where he was running up a dress in purple chiffon for a local bride to wear at the party after the wedding.

The grain *couscous* is made from semolina and is now sold ready to cook. It is available in health-food shops or in grocers' shops in student areas. If you are keen on preparing *couscous* regularly it may be worth bringing back an aluminium *couscousier* from a French hypermarket – they are not expensive.

1½ kg (3 lb) chicken	100 g (3½ oz) chick peas,
1½ kg (3 lb) shoulder of	soaked and half-cooked
lamb, boned	1 tablespoon salt
3 tomatoes, peeled and	1–2 tablespoons cayenne
chopped	pepper
3 artichoke bottoms	½ teaspoon ground cumin
3 courgettes, cut in chunks	2 cloves
1–2 turnips, cut in pieces	
1–2 onions, chopped	*Sauce royale*
1–2 green peppers, seeded	1–2 tablespoons *harissa*
and sliced	(see p. 101)
225 g (8 oz) broad beans	1 kg (2¼ lb) couscous grain

Cut the chicken into portions and discard the skin. Cut the lamb into large pieces. Cover with water in a large pan and bring to the boil. Skim off any froth and discard.

Add all the remaining ingredients (I think the recipe is improved if artichokes, courgettes, green peppers and broad beans are added half-way through the cooking time), cover and cook for 1 hour.

Place a colander or the top of the *couscousier* on top of the pan and add the grain. Cook for a further ¾–1 hour, stirring the *couscous* grain with a fork half-way through the cooking.

Turn the grain into a hot serving dish and the stew into another. Mix about 300 ml (½ pt) of the meat juices with the *harissa* and pour into a bowl to hand separately as a sauce.

Rognons aux Anchois

KIDNEYS WITH ANCHOVY BUTTER

Anchovy butter	finely chopped parsley
4–5 anchovy fillets	6–8 lamb's kidneys
55 g (2 oz) butter, softened	olive oil
lemon juice	breadcrumbs, fairly dry

Rinse the anchovy fillets in warm water, and chop them very finely. Mix with the butter, a dash of lemon juice and the parsley.

Remove the thin skin from the kidneys, cut each in half and remove the core. Brush the kidneys with olive oil and coat with breadcrumbs. Arrange on a lightly oiled grill pan or thread on to wooden or metal skewers. Cook under a hot grill for 5–6 minutes, turning once.

Transfer the kidneys to a hot serving dish and spread the anchovy butter over them. Place under the grill for a few moments until the butter is starting to melt. Serve straight away. Serves 2–3.

Salpicon pour les Rôtis

SALPICON FOR ROAST MEAT

A friend in Haute Provence showed me how she makes her roast pork and lamb so mouthwatering. This mixture is used to baste the meat during cooking and can be used in the same way with oven-baked or grilled lamb or pork chops.

50 g (2 oz) *lard fumé* or	salt, milled pepper
smoked streaky bacon	5–6 tablespoons olive or
1 clove of garlic, chopped	sunflower oil
small bunch of parsley,	1 tablespoon white wine
chopped	vinegar

Dice the bacon and garlic very finely, add the chopped parsley and season with salt and milled pepper. Mix to a paste with the oil and vinegar.

This *salpicon* can be spread over the meat before or during the cooking. I usually spread half over the fat side of a loin of pork or over the meat side of a boned and butterflied leg of lamb. Leave the joint, covered by an upturned bowl, at room temperature for an hour or so before roasting in the usual way.

Spread the remainder of the *salpicon* on the meat half-way through the cooking time. You'll find the sauce made from the pan juices will be specially good.

VEGETABLES

Bagnol
sur Cège

It may be in the realm of vegetables that we can most easily gain some French culinary wisdom. In many ways it is a comfort to find that some of the best vegetable cuisine in France is in private homes. Too often even highly rated restaurants find getting the vegetables just delectably right a difficult assignment. Rarely content to leave well alone, here a crisp blade is subjected to the will of the chef or there a sensationally lovely leaf is curled or shredded beyond recognition, ruining its looks and its taste. And in lesser establishments far too few vegetables reach your table unblessed by the can-opener.

How reassuring, then, for those about to eat at her table when each day, just before noon, Jeannette Doize leaves her kitchen and crosses the lane to her low walled garden, for they know that they are about to experience one of the finest gastronomic delights: sumptuously fresh vegetables prepared at the last moment and in a manner that respects them.

Walking through the picket gate, past the stone sink of sparkling water that each evening refreshes the plants, one immediately smells the warm, moist soil, black and friable after decades of devotion. The sweet scents of the garden vie with each other as you pass the row of broad beans in blossom, the clumps of purple-flowered chives, the full-blown lettuces waiting to be picked. In the shade of the wall the soldier-like leaves of sorrel stand erect on their red stems, which will melt into a dull green purée, sharp and lemony, the moment they touch the hot foaming butter of the pan.

These are her ingredients. The sorrel purée is served in the centre of a circlet of thinly sliced courgettes. The lettuce is dressed at the last moment with local olive oil and a scattering of chives. And the broad beans, cooked when no bigger than your thumbnail, their eyes still green, are tossed in *crème fraîche* with finely chopped summer savory. The bean pods may also be eaten when tiny or they are turned into a pale green summer soup. The tips of the plants themselves – quickly blanched, chopped and running with butter – are eaten with fish, thereby not only serving as a delicious vegetable but also making the plants more bushy and productive. As an extra bonus, the trick helps prevent an infestation of black-fly. (This works in Britain too.)

Jeannette's vegetable courses are a perfect example of how proper cooking is interrelated. I stand beside her while she cooks in the kitchen of her medieval farmhouse and I notice that her ingredients and dishes are never seen in isolation. Each gains from its proximity to another.

In midsummer, to avoid the heat of the day, Jeannette is at work in her garden soon after dawn and again in the evening. Generations of her family have gardened here before her. Arthur Young, the English agriculturalist, travelling in France in 1787, noted that in the gardens near Le Vigan (Gard) 'Every man has an olive, a mulberry, an almond or a peach-tree and vines scattered amongst them, so that the whole ground is covered with the oddest mixture of these plants and bulging rocks that can be conceived. The inhabitants of this village deserve encouragement for their industry; and if I was a French minister they should have it. They would soon turn all the deserts around them into gardens.'

But however plentiful are the crops from a French country garden, its owner is able to supplement them with supplies from the local market, where the variety and choice of fruit and vegetables is, to us, astonishing. In Pierrelatte (Drôme) market in July there is an onion stall. A stall selling only onions. But it offers fifteen varieties, all named of course; from tiny silver-skinned onions like large pearls to huge, golden Spanish globes and flat, gleaming, white onions, their tops folded over neatly as if on show for a prize, to the garland of ruby, satin-skinned onions. One of these, cut into wafer-thin rings and dressed with oil, looks delightfully pretty and tastes fresh and juicy, almost sweet – not at all bitter – around a platter of potatoes or fish.

Yet this display of allium bounty is regarded as normal by Jeannette, who raised her shoulders in true Gallic fashion and opened her hands: '*Naturellement,*' she says. Such variety, such choice, is regarded almost as a right, as important as clean water or unpolluted air. And we who appreciate it and discover how much our cooking benefits from it do not wish to leave its influence in France.

Every town or village has a shop selling seeds. The highly coloured packets, each with a picture of the vegetable, herb or flower, are all you need to be able to give yourself this welcome variety when cooking in Britain: the long-leaved red *radicchio* from Treviso or the round crumpled variety from Verona; white carrots, yellow beetroots, three kinds of globe artichokes, *feuille de chêne* or oak-leaf lettuce, a large-leaved salad rocket or more varieties of pumpkin than you'd have room or appetite for.

Even if you have no garden you may have a terrace, back yard or windowbox; wonders can be performed in a Gro-bag placed on a windowsill. And then there are allotments or friends' allotments. The two kinds of basil seed that I bring back from France flourish in pots on the windowsill as no English seed seems to. This is in the tradition of John Evelyn, the best British salad grower, whose *Acetaria* (1699) still inspires us with a sense of adventure in the kitchen garden, his own sown with seeds from Italy, France and Spain.

A few decades ago Elizabeth David pointed out that, 'It is in the matter of vegetables and fruit that a country's eating habits evolve most rapidly.' Since that was written there have been changes in our eating habits but many of them have been foisted on us by commercial interests. Huge sums are spent on advertising and boosting the future of the avocado, the kiwi or the sharon fruit, but providing a real choice of lettuce, or carrots with a proper flavour, are matters ignored. By recovering John Evelyn's spirit of adventure we can bring back from France seeds (plants are subject to certain regulations) and the enthusiasm which can help us regain our appreciation of vegetables and enliven our eating.

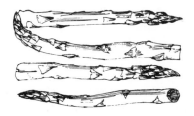

ASPERGES EN SAUCE MOUSSELINE

ASPARAGUS WITH MOUSSELINE SAUCE

In a warm sleepy village where two small cats sitting at the top of a flight of stone steps narrowed their eyes at us, we discovered a gem of a restaurant – small, quiet and good. It was May, there was lily of the valley on the table and we had our first asparagus of the season. And it was delightful with this sauce. But to my mind, French white-stemmed asparagus lacks the flavour of the green spears we grow here. Just occasionally you meet a Frenchman who admits it. And I notice that some growers in the south are starting to plant the green variety.

680 g (1½ lb) fresh asparagus
salt

Sauce mousseline
3 egg yolks
1 tablespoon white wine vinegar, ideally a herb vinegar like tarragon or rosemary

salt, ground white or green pepper
225 g (8 oz) butter
juice of a small lemon
100 ml (3½ fl oz) *crème fraîche* or whipped cream

Trim the end of each stick of asparagus. In France you may need to scrape away the skin on the lower end of the stalks. If you grow your own and cut it young this should not be necessary.

Cook the asparagus in salted water, stalks down, with a hood of foil over the spears so that they cook in the steam. Home-grown asparagus takes 6–12 minutes depending on the size. Bought asparagus which has dried out a little may need up to 20 minutes. Test the end of a stalk with the point of a knife now and again but do not overcook. Drain the asparagus and keep it hot, wrapped in a cloth while you make the sauce.

Whisk together the egg yolks with the vinegar and a little salt and pepper in a bowl over hot water. Add the butter in small lumps, whisking in each addition. The butter should soften but not melt. If the bowl gets too hot stand it in a bowl of iced water to cool and then replace over the hot water. Continue whisking the sauce, which should mount and thicken like a mayonnaise or *hollandaise* sauce.

Remove the bowl from the heat and gradually whisk in sufficient lemon juice to sharpen the flavour agreeably. Fold in the cream, check the seasoning and serve with the asparagus. Serves 4.

CONFITS DE POIREAUX AUX PETITS LARDONS

BRAISED LEEKS WITH BACON

With tender, young leeks the whole vegetable can be used in this dish. With older leeks it's probably best to cook only the white fleshier parts, keeping the green part for soups.

680 g (1½ lb) young tender leeks	2–3 slices of smoked streaky bacon, diced
2 tablespoons olive oil	salt, milled pepper
1 onion, chopped	55 g (2 oz) Gruyère cheese, grated
1 clove of garlic, crushed (optional)	

Trim the leeks and wash them really carefully under cold running water. Cut across into narrow slices.

Heat the oil in a pan. Stir in the onion, garlic and bacon for 3–4 minutes, and then add the leeks. Stir until coated with the oil. Cook over moderate heat, stirring now and again until the vegetables are cooked and almost all the liquid from them has evaporated from the pan. Season with a little salt and pepper.

Spoon the mixture into a hot ovenproof dish and sprinkle the cheese over the top. Place under a hot grill or in an oven for a few minutes until the cheese has melted and is bubbling. Serves 4. Very good with poultry and game.

HARICOTS À LA TOMATE

DRIED HARICOT BEANS WITH TOMATOES

Dried haricot beans in a tomato sauce with a spicy sausage make a good, cheap, nourishing meal. It works equally well with other dried beans if you prefer.

225 g (8 oz) dried haricot beans
a bay leaf and a clove of garlic
2 tablespoons olive oil
1 onion, chopped
1 clove of garlic, chopped
a little thyme and marjoram, chopped

400 g (14 oz) tomatoes, peeled and chopped
½ teaspoon sugar
a splash of red wine
1 or 2 *chorizo* or other highly spiced sausages
finely chopped parsley

Soak the haricot beans for 2 hours in warm water until swollen. Drain, cover with fresh water and simmer with the bay leaf and the clove of garlic, adding more water if necessary, for 40–60 minutes or until cooked. Drain well.

Meanwhile, heat the oil in a pan and cook the onion and the chopped garlic in it until soft. Add the thyme and marjoram, and the tomatoes, sugar and wine, and cook over moderate heat for 20 minutes, when the sauce should be thick and aromatic. Mash the tomatoes with a fork to give an even consistency and add the sausages, cut into chunks. Cook together for 10 minutes.

Mix in the hot drained beans and then turn into a warmed pottery dish; sprinkle with finely chopped parsley and serve. Follow with a green salad. Serves 3–4.

RAGOÛT DE FÈVES VERTES

RAGOUT OF BROAD BEANS

Broad beans invariably need a sauce, I think. This one is light and quickly made with egg yolk and olive oil.

> 340 g (12 oz) young broad
>   beans, shelled
> salt
> a few sprigs of summer
>   savory
> a few sprigs of fresh thyme
> 2 tablespoons olive oil
> 1 large egg yolk

Cook the broad beans in the minimum of salted boiling water with the savory and thyme.

Drain the beans but reserve 2–3 tablespoons of the cooking water. Discard the herbs. Mix the cooking water with the oil and the egg yolk.

Return the mixture to the pan with the beans and cook gently, stirring all the time until slightly thickened, but do not allow to boil. Serves 3–4. A little very finely chopped fresh savory on top is a nice garnish.

ARTICHAUTS AU CRABE

ARTICHOKES WITH CRAB

This is a really delicious filling for artichoke bottoms but it also might be served in crisp curved lettuce leaves. I have also replaced the crab with slivers of smoked trout with equally good results.

4 fresh artichokes
salt
a slice of lemon or a splash
    of vinegar
1 stick of celery
a handful of flat parsley
4 tablespoons mayonnaise

a squeeze of lemon juice
a good pinch of curry
    powder
140 g (5 oz) fresh or tinned
    white crabmeat
1 egg yolk, hard-boiled

Cook the artichokes in boiling salted water with the lemon or the vinegar for 25–40 minutes depending on size and freshness. They are cooked when a leaf pulls away easily. Drain, trim off all the outer leaves (I scrape off the soft green part and add it to soup) and remove the choke to give you four neatly trimmed artichoke bottoms. Leave to cool.

Remove any tough outer strings from the celery and chop it finely. Mix into the mayonnaise with the lemon juice and the curry powder. Fold in the crab meat.

Spoon the filling into the artichoke bottoms and push the egg yolk through a sieve over the top of each to give a pretty effect. Serves 4.

SALADE COMPOSÉE

Sometimes one especially fine vegetable inspires a *salade composée*. Here I started with the artichoke hearts but, of course, a different vegetable could take the starring role.

6–8 artichoke hearts,
    freshly cooked but
    cooled
1 green pepper
a few slices of *jambon cru*
    or a mild *saucisson sec*

olive oil
seed mustard
lemon juice
salt, milled pepper
a handful of green olives

Cut the artichoke hearts in half downwards. De-seed the pepper and cut in thin slices. Slice the *jambon* or *saucisson sec* in narrow strips and dress with a little olive oil.

Make a dressing for the salad by mixing the mustard with some olive oil and lemon juice in the proportions you prefer. Season with salt and pepper.

Half the charm of this salad is the way it is arranged.

Place a ring of green pepper on each of three or four plates and arrange 4 artichoke halves around it. Fill in the gaps with strips of green pepper radiating like curved spokes. Spoon the *jambon cru* into the centre of the plate and arrange a few olives around the plate. Spoon some dressing over the salad. Serve with French bread. Serves 3–4.

POMMES DE TERRE FONDANTES

FONDANT POTATOES

If you select tiny new potatoes, gob-stopper size, for this excellent dish, I'm sure you'll be delighted with the result. The potatoes are golden and crisp outside and meltingly soft as soon as you cut into them.

> **450 g (1 lb) new potatoes**
> **30 g (1 oz) butter**
> **coarse sea salt**

Scrape the potatoes, rinse and dry them in a cloth. Melt the butter in a wide, heavy-based pan, add the potatoes and shake to coat them with butter.

Cover the pan and cook over moderate to low heat for 20–30 minutes, shaking the pan now and again to prevent the potatoes sticking.

When cooked, remove the lid and sauté the potatoes briefly over high heat to drive off any water and to give the potatoes a crisp finish. Turn the potatoes into a very hot serving dish, sprinkle with the salt and serve straight away. Serves 3–4.

GRATIN DE COURGETTES

COURGETTE GRATIN

How many vegetable gratins have we in our national cuisine? Well, there's Cauliflower Cheese (hardly a triumph, I feel) and . . . could you call Pan Haggerty a gratin? Clearly we are not over-endowed with the things, which is why we seize on what the French do. This courgette gratin is superb served straight from the oven: the courgette tender but faintly crisp in an egg custard that is just set. A dish worth perfecting so that you don't deprive yourself of the real joy of it.

about 250 g (8–9 oz) slim
   courgettes
a little fruity olive oil
85 g (3 oz) Gruyère cheese,
   finely grated
2 large eggs

6 tablespoons milk
1 clove of garlic
salt
30 g (1 oz) fresh white
   breadcrumbs

Wipe the courgettes and remove the stem ends. Slice thinly and make a layer of the slices in the base of each of four lightly oiled small gratin dishes. Sprinkle the courgettes with a little cheese and make a further layer of courgettes.

Beat the eggs with the milk, using a fork with a clove of garlic impaled on its tines to flavour the mixture subtly – Escoffier's trick. Season with just a little salt and stir in half the breadcrumbs.

Divide half the egg mixture between the dishes, sprinkle with a little more cheese and add a final layer of courgettes. Pour over the remaining egg mixture and sprinkle the rest of the cheese mixed with the rest of the breadcrumbs on top of each dish. Trickle a little olive oil over the top. Bake the dishes in a moderate oven (Mark 4, 180°C, 350°F) for 25–30 minutes. Serve straight away. Serves 2–4.

SOUPE À L'OIGNON D'ANNONAY

ANNONAY ONION SOUP

Charles Forot in his affectionate portrait of the Ardèche, *Odeurs de forêt et fumet de table*, gives this recipe for a creamy-white onion soup. Such a simple soup depends on well-ripened onions and a beautifully flavoured home-made stock. We find it excellent late at night on the day after Boxing Day, as a restorative.

450 g (1 lb) yellow-skinned
  onions
55 g (2 oz) butter
2 tablespoons flour
570 ml (1 pt) chicken or
  turkey stock

275 ml (½ pt) creamy milk
salt, milled pepper
croûtons fried in butter

Peel and chop the onions and stir into the butter, melted in a pan, until well coated. Cover the pan, lower the heat and allow the onions to sweat in the butter for 10–15 minutes until yellow and pulpy. It is important that the onions do not brown at all because the flavour would be totally altered.

Stir in the flour and cook for 1–2 minutes. Gradually mix in the stock and the milk. Cook, stirring now and again, for 10–15 minutes until thickened and there is no trace of the taste of flour. Sieve or process the soup until smooth. Return to the pan and reheat; season with salt and pepper. Serve with hot croûtons. Serves 3–4.

PÂTE NIÇOISE

NIÇOISE PASTA

I was given this recipe for green gnocchi but found the pasta more delicious rolled out thinly, cut into strips and served as tagliatelle with butter, oil and Parmesan cheese. But if you wish, the mixture can be rolled into small balls and cooked in bouillon or around the meat in a *daube* for the final half-hour of the cooking time.

85 g (3 oz) fresh spinach
85 g (3 oz) leaves of Swiss
  chard
55 g (2 oz) leaves of lettuce
salt

55 g (2 oz) Parmesan
  cheese, finely grated
285 g (10 oz) flour
1 tablespoon olive oil
2 eggs

Wash the spinach, Swiss chard and lettuce; drain well. Shred all the leaves, sprinkle with salt and leave in a bowl for 30 minutes. Rinse in cold water, drain well and dry by wrapping tightly in a cloth.

Chop the leaves very finely, with a knife or in a processor. Mix with the cheese, flour, oil and eggs and just a little salt. Add a splash of water, if necessary, until the dough is soft but malleable. All the chopping and mixing can be done very quickly in a processor.

Form the dough into a ball and leave under an upturned bowl for 30 minutes. Roll out on a floured surface until very thin indeed. Cut narrow strips as for tagliatelle.

Cook the pasta in salted, boiling water for 3–5 minutes. Drain well and turn into a hot serving dish. Serve with butter or oil and Parmesan cheese and freshly milled black pepper. Serves 3–4.

CRIQUE

Many parts of Europe have their own version of this potato dish. The Ardéchois version is known as *la crique*. Jean-Paul Barras in his delightfully personal book, *Le Coeur et la fourchette*, gives four recipes for the dish: one for those in a hurry, one for the rich, one for the impoverished and his own. I find *la crique des pauvres* the best and this is the version I watched Jeannette make for us the evening she prepared a specially authentic Ardéchois meal.

450 g (1 lb) potatoes	salt
1 clove of garlic, crushed	oil for frying
1 tablespoon finely chopped parsley	

Peel the potatoes and grate into a bowl. Add the garlic, parsley and salt. Mix well.

Heat a little oil in a pan until almost smoking. Add tablespoonfuls of the mixture to the pan, making three or four flat heaps. Cook until golden-brown on both sides. Drain well on kitchen paper and serve straight away.

Alternatively pile the mixture into the pan and make one large potato cake, turning it over once. Serve cut into wedges. Serves 3–4.
Variations
La crique des gens riches: add 2 eggs and 150 ml (¼ pint) of *crème fraîche* to the mixture.

La crique de Jean-Paul Barras: omit the garlic and parsley from the recipe for the poor.

IMAN BAYILDI

STUFFED AUBERGINES

The title of this famous aubergine dish translates as 'the Iman fainted' – whether at the scent or savour of the dish is not certain; some have reckoned it was the cost which caused the dramatic reaction. Though the price of olive oil goes up, aubergines seem to be cheaper every year, and I have managed to grow them surprisingly well under glass in England. In France, in the south, like most vegetables, they are good value.

I prefer to halve the aubergines and cut into them like the leaves of a book, but the vegetable could as easily be hollowed or have the cuts made on the outside. Iman Bayildi makes an excellent but surprisingly filling preliminary to a summer meal.

2 medium-sized aubergines
salt
2 medium onions, finely
  chopped
1 clove of garlic, finely
  chopped
2 tablespoons olive oil
2 tomatoes, skinned and
  chopped

45 g (1½ oz) currants
1 tablespoon finely
  chopped parsley
¼ teaspoon ground allspice
salt, milled pepper
a little olive oil

Halve the aubergines lengthways. Make 3 or 4 cuts into the cut surface but not all the way through so that the sections of aubergine resemble the pages (very thick ones) of a book. Sprinkle all the cut surfaces with salt and leave the aubergines in a colander for 30–45 minutes for any bitter juices to seep out. Rinse in cold water and dry well on a cloth or kitchen paper.

Meanwhile soften the onions and garlic in the olive oil over moderate heat. Add the tomatoes, currants, parsley, allspice, salt and milled pepper and cook together for 15–20 minutes until you have a thick, mushy sauce.

Spoon the sauce into all the gaps in each half of aubergine. Place them skin side down in a casserole and spoon the remaining sauce on top.

Dribble some olive oil over the vegetables, add a coffee cup of hot water and cover tightly.

Cook in a slow oven (Mark 3, 160°C, 325°F) for about 1 hour until the aubergines are completely cooked and there is little liquid in the casserole. Add a little more liquid during the cooking if necessary. (Earlier recipes give a huge quantity of olive oil – enough to make you faint at today's prices – for the cooking stage but I think it needs to be cut down to the amount I've given for present-day taste.)

Remove from the oven and allow to cool. Serve at room temperature. Serves 4.

Navets à la Moutarde

TURNIPS WITH MUSTARD

Turnips with mustard is a classic combination in French country cooking. One Christmas I was inspired by the field of turnips opposite the house to serve this dish with goose. We find it provides the right balance of sharp and sweet flavours that goes so well with rich poultry and game.

450 g (1 lb) baby turnips	**150 ml (¼ pt) soured cream**
salt	**or *crème fraîche***
1–2 teaspoons Dijon seed	**a squeeze of lemon juice**
mustard	

Peel the turnips and shape each neatly so that they are all the same size. Cook in salted boiling water for 7–10 minutes or until tender. Drain and keep hot.

Stir the mustard into the soured cream with the lemon juice over moderate heat. Add the turnips and when coated with the sauce turn the vegetables and sauce into a serving dish. Serves 4.

OIGNONS ÉTUVÉS AU BEAUJOLAIS

ONIONS STEWED WITH RED WINE

Beaujolais Nouveau arrives here at about the same time in November as the first pickling onions. The two work exceptionally well together. But any of the other *primeurs*, especially Côtes du Rhône, are just as acceptable in this dish and are often cheaper.

450 g (1 lb) small onions, pickling size	salt
	2 bay leaves
55 g (2 oz) butter	a little brown sugar
1–2 teaspoons flour	(depending on the wine)
275 ml (½ pt) Beaujolais Nouveau	a little ground allspice

Peel the onions. Melt the butter in a flameproof casserole, add the onions and cook, stirring from time to time, until well coated with butter and just starting to change colour.

Stir in the flour then add the wine. Season lightly with salt and tuck the bay leaves between the onions.

Cover and cook over moderate heat or in a moderate oven (Mark 4, 180°C, 350°F) for 30–40 minutes until the onions are cooked but are not mushy.

Transfer to the hob, add a little sugar and a trace of allspice. Bubble the sauce until thick, and serve. This dish is splendid with game and roast meats. Serves 4.

UN PLAT D'AUBERGINES ET DE TOMATES À M. CHABRIER

M. CHABRIER'S DISH OF AUBERGINES WITH TOMATOES

Eighty-year-old M. Chabrier was my neighbour in Vézénobres. And whenever we met we talked about food; sometimes we sat on the high terrace overlooking the valley below and, at other times, in front of the brick fireplace which his wife had waxed for fifty years until it looked like glass and of which he was very proud.

'This land around here is aubergine country,' he said one morning, 'so I'll tell you a good way of eating them.'

Wipe some medium-sized aubergines with a cloth, then cut into slices and place in a sieve, covered with a plate, to drain for about half an hour.

Dry the slices on kitchen paper and toss them in seasoned flour. Shallow-fry the aubergines on both sides in olive oil and then drain on paper.

Take a large serving plate and arrange the slices of aubergine in a circle towards the edge of the plate. Slice some large tomatoes and arrange in overlapping rings in the centre. Chill the plate for up to one hour. Then, just before serving, dribble a little olive oil over the tomatoes, season and sprinkle some chopped basil or parsley on top.

OEUFS BROUILLADE AUX TROIS POIVRONS

SCRAMBLED EGG WITH THREE PIMENTO PEPPERS

I make the best scrambled eggs when I bake an angel cake or meringues, because then I can add extra egg yolks.

3 small sweet peppers, red, green and yellow	2–3 egg yolks
55 g (2 oz) butter	4 tablespoons single cream
3 eggs	salt, milled pepper
	finely chopped chives

Seed and dice the peppers and cook in half the butter until soft. Lift out with a slotted spoon and keep hot.

Add the remainder of the butter to the pan and leave to melt slowly. Lightly beat the eggs with the egg yolks and the cream. Season with salt and pepper.

Place the pan over moderate heat and, when the butter is hot, pour in the eggs. Cook gently until a layer of egg is set, then stir to allow a fresh layer of liquid egg to come in contact with the base of the pan.

Add the cooked peppers and the chives. Cook, stirring gently until all the mixture is *just* set. Serve straight away. Serves 2–3.

POIS CHICHES GRILLÉS

TOASTED CHICK PEAS

A young classics master once explained to me in great detail how ancient Rome would have collapsed without beans. Certainly the Romans introduced chick peas to Britain and, doubtless, they strewed them through France on the way. During the last ten years the chick pea, one of the staples of the Middle East and North Africa, has made a comeback in France, accompanying the immigrants from those cultures. As a result, a French market, especially in the south, usually has a sizeable stall displaying a good variety of pulses – beans, peas and seeds, whole and ground, along with the exciting spices that are usually necessary to give some taste to these otherwise bland vegetable proteins. Chick peas, though, have a more pronounced flavour; flat and earthy, they are probably at their best puréed in hummus or whole in salads. But it was in Israel that I first came upon chick peas, soaked, cooked and toasted, sold as a snack like roasted peanuts. I've now worked out how to prepare them at home for serving with a dozen or so small bowls of other nibbling foods to munch with wine as part of a light lunch eaten in the midday shade. Only some cheese and fruit is needed to complete the meal.

115 g (4 oz) chick peas
1 tablespoon nut or
sunflower oil
salt

Soak the chick peas in warm water to cover for 2 hours. Turn into a pan and cook, covered, over moderate heat for 30–40 minutes, depending on their age, until tender.

Drain the peas and while still warm remove their skins. Spread the peas in a single layer on a baking sheet. Dribble the oil over them and toast under a hot grill, shaking them from time to time, until golden.

Remove from the heat, sprinkle with salt and serve warm or cold.

TOURTE DE BLETTES

SWISS CHARD PIE

After some discussion with three generations of Niçois, everyone agreed that this pie is the main speciality of Nice. And traditionally *tourte de blettes* is served as part of the Provençal Grand Dessert at Christmas Eve. The recipe is slightly adapted from Jacques Méde-cin's *Cuisine du comté de Nice*. How recipes change with time and place is always fascinating; Médecin says his recipe is traditional while Prosper Montagné, writing fifty years earlier, omits an important ingredient, the apples, from his version. I prefer the pie made without the sugar; it is then suitable for serving warm at the start of a meal.

Pastry
340 g (12 oz) flour
200 g (7 oz) butter, softened
1 large egg

Filling
55 g (2 oz) seedless raisins
55 g (2 oz) currants
6 tablespoons *eau-de-vie*
570 g (1 lb 4 oz) green part
    of Swiss chard (*blettes*)

55 g (2 oz) Parmesan
    cheese, freshly grated
2 eggs
115 g (4 oz) pine nuts
2 tablespoons olive oil
30 g (1 oz) caster sugar
    (optional) *or* salt, milled
    pepper
225 g (8 oz) Reinette or
    Cox's Orange apples,
    peeled and sliced
2 tablespoons dark rum

Sift the flour on to a cold working surface or a wide shallow bowl (which can be chilled in the fridge first). Make a well in the centre, add the butter and egg and, using the fingertips only, draw the flour into the centre and gradually mix with sufficient cold water to make a soft dough. Wrap and chill for 30 minutes.

Soften the raisins and currants in the *eau-de-vie* over a low heat and leave in a warm place until needed. Wash the leaves of the Swiss chard and then cut into narrow strips and wash again in plenty of cold water until all traces of green in the water have disappeared. This makes the vegetable less bitter. Obviously use your judgement about all this washing. I find Swiss chard straight from the garden is not at all bitter but if your leaves are huge and a touch elderly it may be wise to follow the instructions given. Cook the leaves in boiling salted water until tender but still bright green. Drain well, wrap in a clean cloth and wring out all the surplus water.

Chop the leaves finely and turn into a bowl with the dried fruit mixture, the cheese, eggs, pine nuts, olive oil and sugar or salt and pepper. Mix well.

Roll out two thirds of the pastry and line a buttered 25 cm (10 in) flan dish or tin; it should be rather deeper than a tart tin. Spoon half the filling into the pastry case, add a layer of the sliced apples and cover it with the remainder of the filling. Sprinkle the rum over the top and cover with a lid of pastry. Squeeze the edges together firmly and cut a few steam vents in the lid.

Bake in a moderate oven (Mark 5, 190°C, 375°F) for 30–40 minutes until the pastry is golden and crisp. Serve warm or cold. Serves 6.

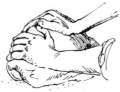

SAUCE FROIDE DE MOUTARDE POUR ASPERGES ET ARTICHAUTS DE MME VIGNON

COLD MUSTARD SAUCE FOR ASPARAGUS AND GLOBE ARTICHOKES FROM MME VIGNON

I had arrived to talk to M. Vignon about his chestnut bread. As we walked into the bakery to check some details on the flour bags we met Mme Vignon in her tiny, neat *cuisine de coin* tucked in behind the shop. She was scraping some fat white sticks of asparagus to serve for lunch. We discussed sauces for asparagus and she insisted on making her own mustard sauce straight away for me to taste. Once the asparagus is over, I find it goes well with globe artichokes too.

1 teaspoon smooth Dijon
  mustard
3–4 tablespoons fruity
  olive oil
a little white wine vinegar

2 tablespoons *crème fraîche*
salt, milled pepper
freshly cooked asparagus
  or globe artichokes

Blend the mustard with the oil and add just a little wine vinegar with the *crème fraîche* and salt and pepper to season. Spoon the sauce into small cocotte dishes and serve with the asparagus or artichokes.

THE CHESTNUT, ALMOND AND WALNUT

Towards the end of his journey in *Travels with a Donkey in the Cevennes*, Robert Louis Stevenson spends a night in a chestnut grove. The ledge he has chosen is too narrow for his sleeping bag, his sleep is disturbed by ceaseless rustling noises – later revealed to be rats – and his morning departure is interrupted by two inquiring peasants who have arrived early to prune the trees. None of this detracts from his admiration for the magnificent trees. When he wrote that 'their individuality, although compounded of so many elements, is but the richer and the more original', he could have been speaking of the dishes of France.

At this time, during the latter half of the nineteenth century, the fruit of the sweet chestnut was still an important ingredient in the food of rural France. It was known as the 'bread tree' because the flour made by pounding the chestnuts with a club studded with nails was made into bread, soup and a kind of sustaining porridge known as *le cousinat*. In the non-grain-producing regions of the Ardèche and the Cévennes, chestnut flour was a vital part of the domestic economy.

Gradually, as transport improved and wheat flour became more widely available, chestnut bread disappeared from country food. Until ten years ago, when the Ardèche Chamber of Agriculture, in an imaginative scheme, delivered to each *boulanger* in the *département* a five-kilo bag of chestnut flour with a request to develop a recipe for chestnut bread. This bread, it was thought, could be a regional speciality and would also utilize surplus chestnuts.

Jean-Paul Coste, a baker at Joyeuse, rose to the challenge to devise a loaf that contained sufficient chestnut flour to give a distinctive taste yet not so much that the sugar in the flour (in contrast to the almond, hazelnut and the walnut, the chestnut has a high sugar but low oil content) would caramelize and impede the final rising of the dough. At last, Jean-Paul was happy with his experiments and produced a chestnut loaf that he was proud of. 'There should be no more than 20 per cent chestnut flour in the dough,' he declared, adding that normally he did not like to reveal his recipes. 'And anyway,' he continued, giving nothing away, 'the real skill is in the *tour de main* and the baking.'

Since then other bakers in the Ardèche have started to bake chestnut bread for the locals and visitors. My local baker showed me the flour bag from his miller, which specified one third chestnut flour and two thirds white flour as the blend. I have been experimenting with chestnut bread in England and the recipe that comes closest to the loaves I like most in France is given below.

At just about the same time that Robert Louis Stevenson and Modestine, his donkey, were making their way along the tracks of southern France, further north and to the east M. Clément Faugier and some associates formed a group of marron glacé manufacturers. A century later, Privas is the marron glacé capital of the world; each year it produces some ten thousand tons of the sweet, sticky delicacy.

Jacky Reyne in his book Marrons et Châtaignes d'Ardèche answers the question that I'd been asking for years. What is the difference between a marron and a châtaigne? After all, they are both chestnuts. Very little, is the answer, apart from their size. In fact a marron is a superior châtaigne but can only become one if considered to be sufficiently large and splendid to crystallize.

This process – which at Clément Faugier is still hidden from public gaze – requires at least sixteen stages of cooking and sugaring in the vanilla syrup before the shiny, brown-skinned sweet chestnut makes it from the tree to the padded recesses of a paper-covered tin and finally becomes a delicious sensation for the palate. According to Jacky Reyne, each year every French person consumes on average thirty chestnuts (mainly roasted), about six tablespoons of purée (in those scrumptious Mont Blancs, I hope), a few fresh raw chestnuts and about one marron glacé. It's slightly daunting to discover that every year I clock up the same amount as about a dozen French on the marron/châtaigne front.

A small sign outside Mme Marquet's house says: AMANDES, MIEL, OEUFS. If you go in early summer the almonds will still be green. Fresh green almonds are a fleeting springtime treat. By the autumn, the dried brown shells will have the familiar look of the almonds we buy at Christmas. The Marquets' almonds come from the delicately wispy trees, entrancingly pretty in flower, that fringe one or two of their vineyards. They no longer grow them as a commercial crop but simply harvest them in July for their own and the occasional visitor's eating.

It has been said that if you held a magnet sensitive to almonds outside the windows of every pâtisserie in Paris nearly all the cakes would collapse. It is wonderfully true. Ground almonds replace much of the flour that we mix into our own cakes. Hence the superb taste of French *pâtisserie*. If only for the invention of *praline* – a mixture of almonds and caramel – French *pâtisserie* is assured of a place at the pinnacle of the world's baking pyramid.

The oil produced from almonds has the colour of pale straw and a most delicate taste. I keep some in the kitchen, but this oil is not widely available since it is more commonly used in cosmetics.

Because almonds are an expensive ingredient, they are replaced at times by hazelnuts whose more pronounced and less subtle taste is hardly less delightful. Hazelnut oil from filberts grown in the Vendée usually costs about the same as walnut oil. It tastes strongly of the nuts and very little is needed to give great interest to salads and vegetables. But due to its expense you may prefer to mix either hazelnut or walnut oil with a mild oil like sunflower, safflower or grapeseed.

When you arrive at Le Pradel, near Villeneuve-de-Berg, the birthplace of Olivier de Serres, a splendid avenue of walnut trees greets you. The trees were planted to honour this visionary French agriculturalist, who introduced not only the white mulberry and hence the silk industry to France, but also a vast number of trees, shrubs and plants, and the best systems for growing them, much of which is still of great economic importance for France.

Walnuts are grown commercially in the *départements* of Lot and Dordogne. And as you walk through the well-kept groves, the green light cast by the leaves is unforgettably lovely. In the past the cooking of the Périgord was mainly founded on the oil from their walnuts, which has an exceptionally fine flavour. After the walnut harvest, the nuts were spread out to dry on the wooden balconies of farmhouses. Then they were tipped into sacks and taken to the mill for crushing. On the way everyone left a smaller bag in the churchyard, and the oil from these nuts lit the church during the winter.

At the mill, the walnuts are crushed by a huge millstone. Then warm water at a carefully controlled temperature is added to the crushed nuts. If the water is too hot the fine flavour of the oil is lost, if too cool insufficient oil is driven from the kernels. Most of the oil is now bottled but in the past some was stored in large, two-handled earthenware jars called *melards* because they are also used for storing honey. All the oil was kept in the cool room, beside the brine tubs and the cured sausages. The *torteau* or oilcake sediment was nibbled by children as a special treat on feast days.

Sadly, this fine oil is now expensive, but if you buy it in small amounts and keep it, like all nut oils, in a very cold place – if necessary the refrigerator – it will last some time.

SALADE TIÈDE AU FOIE DE CANARD

WARM SALAD WITH DUCK'S LIVER

This is inspired by a *salade tiède* of Bernard Perrier, who likes to include, when possible, *morilles* brought to the kitchen door by an elderly Ardéchois who knows where to gather them in the wooded countryside around Lamastre. Walnut oil is essential for the delicate balance of flavours in this salad.

a variety of tiny leaves of lettuce, *escarole*, lamb's lettuce (this mixture is known as *mesclun*)
a few sprigs of watercress
a few sprigs of chervil

1 ripe avocado, peeled and diced
3–4 tablespoons walnut oil
3 or 4 duck's livers, sliced
juice of an orange
salt, milled pepper

Arrange the chilled, washed and dried leaves on three or four small plates and scatter the avocado on top.

Heat half the walnut oil and quickly sauté the duck's liver until just browned but still pink inside. Divide the liver between the plates. Add the remainder of the oil to the pan with the strained juice of the orange. Season with a little salt and milled pepper.

As soon as the dressing is hot, spoon over the salad and serve straight away. Serves 4.

POTAGE AU CRESSON ET AUX NOIX

WATERCRESS AND WALNUT SOUP

Watercress in France is sold in huge bundles; it's wonderfully fresh and dark green and makes a first-rate salad. But here I've used it to make a soup with a certain sharpness that goes well with the toasted walnuts.

55 g (2 oz) butter	150 ml (¼ pt) *crème fraîche*
55 g (2 oz) walnuts, finely chopped	or single cream
1 shallot	salt, milled pepper
200 g (7 oz) watercress	a pinch of ground cinnamon
¾ litre (1¼ pt) chicken stock	1 tablespoon walnut oil
1 tablespoon *fécule de pommes* – potato flour	(optional)

Melt half the butter in a pan and add the walnuts. Fry lightly to bring out their flavour and turn on to a plate.

Soften the shallot in the remaining butter. Stir in the watercress and, when it has collapsed, add the stock. Simmer for 10 minutes.

Sieve or purée the watercress and stock and return to the pan with the potato flour blended with a little water. Cook until slightly thickened. Add the walnuts and cream, and bring almost to the boil.

Season with salt, pepper and ground cinnamon to taste, and stir in the walnut oil, if available. Serves 4.

TAGLIATELLE AUX POIVRONS ET AUX PIGNONS

TAGLIATELLE WITH SWEET PEPPERS AND PINE NUTS

Shops selling fresh pasta have spread faster in Britain than in France, perhaps due to the popularity of Italian food here. But recently M. Paul opened his pasta shop under the arches around the Place aux Herbes in Uzès, which is good to know if you are on holiday in the area.

450 g (1 lb) fresh tagliatelle, half plain, half *verde*	1 red pepper, seeded and diced
salt	1 green pepper, seeded and diced
1 tablespoon sunflower oil	
3 tablespoons fruity olive oil	115 g (4 oz) pine nuts
	juice of ½ lemon
1 clove garlic, finely chopped	1 tablespoon chopped chervil or parsley

> **salt, milled pepper**
> **freshly grated Parmesan**
> **cheese**

Cook the tagliatelle in boiling, salted water with the sunflower oil for 3–5 minutes (dry pasta will need 8–10 minutes) or until cooked to your satisfaction.

Meanwhile, heat 2 tablespoons of the olive oil in a pan and sauté the garlic and the red and green peppers for 5 minutes. Add the pine nuts and cook for 2 minutes. Pour in the lemon juice and chervil, season with salt and pepper, and remove from the heat.

Drain the tagliatelle and transfer to a hot serving dish. Toss in the remaining olive oil until evenly coated.

Spoon the peppers and pine nuts over the pasta and serve with Parmesan cheese. Serves 3–4.

SALADE DE POIVRONS AUX TROIS HUILES

SALAD OF SWEET PEPPERS WITH THREE OILS

Aside from olive oil, the nut oils are the most delicious. Those from the walnut, hazelnut and almond add great interest to one's cooking. But, sadly, although cheap, the oil from peanuts (*arachide*) is less delightful. Served this way to those unfamiliar with their flavour, these oils can be quite a revelation.

walnut oil	**celery** ⎱ **cut into**
hazelnut oil	**baby carrots** ⎰ **matchsticks**
almond oil	**cucumber**
3 sweet peppers, red, green	**spring onions**
and yellow	**1 lemon, cut into slim**
salt, milled pepper	**wedges**

Make sure the oils are at room temperature so that their full aroma is released when you pour them. (But replace them in the refrigerator to prolong their life.)

If you wish, blanch the peppers, but I prefer the crisp freshness of unblanched peppers; however, some people find them harder to digest.

Cut a ring from each pepper for each plate. Pour a little oil into the centre of each ring – say almond oil into the ring of yellow pepper and so on. Season the oil very lightly with salt and milled pepper.

Arrange small bundles of the other vegetables between the rings and place one or two wedges of lemon in the centre for those who prefer to sharpen the oil. For me there is sufficient sharpness in the vegetables. Serve as a first course or as a salad course, but before the cheese so that the palate can discriminate.

AILLADE TOULOUSAINE

WALNUT AND GARLIC SAUCE

A large platter of *crudités* – fingers of celery, carrot and chicory with rings of green and red peppers or Florentine fennel, and a few sprigs of cauliflower and watercress – arranged like rays of the sun around two pottery crocks of sauce for dipping into, aïoli in one and this aillade in the other, makes an informal start to an outdoor meal.

> 85 g (3 oz) walnuts
> 2–3 cloves of garlic
> 75–150 ml olive oil
> salt

Cover the walnuts with boiling water, drain and rinse under cold water. If you wish, peel the walnuts but unless the skin is bitter tasting I leave them unpeeled.

Pound the nuts to a purée with the garlic and gradually incorporate the oil and about 60 ml (2½ fl oz) hot water to make a soft consistency. Season with salt and spoon into a bowl. If available a few leaves of fresh coriander, finely chopped and sprinkled on top, gives the sauce an intriguing flavour. This sauce is also good with cold chicken.

PAIN DE CHÂTAIGNE

CHESTNUT BREAD

In the low-beamed *boulangerie* half-way down the Grande Rue, Maurice Vignon has been persuaded by his wife to revive some of the bread of their childhood. This chestnut bread is particularly good, sliced thinly and served with *saucisson sec* or *jambon cru*. By using dried chestnuts this moist, fragrant loaf can be made at any time of the year.

225 g (8 oz) dried chestnuts
2 teaspoons dried yeast
450 g (1 lb) white bread flour
225 g (8 oz) 100 per cent wholemeal flour
1 tablespoon salt
a little olive oil or butter

Rinse the chestnuts in cold water and soak overnight in cold water to cover. Next day, simmer, covered, for 45 minutes or until cooked and floury. Remove from the heat and allow the chestnuts to cool in their cooking water.

Transfer the chestnuts to a food processor. Add some of the cooking water and reserve the rest. Purée the chestnuts until the mixture is smooth but still grainy. Sprinkle the yeast on 150 ml (¼ pt) warm water in a small bowl and leave for 10 minutes until foamy.

In a mixing bowl, stir the white and wholemeal flours with the salt. Add the chestnut purée, the foamy yeast and sufficient of the chestnut cooking water to make a soft dough. Knead the dough on a floured board for 3 minutes and return to the bowl. Cover with a roomy plastic bag and allow to double in volume. This takes 1–2 hours in a warm room or overnight in a cool room.

Knead the dough again for 1–2 minutes. Divide in four and shape each piece into an oval loaf. Place on a greased and floured baking sheet and make a shallow cut down the centre of each loaf. Set aside to prove for 30 minutes.

Bake the bread in a hot oven (Mark 7, 220°C, 425°F) for about 45 minutes or until each loaf sounds hollow when tapped underneath.

Remove from the oven and rub the tops of the loaves with a little oil or butter. Cool the bread on a wire rack.

Sometimes I place one or two of the loaves to prove in a well-floured round or oval basket. When it is risen and puffy, gently turn the loaf, upside down, on to a greased and floured baking sheet, cut a line across the top and leave for 10 minutes. Then bake as above; the basket leaves an attractive design on the crust of a loaf cooked in this way.

ÉPINARDS AUX PIGNONS À L'EAU DE FLEURS D'ORANGER

SPINACH WITH PINE NUTS AND ORANGE-FLOWER WATER

At first sight this appears a most unexpected liaison of flavours but on further acquaintance one discovers it to be firmly in the ancient Italian tradition of savoury combined with sweet elements common to many Niçoise dishes.

450 g (1 lb) fresh spinach
salt
55 g (2 oz) butter
2 tablespoons olive oil
a small handful of pine
    nuts

1–2 tablespoons
    orange-flower water
milled pepper

Cook the spinach in boiling salted water. Drain well in a sieve, pressing out all the water; then chop.

Melt the butter in the spinach pan, add the oil and, when hot, stir in the pine nuts for 2 minutes. Return the spinach to the pan, stirring until the butter and the oil have been absorbed.

Remove from the heat and stir in the orange-flower water. Turn into a serving dish and sprinkle a little more flower water on top. Serve hot or cold as a separate course. Serves 3–4.

MÉDAILLONS DE PORC
À L'HUILE DE NOIX

PORK FILLET WITH WALNUT OIL

This dish is the result of experimenting with marinating lean meat in a well-flavoured oil, but with none of the usual wine, vinegar or fruit juice. The result is a delicate and very clean-tasting meat dish with the full flavour of the oil unmasked. You may like to try something similar with breast of chicken and perhaps a marinade of hazelnut oil and a few toasted chopped hazelnuts in the sauce.

450 g (1 lb) fillet of pork
salt, milled pepper
4–5 tablespoons walnut oil
about 12 walnut halves
2 ripe pears, peeled and
   sliced

2–3 tablespoons *eau-de-vie*
   de poire
4–6 tablespoons double
   cream

Cut the pork into 1 cm (½ in) slices, bat the meat a little thinner and arrange the oval shapes in a single layer in a shallow dish. Season lightly with salt and pepper and spoon 3 tablespoons of the oil over the meat, turning it over until all the surfaces are coated. Cover the dish with cling-film and leave at room temperature for 2–3 hours, or chill overnight.

Heat a tablespoon of the oil in a pan and sauté the walnut halves until slightly browned. Remove to a hot dish. Cook the pear until golden, add to the walnuts and pour the juices into a cup.

Sauté the pork in the pan until lightly browned on both sides and just cooked. Arrange the pork on three or four warmed plates. Deglaze the pan with the *eau-de-vie* and add the pear juices and the cream. Simmer for 2–3 minutes; adjust the seasoning. Place the walnut halves on the larger medaillons of pork and arrange the sliced pear in fan shapes on each side of the meat on each plate. Spoon over the sauce and serve straight away. Serves 3–4.

TURINOIS
CHOCOLATE CHESTNUT PUDDING

Towards Christmas, tins of the new season's chestnuts appear in shops. For this pudding I prefer the unsweetened purée. The *turinois* freezes well and is very good served *semi-freddo* or completely frozen.

115 g (4 oz) butter	450 g (1 lb) unsweetened
115 g (4 oz) caster sugar	chestnut purée
1 teaspoon vanilla essence	30 g (1 oz) flaked almonds,
140 g (5 oz) plain dessert	toasted
chocolate	a drop of mild oil
4 tablespoons dark rum	

Soften the butter in a slightly warmed bowl and beat until light. Gradually beat in the sugar until the mixture is fluffy, then beat in the vanilla essence.

Melt the chocolate with the rum in a bowl over hot water; then cool slightly. Sieve the chestnut purée.

Gradually beat the chocolate and the chestnut mixtures into the butter until the mixture is smooth and soft.

Line a lightly oiled 15 cm (6 in) square cake tin with cling-film. Sprinkle the base with the toasted almonds and spoon the mixture on top. Spread level and chill or freeze.

To serve, unmould and cut into fingers. Serves 8–10.

TARTE AUX NOIX ET AU RHUM
RUM AND WALNUT TART

In the Périgord the walnut trees lining the roads south from Brive are a fine sight. If you are there in the autumn take advantage of the new season's crop. The ripe walnuts which fall overnight must be collected every day to prevent their blackening on the ground. After a short spell drying in the sun they are packed in lacy sacks for sending to other parts of France or Britain. But it's even nicer to bring your own home, if you can, for eating with cheese or to make a walnut tart.

Pastry	Filling
170 g (6 oz) flour	85 g (3 oz) butter
30 g (1 oz) caster sugar	85 g (3 oz) muscovado sugar
85 g (3 oz) butter	1 large egg
grated rind and juice of	2 tablespoons rum
half an orange	170 g (6 oz) broken walnuts
1 egg yolk	

Sift the flour and sugar into a bowl. Rub in the butter and mix to a dough with the rind and juice of the orange mixed with the egg yolk. Chill for 15 minutes and roll out on a floured board to line a greased 24 cm (9½ in) tart tin. Prick the base all over.

Bake in a moderately hot oven (Mark 6, 200°C, 400°F) for 10–15 minutes until lightly coloured.

For the filling, cream the butter with the sugar until light and fluffy, and then beat in the egg and rum. Fold in the chopped walnuts and spread the mixture level in the pastry case.

Bake in the centre of a moderate oven (Mark 4, 180°C, 350°F) for 25 minutes.

Cool, and then serve with *crème fraîche* or soured cream. Serves 8.

PÂTE D'AMANDES

ALMOND PASTE

This almond paste – which is quite different from marzipan – is a sweet, served in small paper cases, with coffee at the end of a meal.

225 g (8 oz) almonds, unblanched	a drop or two of *fleurs d'oranger* or
2 egg whites	orange-flower water
140 g (5 oz) caster sugar	a little icing sugar
30 g (1 oz) honey	

Blanch the almonds by covering with cold water in a pan. Bring to the boil. Remove from the heat, pour off the hot water and replace with cold. The brown skins should now slide off easily. Dry the blanched almonds on a baking sheet in a low oven for 15–20 minutes but do not let them change colour.

Either pound the almonds a few at a time in a mortar or grind them in a food processor. Turn the ground almonds into a pan, preferably glass or enamel, and mix in the egg whites, caster sugar and honey. Gently heat the mixture over very low heat, stirring all the time, until the mixture starts to come away from the sides of the pan. Add the orange-flower water and remove from the heat.

Drop teaspoons of the mixture on to greaseproof paper sprinkled with icing sugar. When set place in paper cases.

GÂTEAU DE MARRONS DE L'ARDÈCHE

ARDÉCHOIS CHESTNUT GÂTEAU

In *Le Trésor de la cuisine du bassin méditerranéen* Prosper Montagné revised and prefaced a collection of recipes from seventy French doctors. Enlivened by many small woodcuts and one gruesome advertisement for the digestive medicines of Dr Zizine, the recipes are interesting. This is Dr Cleu's recipe which I have adapted only slightly.

450 g (1 lb) large chestnuts, preferably from the Ardèche
¼ teaspoon salt
1 teaspoon sunflower oil
85 g (3 oz) plus 2 tablespoons caster sugar
150 ml (¼ pt) single cream or creamy milk
½ vanilla pod
1 large egg, separated
a small knob of butter
1 tablespoon rum
vanilla- or chocolate-flavoured pouring cream

Make a small cut in the outer skin of each chestnut. Cover with cold water, add the salt and oil and bring to the boil slowly. Simmer for 5 minutes. Remove from heat and, when cool enough to handle, peel the chestnuts carefully, removing the outer and inner skin.

Make caramel by dissolving 85 g (3 oz) sugar in 2 tablespoons water over low heat. Turn up the heat and cook until orange-brown. Pour into a buttered straight-sided mould of 570 ml (1 pint) capacity and coat the base and half-way up the sides. When cool rub a little butter over the caramel.

Heat the cream or milk with the vanilla pod, stirring to extract the flavour. Remove the pod and add the chestnuts. Cook together, stirring, for 5 minutes. Purée the mixture by sieving or processing with 2 tablespoons sugar and the egg yolk until almost completely smooth.

Whisk the egg white until stiff and fold into the chestnut mixture. Turn into the mould and smooth level. Cover with a buttered paper cut to fit.

Cook in a bain-marie in a moderate oven (Mark 4, 180°C, 350°F) for 25–30 minutes until the gâteau is set. Remove from the oven and allow to cool in the bain-marie. Chill until ready to serve.

Run the blade of a knife around the gâteau and turn out on to a flat serving dish. Pour over the rum and serve, cut into wedges, with a little of the pouring cream. Serves 6.

Autreterre

Sunday evening in Annonay, as its inhabitants are quick to point out, is hardly likely to knock you off your feet with its pace of life. I had spent the afternoon discovering the back streets of the town after glimpsing the letters FAST followed by FOOD running down the side of a café-restaurant. Until then I had seen these dreadful words, which have now seeped into French gastronomy, only in Paris. Was nowhere safe? Here in the heart of provincial France, where plenty of proper fast food such as an *omelette*, an *assiette anglaise* or a plate of *fruits de mer* had been available for generations, the pallid hamburger and the sesame bun had been imported in the name of American chic.

I walked on into the centre looking for a decent restaurant. I came to the Place aux Cordeliers where a brass plaque marks the spot from which, in 1783, the Montgolfier brothers first demonstrated balloon flight. I thought about devising a commemorative soufflé. Down by the river the town has the feel of our own northern wool towns with huge, empty mills, becalmed, grey and cold. At last I came upon a restaurant with a simple menu described as Ardéchois. Indeed it was. The omelette was inspiriting; crisp, buttery croûtons made a satisfying contrast to the soft dark *cèpes*. It was followed by an endive salad dressed with walnut oil. And then a treat – a local, freshly drained cheese which sent the owner-chef's wife running back to the kitchen to find the label for me. I decided to see for myself how this delicious cheese had been made.

Next day, straight after breakfast, I drove out of Annonay on the St Marcel road through clouds of wild cherry blossom to find M. Girard in his *fromagerie*. Two lorry-drivers and their restaurant-owning friend from Lyons had arrived ahead of me. We were all conducted into the various rooms of M. Girard's cheese-making enterprise where for twenty years he had been producing the best cheese in the neighbourhood. The milk comes from local farms – some is cows' milk and some from herds of goats. In fact, farmers round here often run the two animals together. But for his cheese-making M. Girard keeps the milks separate. The milk is run into large rectangular tanks for the rennet to be added. It is then decanted into smaller bucket-shaped containers for twenty-four hours, to give the rennet time to work and to allow the flavour to mature.

From here each cheese starts its journey to the plate. The curds or *cailles* are ladled into individual *faiselles* or pierced moulds. The design of these moulds has remained unchanged for centuries: made of red earthenware or a grey stoneware, you can still buy them to make a drained cheese at home. But the larger farms and M. Girard use modern plastic moulds, which are unbreakable and last longer. Sometimes a very fresh cheese is sold still in its plastic mould. Once in the mould, the whey or *petit lait* drains out and is collected for feeding to the local pigs. And the curd solidifies to form the cheese.

Eaten fresh, only one to three days old, the cheese has a smooth lusciousness. Full cream, freshly drained cheeses are served alone or with a light powdering of salt and pepper. In the Haute Ardèche a cheese may be served in a small pool of fresh cream. And with a scattering of wild strawberries on top, my Ardéchois friends declare the combination *régal*.

But most of the cheeses are emptied from the moulds to be matured for two to three months before eating. They are stored first on wooden slats in the humidifying room for two to four weeks, to allow the mould to develop – it starts white and changes to grey. Then the cheese is moved to a cold store for at least four weeks. Each cheese is growing smaller all the time but it is developing a superb flavour. This is an interesting refutation of the law of diminishing returns in terms of weight, for the older, smaller cheeses sell at a higher price than the heavier, younger sort.

Because cheese is so highly valued in France it is easily available. Every market has a stall, sometimes a long van with sides that fold down to reveal a counter above a capacious display of local and national cheeses. In small places a local farmer's wife brings in her cheeses to sell. In the Rhône area of Drôme and the Ardèche she will probably sell her *picodon* cheeses, some of them wrapped in chestnut leaves. The name comes from the word *piquant* and the small round cheese is made from goats' milk. Further west in the Auvergne, you may be lucky enough to track down a *péraldoux*, the sheep's milk equivalent of the *picodon*. *Péral* means sheep's milk cheese ripened on straw and *doux* here means sweet.

But there is another sheep's milk cheese which is rare and fine. It is a *brousse*, which is a light, freshly made cheese with an almost junket-like consistency. Mme Dumas at Le Vaccarès in Arles introduced this cheese to me, of which I had only read in M. F. K. Fisher's *Map of Another Town.*

. . . and I said now and then the shepherdess made us a *brousse*. This is a delicate kind of bonny-clabber made from fresh ewe's milk left to 'set' and sweetened and faintly spiced with nutmeg and perhaps ginger. It is as light and fresh as brook water, leaving one feeling light and fresh too.

A *brousse* is usually served straight from the *faiselle;* these moulds are long and tapering and a clutch of them stands upright,

draining into a bowl. Mine was served plain but clearly the cheese can be sugared and spiced if you wish. So be sure not to pass it by – a *brousse* in any form is truly memorable.

In remote country areas a farmer's wife on occasion prepares her own rennet by steeping small pieces of pig's stomach in vinegar, or she keeps the rennet collected from the stomach of a kid when surplus male kids are killed for eating. This happens because it's reckoned that one billy-goat can satisfy a herd of up to fifty nanny goats – an impressive and cost-effective *tour de force*.

My friends, the Marquets, aim to produce their goat kids around Easter when the grass is richer and the cheese-making can start. A few drops of rennet are sufficient to curdle the still-warm milk from the morning's milking. After lunch the curds are spooned into the moulds on the draining rack and in the evening the cheese is salted on both sides. On the morrow the cheeses are firm enough to be turned on to straw mats or *pallou*, and they can be eaten the following day. But to develop a fuller flavour the cheese is left on the straw mats in a cool, airy place, or in a cellar, to mature for up to one month. Fifty years ago cheeses were stored for this longer period in upright baskets with shelves and a door like a cupboard (there is a beautiful example in the museum at St Jean du Gard) and hung from a beam.

Seeing that most of the cheese made in the Midi starts with goats' milk, it is not uncommon to come upon a herd grazing in a vineyard. Pierre Androuet advises us to stop and buy the local cheese straight away, because, he says, '*C'est le lait de chèvre des "terres à vigne" qui donne le meilleur fromage.*'

AUBERGINES AU FROMAGE

AUBERGINES WITH CHEESE

This excellent way of preparing aubergines comes from the booklet of recipes supplied by the Beaumes de Venise olive oil cooperative.

3 or 4 medium-sized
aubergines
olive oil
225 g (8 oz) Gruyère cheese,
finely grated
4–5 tablespoons fresh
breadcrumbs

6 tablespoons milk
salt, milled pepper
3 or 4 tomatoes, sliced
herbes de Provence
(see p. 19)

Wipe the aubergines and cut in half lengthways. Heat some olive oil in a cast-iron pan, large enough to hold the halved aubergines in a single layer. Turn each aubergine over in the oil and place cut side down and sauté until lightly browned. Transfer to a moderate oven (Mark 5, 190°C, 375°F) and bake for about 15 minutes until the aubergines are almost cooked.

Meanwhile mix the cheese with the breadcrumbs and milk, and season lightly. Divide the mixture between the aubergines, spooning it over the cut surfaces. Place the tomato on top, overlapping the slices and sprinkle lightly with the *herbes de Provence*. Place in the oven and cook for about 10 minutes until the aubergines and tomatoes are fully cooked and the cheese layer has melted. Serve hot. Serves 3–4.

SALADE FRISÉE AU ROQUEFORT

CURLY ENDIVE SALAD WITH ROQUEFORT

The superb flavour of the king of French cheeses goes a long way in cooking. Try just a little in a cheese sauce for serving with root vegetables; or a Roquefort cheese soufflé is a fine dish. Here, this beautiful cheese gives the flat bitter taste of curly endive a fabulous lift.

1 head of curly endive
100 g (3½ oz) Roquefort
  cheese
2 tablespoons lemon juice
2 tablespoons hazelnut or
  walnut oil

100 ml (3½ fl oz) *crème
  fraîche*
salt, milled pepper

Trim the stalk from the endive, wash the leaves and drain well. Dry in a salad spinner or basket or on a clean teacloth.

Use a wooden spoon to blend the cheese with the lemon juice and the oil in the salad bowl. Gradually whisk in the *crème fraîche* and season to taste.

Add the leaves, torn into smaller pieces if necessary, and toss lightly in the dressing. Serve straight away. Serves 4–6.

FROMAGE DE PRINTEMPS
À LA MODE DE PÈRE HOUGHTON

FATHER HOUGHTON'S SPRING CHEESE

In early May an English priest domiciled in France for many years looks down from his high windows to the rushing Rhône below. The river here is wide and blue-grey and in calm weather reflects the orange T G V train as it flies south. Father Houghton waits until his apricot tree is in blossom and then sets off for the market, hoping to find some of the first strawberries of the season, probably ripened under glass near Carpentras. If he is lucky he hurries back with strawberries and a couple of freshly drained – *en faisselle* – goats' cheeses to make his Vivarais variation of English strawberries and cream.

2 very fresh goats' cheeses
4–6 tablespoons *crème
  fraîche*

a little caster sugar
450 g (1 lb) ripe
  strawberries

Use a fork to mash the goats' cheese and add sufficient *crème fraîche* to give a soft dropping consistency rather like whipped double cream. Sweeten to taste with a little sugar but don't lose the delightful taste of the fresh cheese.

Serve with whole or halved strawberries. Serves 4.

SOUPE AU FROMAGE DE CANTAL

CANTAL CHEESE SOUP

Cantal, the cows' milk cheese from the Auvergne with a creamy, nutty flavour, looks like a mature Cheddar. At its best in summer and autumn after maturing for three to six months, this cheese is worth sampling. You may find such a fine Cantal that you would only wish to eat it on its own. At other times you may like to try this cheese soup from the Auvergne which is most reviving late at night and is traditionally served at Christmas after midnight mass.

225 g (8 oz) onions, sliced
2 cloves garlic, finely
  chopped
30 g (1 oz) butter
salt
570 ml (1 pt) chicken stock
  or water

bread, cut into rounds or
  diced and lightly toasted
100 g (3½ oz) Cantal
  cheese, grated

Brown the onions and the garlic in the butter. Salt lightly and add the stock or water. Bring to the boil and simmer for 5–10 minutes.

Divide the bread between two or three soup bowls and pour the onion mixture on top. Sprinkle the cheese on the onions.

Place the bowls under a hot grill or in a hot oven and cook until the cheese has melted and the soup is piping hot. The soup should be very thick. Serves 2–3.

My family *font chabrot* when they have almost finished the soup by adding a dash of wine to the hot bowl and then supping from it, unfortunately, as noisily as possible, which they claim is in tribute to the cook.

Faux-filet au Roquefort

FILLET STEAK WITH ROQUEFORT

When eating in provincial France it is always interesting to see the influence of past and present chefs on today's cooks. The volumes of Escoffier and Pellaprat, often lovingly covered in protective plastic or brown paper, still sit in the kitchens of restaurants and small hotels. But Troisgros, Bocuse and Guérard are now leaving their mark, at times quite openly on the menu, at others as a more subtle but pervasive presence in the cooking and presentation of the food.

In the small hotel in Carcès, where I have spent some happy times, Escoffier is revered – as this rich dish shows.

2 slices of *faux-filet* or fillet steak	55 g (2 oz) Roquefort cheese
a knob of butter	150 ml (¼ pt) *crème fraîche*
100 ml (3½ fl oz) brandy	milled pepper

Cook the steak in the melted butter according to your preference. Flame with the brandy and transfer to a hot serving dish.

Add the Roquefort to the pan and stir until melted. Stir in the cream and allow the sauce to bubble and thicken. Season with a little pepper.

Spoon the sauce over the steak and serve with puréed potatoes. Serves 2.

Oeufs au Fromage

EGGS WITH CHEESE

A nineteenth-century version of scrambled eggs that makes an admirable lunch or supper.

a small lump of butter	1 tablespoon finely chopped parsley
115 g (4 oz) Gruyère cheese, grated	

1 tablespoon finely chopped chives	6 eggs, lightly beaten
a little grated nutmeg	hot, buttered triangles of toast.
½ wineglass dry white wine	

Melt the butter in a pan over moderate heat. Add the cheese, parsley, chives, nutmeg and wine, and stir until the cheese has melted.

Add the eggs and stir gently until set. Serve with or on the toast. Serves 2–3.

FOUDJOU

ARDÉCHOIS POTTED CHEESE

Foudjou is a *fromage fort* or strong-flavoured potted cheese which is much appreciated by those with a well-developed palate. Made in farmhouses of the Ardèche, *foudjou* comes from the Basse Ardèche; elsewhere it is known as *miramande*. The mixture should be stored in a cool room or, in a small house, in the refrigerator, for six months for the flavour to mature. Charles Forot says that a little *foudjou* should be left in the jar to start the fermentation of the new cheese. In some families, he writes, the bottoms of some cheese crocks have not been sighted for fifteen years.

1 or 2 well-matured goat cheeses	*eau-de-vie de marc*
1 or 2 fresh goat cheeses	olive oil
1 clove of garlic, crushed	salt, milled pepper
a little *serpolet* or wild thyme, finely chopped	

Grate or crumble the dried goat cheese into a bowl and mix in the fresh cheese with a fork. Gradually work in the other ingredients until the consistency is a thick cream. Check the taste and adjust the seasoning.

Spoon into a lidded stoneware pot – one made for *confit d'oie* is ideal. Smooth the top of the cheese level, cover with the lid and store in a cool room for at least one month before serving. In mountainous areas of the Ardèche *foudjou* is served with whole boiled potatoes. It is also splendid on halved jacket potatoes.

POULET AU FROMAGE

CHICKEN WITH CHEESE

An appetizing-looking dish, the cheese sauce bubbling around the tender chicken on a dark dish, if possible. I like those dark green glazed oval dishes from Berry.

a walnut-sized knob of butter	***beurre manié*, made by blending ½ teaspoon**
1½ kg (3–3½ lb) chicken	**butter with ½ teaspoon**
salt, milled pepper	**flour**
½ wineglass dry white wine	**70 g (2½ oz) Gruyère cheese, finely grated**
bouquet garni	

Melt the butter and lightly brown the chicken all over in a cast-iron casserole. Season lightly with salt and pepper. Add the wine, the bouquet garni and sufficient water to cover the first joint of your finger. Bring to the boil.

Cover tightly and turn down the heat. Simmer gently for 45–60 minutes until the chicken is cooked.

Lift out the chicken, joint it and arrange the pieces on a hot oven dish; keep hot while you make the sauce. Remove any surplus fat from on top of the cooking liquid by floating a sheet of kitchen paper on the liquid to absorb the fat.

Remove the bouquet garni and add the *beurre manié* in small pieces, whisking over medium heat until the sauce has thickened. Add the cheese and spoon over the chicken.

Place the dish under a very hot grill until the sauce is bubbling and is just turning golden. Serves 4.

FROMAGE DE CHÈVRE EN VINAIGRETTE

GOATS' CHEESE WITH VINAIGRETTE

This highly seasoned cheese spread is at its best spooned on to halved jacket potatoes and eaten in front of the fire.

100 g (3½ oz) fresh goats' cheese
2–3 tablespoons olive oil
2–3 teaspoons white wine vinegar

1–2 cloves of garlic, crushed
salt, milled pepper
cayenne pepper

Mash the cheese in a bowl. Gradually beat in the other ingredients. Taste and adjust the seasoning if necessary. Spoon into a dish.

Serve the seasoned cheese with jacket or boiled potatoes or on toast. It also goes well with parsnips.

SARRASSOU

Sarrassou is an ancient preparation, originally given by Olivier de Serres as a mixture of buttermilk and full cream milk blended together to make a cream for serving with potatoes. This present-day recipe appears to have strayed somewhat from the older version but, in fact, tastes very good in its own right.

2 fresh goats' cheeses, up to 3 days old
4 tablespoons buttermilk or plain yoghurt
1–2 teaspoons Dijon mustard

1 tablespoon white wine vinegar
salt, crushed peppercorns

Mash the cheeses with a fork and add the remaining ingredients until well combined.

Spoon into a small lidded stoneware pot. Store in a very cold place or the refrigerator for up to 6 weeks.

Serve the cheese on fingers of toast or on plain boiled potatoes.

ALIGOT

The name *aligot* can cause confusion; it is not only a cheese but also the potato dish which includes the cheese. (Leave aside an accented é, which would make it *aligoté*, that delicious, flinty wine which is an essential ingredient of the concoction that Canon Kir devised to help the ailing blackcurrant growers of Burgundy.) To confuse matters further, *aligot* is also known as *tomme d'aligot* or *tomme fraîche* and is a very good cheese in its own right. Try it in late spring through the summer when the cows are grazing on higher pastures. *Aligot* is a substantial dish best served in cold weather. I usually add the smaller amount of cheese but it largely depends on the nature of the rest of the meal; it's possible that vegetarians would prefer to add more. In Britain the *aligot* cheese could reasonably be replaced with Caerphilly.

1½ kg (2–3½ lb) floury potatoes	340–680 g (12–24 oz) *tomme d'aligot* cheese
225 g (8 oz) butter	1–2 cloves of garlic, very finely chopped (optional)
275 ml (½ pt) *crème fraîche*	
milled pepper	

Scrub the potatoes and cook them in their skins in salted water until tender. Drain and peel.

Purée the potatoes through a *mouli-légumes* on the finest setting or push through a fine sieve.

Melt the butter in the potato pan and add the *crème fraîche* and the puréed potatoes. Season with pepper and add the cheese. Cook, stirring over medium heat, for 7–10 minutes or until the cheese starts to make strings. Add the garlic if desired and turn into a hot serving dish. Serves many.

TRUFFADE

AUVERGNE POTATO CAKE

1 kg (2 lb) waxy potatoes
1 tablespoon *saindoux* or
   pork dripping
salt, milled pepper

thyme or *serpolet*
225 g (8 oz) Cantal cheese,
   diced

Peel the potatoes and cut into rounds. Dry the potatoes on a clean teacloth.

Heat the *saindoux* or dripping in a cast-iron pan. Add the potatoes in overlapping layers, seasoning with salt and milled pepper and a little thyme as you go.

Cover the pan and cook the potatoes over moderate heat for 5 minutes. Remove the lid and cook for 5–10 minutes until the potatoes are tender. Press the layers together with a fish slice now and again so that they stick together.

Add the diced Cantal cheese and when the cheese has started to melt, place the potatoes under a very hot grill and cook until the cheese is browned and bubbling.

Cut into wedges to serve. Serves 6–8.

CRÈME FRAÎCHE

The fresh cream of France has a matured flavour more akin to the way our own used to taste. At last *crème fraîche* is becoming increasingly available in dairies and supermarkets here. But if you cannot persuade your local shop to stock it, you may have to make your own equivalent – it is certainly simple enough.

Mix 150 ml (¼ pt) of soured cream (or for slightly different flavour and lower fat content, buttermilk or plain yoghurt) with 275 ml (½ pt) of double cream in a bowl over simmering water until the cream reaches the yoghurt-making temperature of 45°C (120°F).

Remove from the heat, cover the bowl and leave at room temperature for 8 hours until thickened. Transfer the bowl to the refrigerator where the cream will store well for 1–2 weeks. If a small amount of watery liquid forms on top simply stir it back into the cream.

FROMAGE FRAIS

Fromage frais is a soft, light, smooth cheese with a fat content that varies from nil to over 60 per cent. The low fat kind is popular with *nouvelle cuisine* chefs and with people on fat-free diets as a replacement for cream. *Fromage frais* is usually made with cows' milk, and since the cheese so closely resembles the soft cheese that I make from drained yoghurt I find this is the best method for producing a home-made equivalent to *fromage frais*.

Carefully warm 570 ml (1 pt) of fresh milk to just above blood heat (45°C, 120°F). Remove from the heat and stir in 2 tablespoons of fresh plain yoghurt. Set aside, covered, in a warm place for about 8 hours until the mixture has thickened. If you have time, chill the yoghurt for 24 hours to firm up the curd.

Next day line a bowl with scalded butter muslin or very fine net and spoon the yoghurt into it. Pull up the corners of the muslin, tie with a string and suspend from a hook or the upturned legs of a chair so that the yoghurt drips into the bowl placed directly underneath. When the whey has completely drained from the curds, which usually takes about 6 hours, take down the muslin and tip the cheese into a bowl.

The cheese is now ready for use. Use the whey when making scones or soda bread – it can be frozen for later use.

If you prefer a softer cheese, mix a little of the whey into the cheese. Or for a richer cheese add milk or some cream. Alternatively, to lighten the cheese, fold in a little stiffly whisked egg white.

For a delightful pudding sweeten the home-made *fromage frais* with a little vanilla sugar and, if you wish, fold in some whipped cream or serve plain with a few halved strawberries or a powdering of finely ground coffee. *Fromage frais* mixed with cream and drained overnight in heart-shaped moulds makes the charming and traditional *coeurs à la crème*.

FROMAGE DE CHÈVRE

GOATS' CHEESE

It is now easier to obtain fresh goats' milk, certainly in the West Country. So I occasionally follow the instructions of my cheese-making friends in France and produce a home-made *picodon*.

> 1 litre (1¾ pt) fresh goats'
>   milk
> 2 teaspoons (or follow the
>   maker's recommendation)
>   cheese rennet

Slowly bring the goats' milk to just above blood heat (45°C, 120°F). Remove from the heat and stir in the rennet. Set aside at room temperature until curds have formed.

Pour into a ceramic or plastic cheese drainer and leave in a cold place for 24 hours or overnight to allow the whey, *petit lait*, to drain away and the curds to set.

For freshly drained goats' cheese or *fromage en faisselle*, turn out the cheese and serve with salt or cream. Alternatively turn the cheese out on to a draining board or a straw pallet or a layer of dry hay (which will perfume the cheese beautifully) and store in a cold, dry place for 1–8 weeks. Turn the cheese every day. The cheese will shrink as it ages but the flavour matures and improves.

Some cheese-makers wrap a two- or three-day-old cheese in chestnut leaves or roll the cheese in finely powdered charcoal, or chopped dry herbs, or roughly crushed black peppercorns. These are good ideas for early summer cheeses but later in the year the palate requires the deeper, satisfying flavour of a matured goat cheese.

FROMAGES DE CHÈVRE À L'HUILE

GOATS' CHEESES PRESERVED IN OIL

If there's time, the day before we leave France I pack a preserving jar with two-week-old goats' cheeses, tuck in some local herbs – thyme, rosemary and some bay leaves – and pour over a rich green olive oil. Tie down securely and fasten a spray of leaves from the nearest olive tree on top. The pleasure and satisfaction that one feels a few months later on retrieving the jar from a cool shelf is boundless. The grey-green olive leaves have shrivelled and curled like flowers kept from a wedding bouquet, but the cheese has grown in flavour, rich with the fruity oil and the fragrance of the herbs.

> 8–10 goats' cheeses, 2–3
>   weeks old
> a few peppercorns, lightly
>   crushed
> sprigs of thyme and
>   rosemary
>
> bay leaves
> about ¾ litre (1–1½ pt)
>   olive oil

Pack the cheeses into the jar. Add the peppercorns and herbs and fill the jar with olive oil. The cheeses must be completely covered with the oil.

Place a tight-fitting lid on the jar and secure well. For travelling it is best to seal the lid with plastic parcel tape. Store the jar in a cold place for 1–6 months. Serve the cheeses with warm bread. Use the remaining oil in salad dressings.

An alternative is to replace the olive oil with a dry, white, local wine and store for 3–8 weeks in a cold place.

For most of us on holiday in France, catching sight each morning of the *boulangerie* across the street or in the corner of the square, is a moment of relief. Lunch is assured. For however many delicious waxed-paper packages you've just bought at the charcuterie, or however splendid the cheese in your shopping basket, none of it will taste as it should without bread. A fresh, crisp, golden *baguette*, a larger *flûte* or, for children and those who like plenty of crust, perhaps an *épi* shaped like an ear of wheat, each grain of corn a miniature loaf: all this bread is an important part of every meal in France. It is the frame for the picture each meal represents and one would feel deprived without it.

But not every Frenchman has a *boulangerie* around the corner. Even today there are villages and certainly hamlets without a baker. Although many farmhouses still have their stone or brick bread ovens, they are rarely used for baking. Bread usually arrives each day in a battered grey van, the doors at the back fly open on to dozens of *flûtes* standing on end in paper sacks beside shelves of large round loaves of *pain de campagne*, some shaped into a circle, a *couronne*, that can be carried home on your arm or threaded on to the handlebars of your bicycle.

As with its wine and cheese, the bread of France is a regional food and according to the Parisian baker, Lionel Poilâne, 'The French baker is by nature something of a traditionalist.' For that we should be grateful. There are still at least eighty different breads made across France. And the French value such a richness, particularly since the self-examination that followed the student unrest of 1968, which resulted in a heightened awareness of the cultural history of the country. In baking, as in much else in French food, there is a return to the past. '*Retro cuisine*' means that a baker is now eager to stick a sign on his window advertising his 'bread baked in our wood-fired oven'. The traditional loaves of the south are still to be found: large flat *pain de seigle* made with rye flour; the *pain de Beaucaire*, a long dark loaf made with a mixture of grains that includes barley; the *tête d'Aix* made from folded dough sometimes baked with a dusting of ground olive stones on top; or the *fougasse*, a flat loaf cut into odd shapes and baked on the floor of the oven to test the baking temperature and often burnt black in places as a result, but all the more delicious. The *pain fantaisie* like, for example, the starch-reduced loaf, popular with the young affluent French in the north, is rarely seen in the south (my Ardéchois friends scoff at the very idea) but some bakers produce a few in the summer for the holidaymakers.

Until the end of the last century in towns, and certainly in large villages, there was a communal bread oven to which everyone carried their loaves (and sometimes their meat too, hence the dishes termed *boulangère*) in a cloth-lined basket. When the oven reached a baking temperature, people living near by sent a child along to collect some of the hot charcoal pulled from the floor of the oven to make room for the loaves. The glowing charcoal was rushed home and dropped into an unglazed pottery charcoal burner, a grid was placed over it and on top a dish could be cooked or reheated. These *charbonnières* are now generally in museums; there is a fine example in the Musée Fragonard in Grasse. For some town-dwellers this was their only source of cooking heat. It is perhaps surprising that the art of cooking was not fractured to the same extent as in England during the industrial revolution. Stephen Mennell's fine book, *All Manners of Food*, examines this question among many others when comparing eating in England and France from the Middle Ages to the present.

Whereas town-dwellers and the inhabitants of industrial cities may have had to depend on buying ready-made dishes, the country-man in cottage and farmhouse had an open fire or even a cooking stove and probably wood to burn in it. In the south of France many stone or brick-built *potagers* remain. Most had a central grate in which the fuel was burnt. Some, like the example in the basement kitchen at the château at Entrecasteaux, were beautifully tiled, but the common feature was one or two depressions in the top of the stove to make a hob. The shallow rectangular space was fitted with a metal grid on which hot embers from the firebox below were placed. A cooking pot was balanced on top and the soup or *potage* – hence the name – was gently cooked. Controlling the heat in such a stove must have been a hot and frustrating business, and constantly transferring hot coals or wood embers grimy and possibly danger-ous. What a high degree of devotion to the arts of the kitchen was called for! Presumably it was at least easier to make a sauce or a gently cooked custard on a *potager* than over the full heat of the open fire.

In Arles there is a fascinating kitchen tableau in the Museon Arlaten, which was created by Frédéric Mistral in 1896. The scene is set on Christmas Eve; the *bûche de Noël* burns brightly in the large hearth fireplace. The yule log was intended to last until Epiphany or Twelfth Night. At midnight on Christmas Eve, at the moment when in the Auvergne farmers believed that their animals could talk, the youngest person in the house doused the log with a glass of wine as an offering to the gods of fertility for the season to come. The table is laid with the traditional dishes of the Christmas Eve meal: produce from the countryside – cardoons and celery, snails and a fine fish, the *Treize Desserts* which is still served in Provençal homes at Christmas, composed of dried fruits, almonds, walnuts, hazelnuts, grapes, apples, jams and nougat made with honey. Thirteen foods in all to represent Christ and his disciples. The food is served on octagonal white plates, now, of course, revived by *nouvelle cuisine* chefs but, as any potter knows, it is a design that is far older than the last century. The food in this nineteenth-century kitchen is cooked over the large open fire where a spit is set up for roasting meat, and to the left of the fireplace but quite separate stands the *potager*.

Today's French country kitchen, certainly in a farmhouse, has a continuous burning stove which often, as in the past, burns the cheapest and the most convenient fuel, wood. This stove gives a welcome and constant warmth that is ideal for drying a *saucisson sec* or some wild mushrooms, a handful of herbs or a bunch of flowers. Those who cook on them know that the oven is ideal for baking, especially bread, and the warmth of the kitchen helps the yeast to work and the dough to rise.

In most places in France one can rely on being able to buy bread within a reasonable distance, although I do recall choosing to bake a cake in a particularly remote *gîte*. It is in England that I indulge my enthusiasm for baking and especially for yeast cookery, using French recipes or recreating breads, mainly brioches, and cakes and tarts that we remember enjoying.

When I can I bring back French flour. It *is* different; it tastes and smells different, it seems finer and smoother than English flour and not surprisingly works better in French recipes.

French butter is easy enough to buy here where, by some EEC edict I presume, it is often cheaper than in France. In the past, when it was markedly so, I have taken supplies of it to friends there.

French baking powder, *levure chimique*, which, in any case, is not widely used, is little different from our own, but should you be baking with French recipes you may be glad to know that one packet of *levure chimique* weighs 11 g.

French gelatine, which comes in leaves, is far superior to our powdered variety. If possible bring some back if you use gelatine a fair amount; it is light to carry and you need far less than powdered gelatine. But its chief virtue is the absence of that all too familiar gluey taste. I find that just under three leaves of French gelatine are equivalent to 15 g (½ oz) powdered gelatine.

French sugar is no different, but some French recipes state the quantity in terms of cubes and it can be useful to know that the larger size of sugar cube in France weighs 6 g.

Many French recipes specify vanilla sugar, which is sold in France in 10 g packets. I rarely buy it because it often tastes stale even when fresh. It is so easy to make your own vanilla sugar. French vanilla pods (and all other spices) are of high quality, so buy one or two and break each in half to slide into a jar of caster sugar to flavour it.

While in France, or here, you can easily make your own exceptionally good vanilla flavouring. Snip one or two vanilla pods into small pieces and feed them into a screw-topped jar or bottle. Fill the jar with brandy or eau-de-vie and leave in a warm kitchen, giving the bottle a shake whenever you notice it. Taste after 6–8 weeks, when it should be strong enough to use to flavour cakes and biscuits.

But sugar is not something one has much need of on holiday in France. Honey is preferable as a sweetener. And French honey is always worth buying. A country whose climate ranges from alpine to Mediterranean is able to produce a luscious variety. The flavour of a honey depends on the nectar gathered by the bees. That from chestnut flowers in the Cévennes produces a dark honey with a pronounced resinous taste, while honey made by bees that have worked acacia blossom has a light, flowery and utterly delightful flavour.

Local honeys are always valued and they are frequently offered for sale on market stalls, often by the producers themselves, who are usually happy to discuss their bees, their hives and the season. One beekeeper I know is improving some of her honey even further. Most she sells just as it is, straight from the comb and poured into jars. But some she is mixing with chopped almonds or pounded hazelnuts to make an even more nutritious honey spread. I have since tried this idea at home: the almond honey is nicest if the almonds are blanched and lightly toasted, then chopped or slivered and mixed into some set honey. Hazelnuts can be ground, unblanched, and mixed with set honey and a pinch of ground cinnamon, to make a lovely honey spread for hot crumpets or warm home-made bread.

Brioche aux Fruits

BRIOCHE WITH CANDIED FRUIT

The jewelled look of this brioche, studded with diced candied fruit and shiny with a sugar glaze always catches one's eye in an Ardéchois *boulangerie*. Serve with bowls of piping hot *café au lait* to makes a perfect Christmas breakfast.

15 g (½ oz) fresh yeast *or* 2
    teaspoons dried yeast
225 g (8 oz) strong white
    flour
2 large eggs
½ teaspoon salt
2 tablespoons caster sugar
85 g (3 oz) melted butter
grated zest and juice of an
    orange

Filling
85 g (3 oz) mixed candied
    fruit and peel, diced
45 g (1½ oz) angelica, diced
45 g (1½ oz) glacé cherries,
    natural colour

In a wide mixing bowl, cream the fresh yeast with 2 tablespoons warm water or sprinkle the dried yeast on to the water. Leave the bowl in a warm place for 5–10 minutes until foamy.

Add the flour to one side of the bowl. Pour the eggs, beaten with the salt, into the centre and add half the sugar, the butter and the orange zest to the other side.

Use a wooden spoon to mix everything together. Then beat for 5–10 minutes, stretching the dough as much as possible until it becomes elastic and less sticky. Alternatively, mix the dough in a processor for 1 minute.

Cover the bowl with a plastic bag and leave at room temperature for 1–2 hours until the dough doubles in bulk.

Meanwhile soak the diced candied fruit, peel, angelica and cherries in the juice of the orange to soften slightly. Pour off the juice and heat in a small pan with the remainder of the sugar until dissolved. Set aside.

Turn the dough on to a floured surface and knead lightly for half a minute. Roll out to make a rectangle about 25 × 20 cm (10 × 8 in).

Brush with some of the sweetened orange juice and spread almost all of the diced candied fruit over the dough. Press into the dough slightly with a rolling-pin.

Roll up the dough from the longest side to make a sausage. Cut into seven even slices.

Rub a little butter over the inside of a 15 cm (6 in) cake tin. Arrange six of the slices, cut side down, around the outside with the seventh in the centre. Press the remaining candied fruit on top of each slice of dough. Set the brioche aside in a warm place for 30–45 minutes until the dough is puffed up.

Bake in a moderate oven (Mark 5, 190°C, 375°F) for 25–30 minutes. The top should be golden, not brown.

Meanwhile simmer the orange juice and sugar until thick and syrupy. Remove the brioche from the oven and transfer to a wire tray. Brush the top with the orange syrup. Cool slightly before serving or freeze when completely cold and reheat in a warm oven to bring out the flavour before serving.

CRÊPES FRISÉES DE TANTE JEANETTE

AUNT JEANETTE'S CURLY PANCAKES

I've always adored pancakes and crêpes, making them and eating them. But I've never thought of doing this: making crêpes with holes in them. I came across the recipe in *La Bonne Cuisine du Périgord* by La Mazille; it makes a crêpe with a crisp lattice that only needs a dusting of vanilla sugar. The method gives plenty of scope for artistry since I've found it possible to make faces, dinosaurs or mysterious creatures from outer space in the same way, so naturally these crêpes are highly popular with children, who also enjoy trailing the batter into the pan themselves.

2 eggs
75 ml (3 fl oz) milk
85 g (3 oz) flour
1 tablespoon vanilla sugar
a pinch of salt

2 tablespoons *eau-de-vie*
a little sunflower oil
vanilla sugar for sprinkling
wedges of lemon

Beat the eggs with the milk and gradually whisk in the flour, sugar and salt. If you have time, set aside for up to an hour to thicken. With admirable prudence French cooks insist on this, because that way you'll get more crêpes from the mixture.

When ready to cook the mixture, stir in the *eau-de-vie*. Heat a dribble of oil in a crêpe pan and tilt to coat the base.

Take a tablespoon of the mixture and trickle it into the pan, moving it around as you do so to make a pattern. Add a little extra to make cross lines. The idea is to leave holes in the crêpe and form unusual patterns with the mixture.

As soon as the mixture is set and the underside is golden, flip or turn the pancake over and cook until golden-brown.

Serve straight away with a sprinkling of sugar and a splash of lemon juice. Makes about 12 pancakes.

GÂTEAU AUX AMANDES DE MME MARQUET

MME MARQUET'S ALMOND CAKE

Mme Marquet uses her own almonds to make this lovely, delicately flavoured cake, the recipe for which came from her niece, Suzanne. I'm usually given a huge bag of almonds to bring home, *'pour les gâteaux'*, she says, knowing my fondness for baking. This cake is nicer if you blanch and grind the almonds yourself; they have far more flavour than bought ground almonds.

115 g (4 oz) flour	200 ml (7 fl oz) *crème*
115 g (4 oz) ground	*fraîche*
almonds	1 egg, beaten
100 g (3½ oz) caster sugar	1 tablespoon caster sugar
1 teaspoon baking powder	30 g (1 oz) flaked almonds

Sift the flour, almonds, sugar and baking powder into a bowl and mix to a dropping consistency with the *crème fraîche* and the egg.

Spoon the mixture into a 20 cm (8 in) buttered and base-lined cake tin. Smooth level and sprinkle the caster sugar and the almonds on top.

Bake in a moderate oven (Mark 5, 190°C, 375°F) for 30–40 minutes or until the cake is firm in the centre. Turn out on to a wire rack to cool.

OEUFS À LA NEIGE

SNOW EGGS

This is a pudding from my childhood and properly made, probably at home, it is delightful. Unfortunately there are a great many *oeufs à la neige* along with the bought-in *crème caramel* served in hotels and restaurants in provincial France that are not worth slipping your spoon into. So I include it here for all the children I know in France and England to whom this pudding is the tops.

570 ml (1 pt) milk	few drops French vanilla
3 eggs	essence
70 g (2½ oz) caster sugar	55 g (2 oz) granulated sugar
1½ tablespoons kirsch	

Pour the milk into your widest pan and set over a moderate heat.

Separate the eggs and whisk the egg whites until stiff; then whisk in 15 g (½ oz) of the caster sugar. Just as the milk comes to the boil, take rounded dessertspoons of the egg white and drop the balls of meringue into the milk. Poach three or four at a time, spooning hot milk over the *oeufs* until cooked. This is done very quickly – the meringue should need no longer than ½–1 minute in the milk. Lift out each meringue with a slotted spoon and place in a large shallow serving dish. Repeat until all the egg white has been poached.

Whisk the remaining caster sugar into the egg yolks and pour on the milk, stirring all the time. Strain the mixture back into the pan, add any milk that has drained from the *oeufs* and cook the custard carefully, stirring all the time, never allowing it to boil, over moderate heat until just thickened.

Remove from the heat and add the kirsch and vanilla essence according to taste. Cool the custard and gently pour into the shallow dish so that the *oeufs* float.

Dissolve the sugar in 2 tablespoons cold water and boil fast until the mixture turns golden brown. Remove from the heat and spoon a thin trickle of the caramel over the *oeufs* in fine lines. Serves 6.

MADELEINES

I'd like to think that those evocative morsels baked by Françoise and served at Combray were perhaps made to a recipe hardly different from this one from Audot's *La Cuisinière de la campagne et de la ville*. This book, with its splendidly spirited introduction, surely had an enormous influence on domestic cooking in nineteenth-century France. First published in 1818, it appeared in eighty-four editions between then and 1902. The copy that I was so fortunate to study, I read and cooked from in the same kitchen in which the book had inspired *la bonne* when cooking for the *curé* a century earlier.

55 g (2 oz) butter	1 teaspoon orange-flower
140 g (5 oz) caster sugar	water
finely grated zest of ½	115 g (4 oz) flour (if
lemon	possible French)
3 eggs, separated	clarified butter, melted

Cream the butter in a warmed bowl and gradually beat in the sugar with the lemon zest. Beat in the egg yolks with the orange-flower water.

Whisk the egg whites until stiff and fold into the mixture alternately with the sieved flour.

Brush clarified butter into the shell-shaped moulds of a madeleine tin. Place a rounded teaspoon of the mixture in each and smooth fairly level.

Bake in a moderate oven (Mark 4, 180°C, 350°F) for about 15 minutes or until golden and the little cakes are just starting to shrink from the tin. Cool in the tin for 1 minute and then transfer to a wire rack to cool.

Wash the tin with hot water only, dry and brush with clarified butter before baking the next batch of cakes. Makes 24 madeleines.

These days in France, madeleines are coated on one side with chocolate or are pumped full of jam but they are still best, freshly baked and plain. Serve with lime tea, of course.

Shell-shaped tins for baking madeleines are available from David Mellor, 4 Sloane Square, London, and King Street, Manchester.

MINERVES

The baker's wife in Vézénobres showed me how to turn day-old brioche into a kind of biscuit.

Spread slices of brioche, at least one day old, with apricot jam. Whisk an egg white until stiff and whisk in 3 tablespoons icing sugar. Spoon the sugar mixture over the jam and spread to the edges. Place the slices on a baking sheet and cook in a cool oven (Mark ¼, 100°C, 200°F) for 50–60 minutes until the brioche is nicely toasted and the icing is set and just starting to change colour. Cool the *minerves* on a wire tray.

GALETTE ARDÉCHOISE

ARDÉCHOIS YEAST CAKE

This flat brioche cake goes well served at breakfast or tea, either plain or with a fruit jelly. And it easily becomes a fine *galette aux myrtilles*.

**basic brioche recipe
(see p. 242)
a little egg white
caster sugar**

Make the brioche dough, omitting the zest of orange, according to the instructions for the *brioche aux fruits*. Prove the dough in a warm place until double in volume and then turn out on to a floured surface.

Roll out to fit a buttered shallow pizza tin 28 cm (11 in) across. Brush with the beaten egg white and sprinkle caster sugar over the top. Leave in a warm place or at room temperature for 45–60 minutes until well puffed up.

Bake in the centre of a moderately hot oven (Mark 6, 200°C, 400°F) for 20–25 minutes until golden brown. Transfer to a wire rack to cool.

Galette aux Myrtilles: Bilberry Yeast Cake
There are two ways of tackling this cake: either spread the top of the baked *galette* with bilberry jam or slice the cake into two layers and sandwich them with fresh or tinned bilberries, the juice slightly thickened with arrowroot and add, if in the Ardèche, a splash of *liqueur de myrtilles*. Serve warm or cold with *crème fraîche*.

CRÈME BACHIQUE

CREAM OF BACCHUS

A wine and egg custard that is a real delight. It is superb made with the Muscat de Beaumes de Venise but leave out the sugar in that case.

450 ml (¾ pt) sweet white wine like Montbazillac
55–85 g (2–3 oz) caster sugar (the amount depends on the sweetness of the wine)

a strip of lemon zest or ½ stick of cinnamon
6 egg yolks

Bring the wine to the boil, preferably in a glass or enamel pan, with the sugar and lemon zest or cinnamon stick. Simmer for 4 minutes. Remove from the heat and fish out the lemon or cinnamon.

Beat the egg yolks in a bowl and gradually whisk in the slightly cooled wine.

Pour into 4 or 6 cocotte dishes or ramekins and cook in a bain-marie in a moderate oven (Mark 3, 160°C, 325°F) for 20–30 minutes until set. Do not overcook; a knife blade comes clean out of the custard when cooked. Allow the creams to cool in the bain-marie.

Serve very cold with almond *tuiles* or tiny pistachio meringues made from the remaining egg whites. A thin layer of *crème fraîche* spooned on top is an alternative. Serves 4–6.

OREILLETTES

LITTLE EARS

We drove away from Beaulieu-sur-Dordogne after a month's stay at the riverside camp-site beside the bridge. Our four-year-old daughter's lower lip quivered – only a small bag of warm *oreillettes* straight from the *boulangerie* could help offset her disappointment at leaving France until the next year. These crisp nothings, modelled on piglet's ears, are also known as '*bugnes*' and are traditionally made at Christmas in the Ardèche.

255 g (9 oz) flour	½ teaspoon baking powder
55 g (2 oz) butter, softened	½ teaspoon orange-flower
1 egg	water
45 g (1½ oz) caster sugar	oil for deep-frying
pinch salt	vanilla sugar
1 teaspoon sunflower oil	

Sift the flour on to a cold work-surface or into a wide bowl. Make a well in the centre and add the butter, the egg, caster sugar, salt, sunflower oil, baking powder, orange-flower water and 2 tablespoons cold water. Use the fingertips to work all the ingredients together as when making pastry. Gather into a ball and knead slightly. Cover the dough with the upturned bowl and leave for 15 minutes.

On a floured board, roll out the dough until 1–2 mm (⅛ in) thick. Use a toothed pasta wheel to cut strips about 4 cm (1½ in) wide and then cut across to make diamond shapes.

Deep-fry the pastries, three or four at a time, in hot deep fat. This takes only 2–3 minutes and the *oreillettes* will swell up like cushions. Drain on kitchen paper and toss in vanilla sugar. Makes about fifty little ears.

CRÊPES DE BLÉ NOIR

BUCKWHEAT PANCAKES

Blé noir or *sarrasin* grows easily in southern France, even in poor soils. Farmers often grow a strip of the red-stemmed plant for their bees to forage its pink and white flowers. At the end of summer the dried seed is fed to livestock or is ground to make buckwheat flour.

Its distinctive earthy, slightly bitter taste is unique and the flavour goes superbly well with fish, hence *blinis* and caviare. But also try a smoked fish pâté or a selection of smoked fish and a little *crème fraîche* with these easy-to-make crêpes. The recipe comes from Joy Davies and it's far quicker than making yeast-risen *blini*.

115 g (4 oz) buckwheat flour	285–340 ml (10–12 fl oz) warm milk
115 g (4 oz) flour	2 teaspoons lemon juice
½ teaspoon baking powder	55 g (2 oz) butter, melted
a good pinch of salt	a little sunflower oil
1 egg, separated	

Sift the flours, baking powder and salt into a bowl. Stir in the egg yolk and gradually add the milk, lemon juice and melted butter. Whisk the egg white until stiff and fold into the batter.

Heat a few drops of oil in a small crêpe pan until almost smoking. Pour a tablespoon of the batter into the pan and tilt to make a round crêpe about 8 cm (3 in) across. Cook until golden underneath, flip over and cook for 2 minutes more. Transfer to a cloth or kitchen-paper-covered wire rack and keep warm while you make the remainder. Makes about 30 crêpes.

MOUSSE AU CHOCOLAT POUR ERIC

CHOCOLATE MOUSSE FOR ERIC

I had spent the morning in Le Puy, exploring on foot the steep, narrow streets that surround the cathedral. Then I drove south along a high, narrow road that, like an anxious chaperone, never lost sight of the Loire below. Then I came to the village of Cussac and realized that I had misread the map. I sat at the wheel studying the intricacies of a Michelin Route-master when a small head appeared through the open window. 'What are you doing?' a child's voice asked, in English. 'I'm lost and I'm checking the way. Your English is very good. How old are you?' I inquired of this young solemn face. He beamed and boasted that he'd been learning English for just one year and he was now eleven years old. Suddenly the car was surrounded by children of all ages and, seeing my English number plates, they clamoured to know why I was alone and so far from home. I explained that I was interested in French food and asked Eric, my original questioner, for the name of his favourite dish. 'Mousse au chocolat,' he pronounced and then, hearing his mother calling him for lunch, bade me goodbye and ran off shouting 'Mousse au chocolat'. And as I drove away, out of the village, I started to devise a really big chocolate mousse.

285 g (10 oz) plain dessert chocolate
18 boudoir sponge fingers
2 liqueur glasses *marron de l'Ardèche* liqueur or brandy
1 after-dinner cup strong black coffee
2 eggs, separated
275 ml (½ pint) double cream
45 g (1½ oz) caster sugar
150 ml (¼ pt) whipping cream to decorate (optional)

Break the chocolate into pieces and place over hot water to melt.

Line a very lightly oiled 1.5 litre (2½ pt) fluted brioche tin with cling-film; don't worry if there are a few creases, it won't matter. Cut a sponge finger to fit into each flute and arrange a neat pattern of pieces in the base.

Mix one glass of liqueur or brandy with the coffee and brush the sponge fingers with the mixture.

Remove the melted chocolate from over the hot water and beat in the egg yolks. Whisk the double cream with the remaining glass of liqueur until stiff. In another bowl whisk the egg whites until stiff and fold in the sugar.

Now fold first the chocolate and then the egg whites into the cream. Spoon the mixture into the brioche mould and chill until set.

The mousse can be frozen if you wish.

To complete, dip the mould briefly into hot water and then, pulling at the sheet of cling-film, unmould the mousse on to a flat serving dish, preferably on a stand. Whisk the whipping cream until stiff, flavour with a little liqueur, if desired, and then spoon into a forcing bag fitted with a star nozzle and pipe rosettes of cream around the base and top of the mousse. Cut into narrow wedges to serve. The mousse can be served frozen, *semi-freddo* or thawed but chilled. Serves up to 14.

CRÈME ANGLAISE AU FIGUIER

FIG-LEAF CUSTARD

Even if your English figs refuse to ripen – and, denied the southern sun, who could blame them – pluck a leaf or two to give the same, musky scent of the fruit itself to a creamy custard. I first tried this with some wild fig leaves in France after reading about it in Diana Kennedy's *Mexican Regional Cooking*.

275 ml (½ pt) single cream
2 small fig leaves
2 egg yolks
1–2 tablespoons
   vanilla-flavoured sugar

langue de chat biscuits *or*
fingers of toasted brioche

Bring the cream to the boil with the fig leaves. Lift out the leaves and place in the bottom of a glass serving dish.

Pour the cream on to the egg yolks mixed with the sugar. Return the mixture to the pan and cook carefully (ideally in a double boiler) stirring all the time over moderate heat until the custard coats the back of a spoon. Do not allow the custard to boil or it will go grainy.

Strain the custard through a sieve on to the fig leaves. Cover and set aside to cool then remove the fig leaves and chill the custard.

To serve, spoon into small custard cups or stemmed glasses and serve with the biscuits or brioche, which, if hot, is nice dipped into the chilled cream. Serves 3–4.

BEIGNETS DE PRUNEAUX

PRUNE FRITTERS

To my mind, 'prune fritters' sounds too dismal for words, as if a wartime cook has come to the end of her tether. But look to the French name and once you try this slightly adapted recipe from Ethelind Fearon's *The Marquis, the Mayonnaise and Me*, the tale of her days running a villa in Cannes, I suspect you'll be won over.

225 g (8 oz) – about 16 – large prunes
1 wineglass half red wine/half hot water
caster sugar
1 teaspoon arrowroot

Marzipan
55 g (2 oz) ground almonds
30 g (1 oz) caster sugar
30 g (1 oz) icing sugar
1 egg yolk
1 teaspoon brandy

or use 115 g (4 oz) prepared white marzipan

Batter
55 g (2 oz) flour
pinch salt
1 tablespoon sunflower oil
1 egg white
sunflower oil for deep frying

Soak the prunes in the wine and water for 2 hours; cook gently for 15 minutes. Strain off the juice, add a little sugar to sweeten and thicken with the arrowroot over moderate heat until clear. Keep the sauce hot until ready to serve. Remove the stones from the prunes.

To make the marzipan, work the almonds, sugars, egg yolk and brandy together to make a smooth paste. Divide into 16 pieces and roll each into a small egg shape. Tuck one inside each prune.

For the batter: beat the flour and salt with the warm water and the oil until smooth. Whisk the egg white until stiff and fold into the batter.

Dip each prune into the batter, then drop into the very hot deep fat. Fry for 2–3 minutes until golden. Drain on kitchen paper and serve straight away while still crisp with the wine sauce, or dust with vanilla sugar and eat with the fingers. Makes about 16 beignets.

QUATRE-QUARTS AUX CASSIS

My fondness for this French version of our pound cake dates from the time that we stayed in a particularly primitive *gîte rural* and I devised some simple balance scales with a stick and a couple of plastic bags so that I could make a *quatre-quarts*. It worked. And now when I have picked a bowlful of blackcurrants in Devon I sometimes make this cake as a reminder of that ill-equipped kitchen in Vaucluse.

4 eggs (in their shells)
flour to the same weight as
   the eggs
caster sugar to the same
   weight as the eggs
butter to the same weight
   as the eggs

zest of lemon, finely grated
   ***or* 1 teaspoon**
   orange-flower water
225 g (8 oz) blackcurrants or
   raspberries (the fruit
   must be dry)

Break the eggs into a bowl and gradually mix in the flour, sugar and butter, first melted in a small pan with the zest of lemon or orange-flower water. Mix well.

Butter a 23–25 cm (9–10 in) cake tin, ideally with fluted sides for the prettiest cake. Place a disc of buttered greaseproof paper in the base. Spoon half the mixture into the tin. Sprinkle the fruit on top and cover with the remainder of the mixture. Smooth level.

Bake the cake in the centre of a moderate oven (Mark 4, 180°C, 350°F) for about 45 minutes until springy to the touch in the centre.

Cool in the tin for 2 minutes, and turn out to cool on a wire rack. The cake is also good served warm with *crème fraîche*.

GLACE AU NOUGAT

NOUGAT ICE-CREAM

In the chapter entitled 'Treasures' in the *Alice B. Toklas Cook Book* there is a recipe for nougat ice-cream which uses honey instead of sugar, and very good it is too. This recipe grew from that idea. However my favourite nougat contains candied fruit and angelica as well as nuts and I wanted to make the ice-cream nougat-white. Incidentally, when buying nougat look at the back of the shelf for the freshest; for the best flavour, nougat should give slightly under thumb pressure – unless you enjoy that other teeth-pulling stuff.

2 egg whites
115 g (4 oz)
   vanilla-flavoured sugar
275 ml (½ pt) double cream
1–2 tablespoons
   orange-flower water
30 g (1 oz) split, toasted
   almonds, slivered

30 g (1 oz) blanched
   pistachio nuts, chopped
30 g (1 oz) angelica,
   slivered
30–55 g (1–2 oz) French
   candied fruits, chopped
   (or undyed glacé cherries
   and pineapple)

Whisk the egg whites with the sugar in a bowl over simmering water until the mixture stands in peaks. Remove from the heat, stand the bowl in cold water and continue whisking for 3–4 minutes until the cooked meringue is cool.

Whisk the cream until stiff, flavour to taste with the orange-flower water and fold in the almonds, pistachios, angelica and candied fruits.

Fold in the meringue mixture and turn into a bowl or plastic box. Cover and freeze until firm. Thaw in a refrigerator for 1–2 hours before turning out on to a serving dish. Serves 6–8.

There were two kitchens at Vézénobres: one shady and vaulted with a mimosa tree at the door, the other on the floor above with one wall almost all window looking out across the valley of the Gardon to the blue Cévennes. In this kitchen it was sometimes hard to concentrate on the cooking. The light constantly shifts across vineyard and olive grove and the flock of milking sheep makes its way up the far hillside. Just below the window a machine like a turquoise scarab moves along every fourth row of vines, spraying against botrytis. It leaves the vineyard looking like neat rows of knitting: three rows of purl where the soil is wet, separated by one of plain where it is light and dusty and dry.

And then there were the comings and goings on the Roman road to Nîmes far below. Once I saw the President of France conveyed along it at speed. His car, which looked as tiny as a toy from the kitchen, was half-hidden in a sea of motor-cycled police whose electronic conversation echoed barbarically amongst the ancient stones of Vézénobres.

In the lower kitchen Mme Romeyer prepared everyone's breakfast: coffee, hot croissants and her home-made greengage jam made from the greenery-yallery *reines-Claude*. She remembered the horses being stabled in this recently converted kitchen which led out to a small sloping orchard of cherry, sweet chestnut, mulberry, persimmon and garden fig. I would lean over the edge of the terrace above and will the fruit to ripen before I had to leave.

Here at Vézénobres, where the weather was always so perfect, my cooking was short and speedy. Meals were quickly prepared and carried outside to be eaten slowly and lazily while contemplating the country of the Camisards below us.

There was fresh pasta from Uzès, served with the new season's creamy garlic and large- and small-leaved basil. I remember a *jambon cru* tasting when we compared a ham from Bayonne with one from the Ardèche and a third from a tiny village near Le Puy in Haute-Loire. M. Petit from Bedarrides had predicted that we would prefer the last kind, and it was so. It was a ham with a depth of delicate flavour that, on this occasion at least, put the others in the shade. It is the long hard winters, explained M. Petit, that account for the outstanding flavour.

Then of course, a salad, followed, perhaps, by some rich, yellow brioches hollowed and filled with pieces of cool, scented melon, some strawberries and a splash of kirsch. Or a basket of apricots given to us as we walked down the hill through a valley of laughter and happy voices where no one was to be seen. The apricot pickers were hidden by leaves. The only person we met was the farmer at the roadside, his donkey waiting patiently and the cart piled high with the golden, blushing fruit. Our small children were amazed to see so many apricots together. And the farmer, laughing, gave them huge handfuls and filled their pockets and mouths with the warm velvety fruit.

For those of us from northern climes, the fruit of the south of France is one of its glories. And because the terrain and the climate that produce this harvest are dramatically different from our own I prefer to arrive gradually. One year I drove south by following the course of the river Mimente from Florac. From the Col de Jalaeste I took the road to St Germain de Calbert through the groves of sweet chestnuts. The road then falls steeply all the way to St Jean du Gard. Around St Étienne Vallée-Française the curved Roman tile appears and there is the odd patch of vines. The house terraces are vine-covered and the road is cream with the fallen blossom of a thousand acacias. This is a road of transition between the Cévennes and the Languedoc. As if to confirm this, just before St Jean du Gard you pass a date palm. And in no time at all, if it's Tuesday morning you are in the midst of the market at St Jean du Gard. There is an open-sided hall for year-round traders who bring in from the countryside fresh charcuterie, local cheeses, and honey from the Cévennes. Here I saw beetroot thinnings sold in bundles so that the leaves could be cooked as a vegetable. On this June morning there were strawberries from Carpentras, the earliest melons no larger than a man's fist, the first figs from Italy, white peaches and a few tiny apricots.

A week later, at Arles, in the magnificent market that stretches all the way down the Boulevard des Lices, the cherries had arrived: the *beulots*, the *coeurs de pigeon*, the *burlats de Ventoux*, the *belles de mai*, the *bigarreaux* and the *reverdons*, the sharp *griottes* and the yellow *boules d'or*.

It seems, though, that such a cornucopia of summer fruit inspires everyone to preserve it for the winter. In Lamastre Bernard Perrier bottles the local pears. And in the Var, Boyaca McGarvie-Munn makes jam in one of the most unusual and versatile country kitchens in France, in the château which her late father, her brother and she have so sensitively restored. Boyaca's lunch cooks quietly at one end of the kitchen, while on the table in the middle she sells admission tickets to the house or a packet of locally made biscuits or sweets. In January she visits her friends near the coast and helps to pick their crop of bitter oranges. Back in the kitchen at Entrecasteaux, she and her brother prepare a vast cauldron of orange marmalade which she flavours with good malt whisky brought back from visits to Scottish relatives. She tells me that French visitors just can't get enough of her orange whisky marmalade, and judging from the jar she gave me it appears to be a delicious example of the Auld Alliance.

Fruit with alcohol is invariably a winning combination and one of the simplest methods of preserving. There is a distillery in Forcalquier in Haute Provence which packs fruit in regimented layers in huge demijohns of *eau-de-vie* so that it looks almost too attractive to break into. At home things can be done more simply.

In country regions sloes, the same sloes that grow in our hedgerows, are collected and put into bottles two thirds full of *eau-de-vie*, and kept for some months to make a fine drink.

Mme Marquet often serves prunes steeped in Armagnac with our afternoon coffee. Some families still own their grandmothers' tiny silver goblets, used for serving cherries preserved in brandy – *griottes au cognac* – a wonderful treat at the end of a meal on a special occasion. Given a generous supply of fruit and wine or spirits there seems no limit to the delectable possibilities.

SORBET DE POIRE

PEAR SORBET

In the neat and tidy village of St Désirat in the parish of St Joseph the elegantly pruned fruit trees – cherries and apricots, peach and pear – grow in every available space. As you drive out towards the Caves Cooperative beside the railway line you'll come upon the distillery of Jean Gauthier. If you've time it is fun to visit his shop to sample the liqueurs and *eaux-de-vie* that he makes from the local fruit. If M. Gauthier is not too busy he may take you across the road to the distillery where he produces these luscious liquids.

I use a Gauthier *eau-de-vie de poire* (some bottles of which contain a whole pear – they make excellent presents) to spoon over a scoop or two of this pear sorbet, to make what Bernard Perrier at Barattero calls a '*trou Ardéchois*'.

1 kg (2 lb) ripe dessert pears, Comice, William or Passa Crassana	a vanilla pod
	1 egg white
50–85 g (2–3 oz) sugar	2 teaspoons caster sugar
a strip of lemon peel	2–4 tablespoons *eau-de-vie de poire*

Peel, core and quarter the pears. Dissolve the sugar in 275 ml (½ pt) water and boil fast with the lemon peel for 4 minutes. Remove the lemon peel and add the vanilla pod.

Poach the pears in the syrup for 10–15 minutes until completely tender. Remove the vanilla pod and cool the pears and syrup by standing the pan in cold water.

Purée the pears and syrup in a processor or blender. Stir in 2 tablespoons of the *eau-de-vie*.

Whisk the egg white until stiff, then whisk in the extra sugar. Fold into the pear purée; turn the mixture into a lidded plastic box and freeze.

To serve, scoop the sorbet into a processor and whizz until smooth. Scoop into small stemmed glasses and spoon a little *eau-de-vie de poire* over the top. Serves 8.

POUDING DE COINGS

QUINCE CUSTARD

Sometimes one comes upon a promising-looking recipe which, cooked, gives a disappointing result. This custard started that way. As a tart it was flabby and undistinguished but I felt that somewhere in the original recipe there was an attractive harmony of flavours that was worth pursuing. Of course, you may have more luck and you will be able to put the custard back in its *pâte brisée* case and triumph, but I prefer the filling on its own. The original recipe for a *Bettelmann de coings* was given by Ginette Mathiot and Lionel Poilâne; the latter runs a smart Parisian *boulangerie* and is the author of the highly entertaining and informative *Guide de l'amateur de pain*.

225 g (8 oz) quinces	⅛ teaspoon ground
115 g (4 oz) sugar	cinnamon
275 ml (½ pt) milk	1 tablespoon kirsch
30 g (1 oz) vanilla-flavoured	55 g (2 oz) fresh white
sugar	breadcrumbs
2 eggs	
a few drops of vanilla	
essence	

Peel and core the quinces, and cut into small slices. Dissolve the sugar in 275 ml (½ pt) water and boil fast for 4 minutes. Add the quinces and cook until tender. Use a slotted spoon to lift out the quinces and make a layer of them in the base of an ovenproof dish or a soufflé dish. Pour the syrup from the quinces into a small jug.

Heat the milk with the vanilla sugar until warm. Pour on to the beaten eggs and whisk in the vanilla essence, ground cinnamon and the kirsch. Stir in the breadcrumbs and pour over the quinces.

Bake the custard in a bain-marie in a moderate oven (Mark 4, 180°C, 350°F) for 30–40 minutes until set. Remove from the oven. Cool a little then serve warm with the quince syrup; or serve it cold. Serves 4.

GELÉE DE VIN DE SUMEAU

ELDERBERRY AND RED WINE JELLY

I started to test a recipe that I'd been given for an elderberry-flavoured red wine but along the way I sensed the concoction might be more pleasing as a jelly. And everyone seemed to agree.

225 g (8 oz) ripe
   elderberries
275 ml (½ pt) Côtes du
   Rhône red wine
55–85 g (2–3 oz) sugar

2 teaspoons powdered
   gelatine
4 tablespoons lemon juice
crème fraîche or single
   cream

If necessary rinse the elderberries in cold water. Remove the main stalks but don't worry about every tiny piece because they will be strained out.

Cover the fruit with the wine and leave, covered, overnight in a cold place.

Next day turn the fruit and wine into a glass or enamel pan, add the sugar and crush the fruit with a wooden spoon. Slowly bring the mixture almost to the boil. Strain through a fine nylon sieve and allow to cool.

Soften the gelatine in the lemon juice in a glass or enamel pan. Heat gently until dissolved and stir into the wine mixture. Pour into 4 wine glasses and chill until set – but note that the jelly does not set firmly and hence the flavour is excellent.

Spoon over a little *crème fraîche* or single cream to make a thin layer on top of the jelly and serve. Serves 4.

FIGUES AUX FRAMBOISES

FRESH FIGS WITH RASPBERRY CREAM

One summer I was delighted to discover a locally produced booklet of fig recipes available in the Syndicat d'Initiative in Vézénobres. This simple recipe from the anonymous authors works specially well.

8–10 fresh, ripe figs	1 tablespoon caster sugar
115 g (4 oz) fresh raspberries	275 ml (½ pt) *crème fraîche*

Halve or, if large, quarter the figs and arrange on a plate.

Sieve the raspberries into a bowl and stir in the sugar. Mix in the *crème fraîche* to make a raspberry cream.

Spoon the cream over the figs and serve straight away or leave in a cold place for up to one hour. Serves 4.

TARTE AUX ABRICOTS À LA FAÇON DE MME CHALENDAR

MME CHALENDAR'S APRICOT TART WITH SHAKEN HOT-WATER PASTRY

Mme Chalendar sells earthenware and stoneware kitchen pots in Lamastre. One year, in the shop, she gave me a lively demonstration of how she makes this unusual pastry. And when I tried it in my own kitchen, it worked. The apricot tart is good, not too sweet or rich.

450–570 g (1–1¼ lb) fresh apricots	½ teaspoon salt
115 g (4 oz) sugar	4 tablespoons mild salad oil like *pépin de raisins*
	½ beaten egg
Pastry	
225 g (8 oz) flour	*Fruit base*
1 tablespoon caster sugar	20 g (¾ oz) flour
½ teaspoon baking powder	20 g (¾ oz) caster sugar

Halve the apricots and remove the stones. (Crack the stones and keep the kernels to replace bitter almonds in other recipes.)

Dissolve the sugar in 150 ml (¼ pt) water over moderate heat. Poach the apricots in the syrup for 2–3 minutes or until the skins can be removed easily.

Use a slotted spoon to transfer the fruit to a plate. Discard the skins and boil the remaining syrup until it measures 3–4 tablespoons. Set aside for glazing the tart later.

Mme Chalendar's method for the pastry is to put all the ingredients with 3 tablespoons of hot water into a plastic lidded bowl and shake them for 1–2 minutes. When you remove the lid of the bowl, the mixture has formed small lumps like coarse breadcrumbs. Use your hand to bind them together to make a ball. On a floured surface roll out the pastry and use to line a 24 cm (9½ in) tart tin.

Mix the flour and caster sugar and sprinkle over the base of the pastry. Arrange the apricot halves in a single layer on top.

Bake the tart in a moderate oven (Mark 5, 190°C, 375°F) for 30–35 minutes until the pastry is crisp.

Remove the tart from the oven and brush the reserved glaze over the apricots. Serve hot, warm or cold. Serves 6–8.

TARTE AUX PÊCHES

PEACH TART

During August and September French peaches are often good value even in England. Here they contrast nicely with the almond pastry and the peaches themselves are rosy with a raspberry sauce.

Pastry	Filling
115 g (4 oz) flour	200 g (7 oz) sugar
45 g (1½ oz) ground almonds	1 vanilla pod
45 g (1½ oz) vanilla sugar	8–10 medium-sized ripe peaches
a pinch of salt	225 g (8 oz) raspberries
70 g (2½ oz) butter, softened	
1 egg yolk	

Sift the flour, ground almonds, vanilla sugar and salt into a wide bowl or on to a cold work surface and make a well in the centre. Place the butter, cut into pieces, and almost all the egg yolk in the middle and work everything together using just the fingertips until well combined to make a dough. Wrap and chill the dough for 30 minutes or put it in the freezer for 10 minutes.

Roll out the dough on a floured board to line a 23 cm (9–10 in) greased tart tin. Brush the base with any remaining egg yolk and prick all over with a fork. Chill in the refrigerator for 10 minutes.

Bake in the centre of a moderately hot oven (Mark 6, 200°C, 400°F) until the pastry is crisp and is just changing colour at the edges. Remove from the oven and cool in the tin.

Dissolve the sugar in 275 ml (½ pt) water and simmer with the vanilla pod for 4 minutes. Wash and halve the peaches (if very large cut into quarters) and poach them in the syrup for 5–7 minutes until tender. Use a slotted spoon to lift out the peaches and the vanilla pod. Place the peaches on a plate and remove their skins.

Reduce the syrup over high heat to one third of the amount. Add the raspberries and remove from the heat. Push the fruit through a sieve to make a purée. (If the raspberries are end of the season and are not specially fleshy you may have to thicken the purée with a teaspoon of arrowroot; cook until the sauce is clear.) Set aside to cool.

No more than one hour before serving arrange the peaches over the base of the pastry case and spoon over the raspberry purée. Leave in a cold place until ready to serve. Serves 6.

CROÛTES AUX FRUITS

TOASTED FRUIT

This toasted fruit on French bread or, even nicer, sliced brioche, is simple enough for children to make; it can provide a welcome contrast at the end of a cold meal.

Spread each slice of French bread with a thin layer of jam, jelly or honey. Arrange halved apricots or sliced peaches, plums or some strawberries or raspberries on top. Dust with caster sugar and place on a baking sheet under a hot grill for 4–8 minutes until the sugar has melted and the fruit has cooked sufficiently for the juice to have seeped into the bread.

Serve the *croûtes* straight away, as they are, or with some *fromage frais* or *crème fraîche* spooned on top.

BOCAL DU VIEUX GARÇON

OLD BOY'S JAR

This is a splendidly simple way of preserving some of the summer's fruit, and I find that boys of any age enjoy it.

Start with a good sized wide-necked jar or bottle. The French make many different shapes and sizes and some are on sale here. Alternatively use a large Kilner jar or even a spaghetti storage jar. Apart from the fruit, the only ingredients are plenty of *eau-de-vie* and sugar.

First of all fill the jar one third full with *eau-de-vie*, and, as necessary, add more as you go, always making sure that the fruit is covered. Every time fruit is added to the jar an equal quantity of sugar must be added, but never more than 450 g (1 lb) at a time. Make a selection from the following summer fruits.

Strawberries: usually the first fruit of the summer suitable for the jar. Wash the fruit and dry well on kitchen paper, leave whole.

Cherries: wash and dry the fruit, stone but leave whole for adding to the jar.

Red currants: wash, dry and sprig – then add to the jar.

Raspberries: as long as the fruit is dry and sound, raspberries go straight into the jar.

Apricots: choose ripe fruit, wash and dry and halve to remove the stones. Add halved or quartered fruit.

Peaches: remove the skin of the peaches by first covering in boiling water for a few minutes. Slice or quarter for adding to the jar.

Pears: peel, core and slice.

Plums and greengages: wash and dry. Then remove the stones and add the halved or quartered fruit.

Grapes: wash and dry black or white grapes, and remove the pips before adding to the jar.

When the jar is full, seal tightly and store in a cold, dark place for at least 3 months. Serve the fruit in small dishes at the end of a meal.

My French guide to this preparation says that it may ferment a little but it is of no importance.

Tarte aux Pommes
à la Clyst William

CLYST WILLIAM APPLE TART

Although first baked in Devon using our own apples, this tart is obviously a variation on many delicious French ones. Properly golden Golden Delicious apples, honey tasting, their skins slightly shrivelled, are excellent in pies and tarts.

Pastry	*Filling*
140 g (5 oz) flour	450–680 g (1–1½ lb) ripe
1 tablespoon vanilla sugar	eating apples
a pinch of salt	55–85 g (2–3 oz) sugar
70 g (2½ oz) butter	45 g (1½ oz) dry white
1 egg yolk	breadcrumbs
	150 ml (¼ pt) double or
	whipping cream
	2 eggs, beaten
	½ teaspoon vanilla essence

Sift the flour, sugar and salt into a bowl, and rub in the butter. Mix to a dough with the egg yolk and 2–3 tablespoons ice-cold water. If the pastry is still very cold roll out to line a greased 20–23 cm (9 in) pie dish about 5 cm (2 in) deep. Otherwise chill the pastry first.

Crimp the edges of the pastry and spread three quarters of the breadcrumbs in the base. Cover with the peeled and sliced apple sprinkled with the sugar.

Mix the cream with the eggs and vanilla essence and pour over the apples. Sprinkle the remaining breadcrumbs on top.

Bake in a moderately hot oven (Mark 6, 200°C, 400°F) for 20 minutes, and then lower the heat to Mark 4 (180°C, 350°F) for 10–15 minutes, until the pastry is golden and the custard is set. Serves 6.

GRIOTTES EN COGNAC

CHERRIES IN BRANDY

Griottes or morello cherries ripen to a bright red but are too bitter tasting to eat fresh and they need plenty of sugar when cooked. They do however make exceptionally good jam and preserve beautifully in brandy.

900 g (2 lb) *griottes* or morello cherries	**285 g (10 oz) sugar** **1 litre (1¾ pt) cognac**

Pick the cherries over, reject any that an unknowing bird has decided to sample, and wash in cold water. Drain well and cut each stalk to about one third of its length to make a handle for eating with.

Fill one or more wide-necked jars with the cherries. Dissolve the sugar in 6 tablespoons cold water in a pan over low heat. Bring to the boil and simmer for 4 minutes. Remove from the heat, cool slightly and then mix with the cognac. Pour the syrup over the cherries, making sure they are covered.

Cover tightly, preferably with a screw-top, and leave in a cold place for at least one month before serving.

To serve: spoon some cherries into a small-stemmed glass and pour over the brandy. Eat the cherries and then drink the liqueur.

EAU-DE-VIE DE PRUNELLES À JEAN MARQUET

JEAN MARQUET'S SLOE EAU-DE-VIE

M. Marquet collects blue-black sloes in December and, instead of the sloe gin I make in England, he produces a beautiful raspberry-pink concoction based on *eau-de-vie*. A few months later a syrup for serving with ice-cream and hot puddings can be made from the same sloes.

1 wineglass sloes	*Syrup*
1 litre (1¾ pt) *eau-de-vie*	up to 1 kg (2¼ lb) sugar
blanche (40° proof)	500 ml (18 fl oz) red wine

In Britain, collect sloes after the first frost, which softens their flesh. Prick each fruit with a pin and pack into a 1 litre (1¾ pint) bottle or jar.

Cover with the *eau-de-vie*, cork the bottle and store in a cool, dark place for at least 2 months and preferably longer, until the *eau-de-vie* has become raspberry pink. Strain into another bottle, cork tightly and store in a cool, dark place for 1–5 years.

For the syrup, dissolve the sugar in the wine and simmer for 5 minutes. Cool slightly and pour over the sloes. Cork the bottle and keep in the kitchen, shaking it every day for 2–4 weeks until the flavour is satisfactory. Strain the liquid into another bottle, add a little of the *eau-de-vie de prunelles* if you wish, and keep for serving with puddings or as a basis for cool summer drinks made with carbonated spring water and ice.

I recommend the syrup served hot, just slightly thickened with a little arrowroot, over a good English sponge pudding – excellent on a frosty day.

PRUNEAUX À L'EAU-DE-VIE

PRUNES IN EAU-DE-VIE

Although *pruneaux d'Agen* are highly thought of and cost more in France, I've found most large prunes (but not the pre-soaked kind – they disintegrate) are particularly good preserved this way.

1 kg (2¼ lb) large prunes	115 g (4 oz) sugar
2 tablespoons dried lime	1 litre (1¾ pt) *eau-de-vie*
flowers	blanche (40°)

Measure the prunes into a bowl. In a jug or teapot make an infusion with the lime flowers and 750 ml (1¼ pt) boiling water. Stir and leave for 5 minutes, then strain over the prunes. Cover and leave overnight. Next day drain the prunes on a cloth and discard the lime tea. Pack the fruit into a jar.

Dissolve the sugar with 2–3 tablespoons water in a small pan over low heat. Pour the syrup over the prunes and fill up the jar with *eau-de-vie*, making sure that all the fruit is covered.

Seal the jar and leave in a cold place for at least 1 month and preferably 6 before serving. As far as I can judge the prunes only improve with time.

Occasionally Mme Marquet replaces the *eau-de-vie* with Armagnac but she declines to use the whisky I take her – that is reserved for M. Marquet to sample along with roasted chestnuts around the fire.

CONFITURE DE REINE-CLAUDE
REINE-CLAUDE OR GREENGAGE JAM

The *reine-Claude* is a fine greengage named after Queen Claude, the wife of François I. My tree in England is not yet mature enough to fruit but as soon as it is I shall make this lovely Vézénobres breakfast jam.

**2 kg (4½ lb) reines-Claude
or very ripe greengages
1 kg (2¼ lb) sugar**

Wash the fruit and dry on a cloth. Halve the greengages and remove the stones. Layer alternately with the sugar in a bowl. Cover and leave overnight.

Turn the fruit and sugar into a preserving pan and cook over low heat until the sugar is dissolved. Raise the heat and cook for 20–30 minutes until a set is reached, at 105°C (220°F). Remove from the heat and pour into warm, dry jars. Cover and label. Makes about 2½–3 kg (5–6 lb).

CONFITURE DE FIGUES

FIG JAM

1 kg (2¼ lb) fresh figs
1 kg (2¼ lb) sugar
2 lemons

Wash the figs and dry them on a cloth, making sure not to damage them. Prick each fig with a knitting needle.

Dissolve the sugar in 250 ml (9 fl oz) water over low heat, and then raise the heat and bring almost to the boil. Add the figs and the juice of the lemons.

Simmer the fruit and syrup for about 1 hour or until a set is reached, at 105°C (220°F).

Remove from the heat; if necessary remove any thick froth from the jam. Pour into warm jars. Makes about 2–2½ kg (4–5 lb).

A friend in Vaucluse makes a delicious September variation on this jam. He picks the second crop of small figs from his trees and adds an equal amount of green tomatoes. I have not made this jam myself but the tomatoes cook to a pale pink and the flavour is delightful, slightly scented.

VINAIGRE POUR LES SALADES

VINEGAR FOR SALADS

An old recipe for herb vinegar which has a peppery undertone.

2 handfuls tarragon
a few sprigs of watercress
or land cress
a small bunch of chervil
a few leaves of salad burnet
2 cloves of garlic, peeled
1 green chilli pepper
white wine vinegar

Put all the herbs, complete with stalks, and the garlic and chilli pepper in a wide-necked jar. Cover with the vinegar, making sure all the leaves are submerged.

Cover tightly and leave at room temperature for 8 days.

Strain the vinegar into bottles, cork and label. Store in a cool place until needed.

CORNICHONS AU VINAIGRE

PICKLED GHERKINS

My mother used to prepare these every year. But it's harder to find the right kind of small dark green gherkin-cucumbers these days. Country markets and WI stalls are often the best bet. It's always worth asking at a WI stall – they may have someone growing just the thing you're after and they can bring it for you next week. That was how I discovered extra supplies of fresh figs to supplement my own last year. In France cucumbers for pickling are on sale from the end of June to September.

1 kg (2¼ lb) firm, dark green gherkin-cucumbers	2 sprays of tarragon
	20 peppercorns
	white pickling vinegar
255 g (9 oz) coarse salt	
255 g (9 oz) small white- or yellow-skinned pickling onions (in France look for *grelots*)	

Wash and dry the gherkins as soon as possible. Turn into a bowl and cover with the salt. Leave for 24 hours for the salt to draw out the water.

Next day, drain them, rinse them in cold water and dry on a clean teacloth. Pack into a jar, adding the peeled onions, tarragon and peppercorns as you go. Pour in the vinegar, making sure that everything is covered. Seal tightly and store in a cool, dark place for at least 2 months before using.

GELÉE DE GROSEILLES FRAMBOISÉE

RED CURRANT AND RASPBERRY JELLY

Fruit from mountain regions of France is highly esteemed, just as we value Scottish raspberries because their flavour is more intense. Perhaps because of its usefulness in pâtisserie there seems to be more jelly in France than here. This kind is especially good.

> **1 kg (2¼ lb) red currants**
> **500 g (1 lb 2 oz) white**
> **currants (if available,**
> **otherwise use red**
> **currants)**
> **500 g (1 lb 2 oz) raspberries**

Don't bother to sprig the red or white currants. Wash briefly in cold water and place in a preserving pan with the raspberries and ½ wineglass water. Cook gently over moderate heat for 10–15 minutes until cooked and the juice runs.

Tip the fruit into a jelly bag or a double layer of fine net and hang up over a bowl to catch the juice. Leave overnight until all the juice has dripped through.

Measure the liquid into a preserving pan and for each litre (each pint) add ¾ kilo (1 lb) of sugar. Dissolve the sugar over low heat, stirring from time to time. Raise the heat and bring to the boil. Boil, not stirring, for 3 minutes. The jelly should then set, with a lovely flavour and colour. Pour into small, hot, dry jars. Cover and label.

MARMELADE DE PÊCHES

PEACH MARMALADE

In my experience most peach jams are delicious but fairly liquid. Mine is usually more of a sauce, wonderful spooned over ice-cream but hopeless on bread. However, in this recipe the peaches are mashed rather than sliced and thus thicken the jam considerably.

1 kg (2¼ lb) ripe peaches
500 g (1 lb 2 oz) sugar
2 lemons
1 tablespoon peach brandy
   or *eau-de-vie*

Cover the peaches, two at a time, with boiling water. Leave for 30 seconds then lift out and peel. Slice all the skinned peaches into a large saucepan or preserving pan.

Crack the stones of half the peaches and simmer the kernels in a little water for a few minutes. Discard the brown skins, chop the white kernels finely and add to the peaches.

Cook the peaches for 10–15 minutes over moderate heat until soft enough to mash with a potato masher.

Add the sugar and the strained juice of the lemons. Stir over low heat until the sugar is dissolved, then boil rapidly for 15–20 minutes, stirring frequently to prevent the jam catching. It may be necessary to lower the heat for the final 5 minutes.

The jam is ready when a teaspoonful cooled on a plate does not run together again after drawing one's finger across it.

Stir in the peach brandy or *eau-de-vie* and spoon the jam into small, hot, dry jars. Cover and label.

PÂTE DE COINGS, OU COTIGNAC

QUINCE PASTE

The exquisitely scented quince is an ancient and distinguished fruit, named the apple of Cydonia (still its botanical name) by the Romans after a town on the north coast of Crete; it was once as familiar in southern Europe as the vine. It is striking to see how often the quince appears on the crisply carved sarcophagi found in the ancient burial ground of the Alycamps in Arles and now moved to the Musée d'Art Chrétien there. Fat, shapely quinces tumble with a few figs, many lemons and a pineapple from a cornucopia, wreathed in flowers and leaves; to me, a far more moving memorial of a life lived and loved than today's headstones.

For centuries in France and Britain quinces have been turned into this lovely sweetmeat. Small, misshapen pieces of quince are fine for this recipe if you are reserving the choice specimens for a pie or compôte.

**1 kg (2¼ lb) quinces
up to 1½ kg (3 lb) sugar**

Wash the quinces in plenty of cold water, rubbing them with your hands to remove the grey down. Cut up the fruit and place in a pan with water to cover.

Cook slowly, uncovered, until the fruit is mushy. Mash gently with a wooden spoon to release all the flavour from the fruit.

Sieve the contents of the pan by rubbing all the fruit and liquid through a nylon sieve. Weigh the resulting purée and return to the pan with an equal quantity of white sugar.

Gradually bring the mixture to the boil, stirring until the sugar is dissolved. Then cook until very thick; stir from time to time, but cover your hand because the mixture can spit.

The paste is ready when the mixture starts to come away from the sides of the pan. At this stage if you draw a wooden spoon across the base of the pan the mixture takes a few moments to flow back.

Remove from the heat and spoon into small pots or moulds to turn out and serve, sliced, with cheese.

But better, I think, is to pour the mixture into a shallow dish or non-stick baking tray. When set cut into squares or diamonds. Roll the pieces in caster sugar and arrange on a small dish for serving with coffee. Quince paste keeps for several weeks, in a cold, dry place and a small jar of pieces rolled in sugar makes a lovely present, especially for town-dwellers.

Confiture de Pastèque

WATER-MELON JAM

A pot of water-melon jam sitting on a sunny windowsill glows orange-red, the sliced fruit rosier than when fresh and lightened by the pale slivers of lemon peel. In late July and August water-melons are remarkably cheap, even in England, and one average-sized water-melon will make up to 4 kg (9 lb) of jam.

4 kg (9 lb) water-melon	2–2½ kg (about 4–5 lb)
3 oranges	sugar
2 lemons	a sherry glass of rum

Halve the melon and scoop the seeds and softer flesh into a sieve placed over a bowl. Press the juice and flesh through into the bowl. Cut the halves into segments and cut the ripe flesh free from the peel. Slice thinly and add to the bowl. Peel the oranges and add the thinly sliced flesh. (Discard the peel.)

Wash the lemons, quarter and slice thinly. Add to the bowl with the sugar. Stir and set the bowl aside, covered, for 24 hours.

Keep the orange and lemon pips and place in a small cloth bag for suspending in the jam as it cooks.

Next day bring the mixture slowly to the boil in a preserving pan, stirring now and again until the sugar is dissolved.

Simmer steadily for 1½–2 hours or until the jam reaches 105°C (220°F) or a tablespoon of the jam cooled on a plate forms a thin skin.

Add the rum and remove from the heat. Allow to cool for 2–3 minutes so that the fruit will be evenly distributed in the jars. Pour into hot, dry jars and cover straight away or when completely cold.

Note that this jam does not set firmly like English jams.

VINAIGRE AUX FRAMBOISES

RASPBERRY VINEGAR

Flavoured vinegars are simple (and far cheaper) to make at home. In recent years raspberry vinegar, in particular, has become the darling of some *nouvelle cuisine* chefs. From time to time a judicious spoonful can certainly give a salad dressing or a sauce a delightful and unusual lift. Incidentally Eliza Acton gives instructions for simmering the vinegar with an equal amount of white sugar to make a syrup for adding to sweet sauces or to chilled water to make a summer drink.

225 g (8 oz) fresh	a few days later, another
raspberries	225 g (8 oz) fresh
white wine vinegar	raspberries

Fill a plastic-lidded jar with the raspberries, pour in the wine vinegar to cover the fruit and cover tightly. Store in a dark place for 3 days.

Strain off the vinegar through a fine nylon sieve. Discard the raspberries and fill the jar with the second batch of raspberries. Pour the vinegar over, cover tightly and store for 3 days, as before.

If you have plentiful supplies of fresh raspberries the steeping process can be repeated yet again – it also depends on how full-flavoured the fruit is.

Finally strain the vinegar through a nylon sieve, lined with a cloth and pour into a bottle. Seal and store in a cool, dark place until needed.

LIQUEUR D'ANGÉLIQUE

ANGELICA LIQUEUR

Even in wine-producing districts of France, there is great interest in making wines and spirits at home, flavoured with fruit and flowers from the hedgerow and garden.

These two recipes appeared in a booklet published by the French equivalent of our magazine *Vole*. I have been able to make the angelica version because angelica seeds everywhere in my herb garden and I am glad to find more ways of using it.

55 g (2 oz) tender young stems of angelica	**1¼ litre (2¼ pt) *eau-de-vie blanche* (40°)**
¼ teaspoon ground nutmeg	**900 g (2 lb) sugar**
¼ teaspoon ground cinnamon	**500 ml (18 fl oz) water, spring or non-carbonated**

Cut the angelica stems into short sections and place in a large jar or wide-necked bottle. Add the nutmeg, cinnamon and the *eau-de-vie*. Seal the jar and leave for 4 days.

Dissolve the sugar in the water over low heat, bring to the boil and simmer for 4 minutes. Cool then add to the angelica mixture. Leave overnight and strain through a very fine sieve or coffee filter.

Bottle up the liqueur and make a pretty label with the name and date. This concoction is recommended as a digestive after meals.

LIQUEUR D'ACACIA

ACACIA LIQUEUR

Once my white-flowered acacia tree from the Ardèche is large enough to flower profusely, I shall make this concoction and discover whether one really can trap the bewitching scent of acacia blossom in a glass. And I hope it will be more successful than the endless experiments with rose petals that I conducted as a child.

450 g (1 lb) fresh white
    acacia flowers
1 litre (1¾ pt) *eau-de-vie*
    blanche (40°)
450 g (1 lb) sugar

275 ml (½ pt) still mineral
    water
½ cinnamon stick
4 cloves

Pack the flowers in a wide-necked bottle or jar. Add the *eau-de-vie*, making sure that all the flowers are covered. Cover the bottle and stand it in the sun for 8 days.

Dissolve the sugar in the water with the cinnamon and cloves and simmer for 4 minutes. Then cool and remove the spices.

Strain the *eau-de-vie* into a dry, clean bottle or bottles and add the cooled syrup. Cork and label.

CONFITURE PHILOSOPHALE

PHILOSOPHER'S JAM

Should you find yourself with one perfect but solitary fresh fig here is an excellent recipe for it. An instant jam of garnet hue with, perhaps, a flavour from the past.

For one person: **1 ripe fresh fig**
10 sweet almonds   **1 tablespoon honey**

If the almonds have bitter skins blanch them by covering with cold water in a small pan. Bring to the boil, pour off the hot water and replace with cold. Peel away the brown skins and discard.

Pound the nuts in a mortar until finely crushed, and then work in the quartered fig and the honey. Or simply chop the almonds in a processor or blender. Add the fig and honey and process to a purée, but don't make it too smooth.

Spread the jam on very fresh bread or toast and serve.

BIBLIOGRAPHY

Amicale des Cuisiniers et Pâtissiers Auvergnats de Paris, *Cuisine d'Auvergne*, 1979.

Andreis, Florence de, *La Cuisine d'aujourd'hui*, Rivages, 1980.

Androuet, Pierre, *Guide de fromages*, Éditions Stock.

Ardagh, John, *France in the 1980s*, Penguin Books and Secker & Warburg, 1982.

Aron, Jean-Paul, *The Art of Eating in France*, Peter Owen, 1975.

Audot, L. E., *La Cuisinière de la campagne et de la ville*, 1818.

Barras, Jean-Paul, *Le Coeur et la fourchette*, Éditions de Plein Vent, 1983.

Bernard, Françoise, *Les Recettes faciles*, Hachette, 1965.

Bocuse, Paul, *The Cuisine of Paul Bocuse*, Granada, 1982.

Bozon, Pierre, *L'Ardèche, la terre et les hommes du Vivarais*, Éditions l'Hermès, 1978.

Catoni, Maurice, *La Cuisine provençale et niçoise*, Presses Pocket, 1980.

Chanot-Bullier, C., *Vieilles Recettes de cuisine provençale*, Tacussel, 1972.

Le Château d'Entrecasteaux, son histoire et sa restauration.

Claustres, Georges, *Connaître et reconnaître les champignons*, Ouest France, 1978.

Dard, Patrice, *Les Fruits et les glaces*, Crealinus, 1983.

David, Elizabeth, *French Country Cooking*, John Lehmann, 1951; Penguin Books, 1959.

David, Elizabeth, *French Provincial Cooking*, Michael Joseph, 1960; Penguin Books, 1964.

David, Elizabeth, *An Omelette and a Glass of Wine*, Robert Hale, 1984; Penguin Books, 1986.

Davidson, Alan, *Mediterranean Seafood*, Penguin Books, 1972.

Durand, *Le Cuisinier Durand*, Laffitte Reprints, Marseilles, 1980.

Durand, Jean, *Augustine centenaire ardéchoise*, Presses Bayle, 1985.

Drysdale, Julia, *Classic Game Cookery*, Macmillan (Papermac), 1983.

Evelyn, John, *Acetaria* (1699), facsimile edition, Prospect Books, 1982.

Evelyn, John, *The Diary of John Evelyn*, edited by John Bowle, Oxford University Press, 1983.

Escoffier, A., *La Morue*, Flammarion, 1929.

Fearon, Ethelind, *The Marquis, the Mayonnaise and Me*, Newnes, 1961.

Fisher, M. F. K., *The Art of Eating*, Hogarth Press, 1985.

Fisher, M. F. K., *The Cooking of Provincial France*, Time Life, 1968.

Fisher, M. F. K., *Two Towns in Provence*, Hogarth Press, 1983.

Forot, Charles, *Odeurs de forêt et fumets de table*, Seilc, 1975.

Francus, Docteur, *Voyage fantaisiste et sérieux à travers l'Ardèche et la Haute-Loire, Tome I et Tome II* (1870), reprinted Éditions Simone Sudre, 1983.

Girardet, Fredy, *Cuisine Spontanée*, Macmillan, 1985.

Grigson, Jane, *Charcuterie and French Pork Cookery*, Michael Joseph, 1967; Penguin Books, 1970.

Grigson, Jane, *The Mushroom Feast*, Michael Joseph, 1975; Penguin Books, 1978.

Kennedy, Diana, *Mexican Regional Cooking*, Harper & Row, 1972.

Lamaison, P. A., *Recettes et paysages, sud-est et méditerranée*, 1951.

Leblanc, M., *Nouveau Manuel complet du pâtissier*, Manuel-Roret, reprinted 1985.

Mathiot, Ginette, *Les Conserves pour tous*, Albin Michel, 1948.

Mathiot, Ginette, *Je sais faire la pâtisserie*, Albin Michel, 1938.

Mathiot, Ginette, et Poilâne, Lionel, *Pain, cuisine et gourmandises*, Albin Michel, 1985.

Mazille, la, *La Bonne Cuisine du Périgord*, Flammarion, 1929.

Mazollier, Julien, *La Cuisine ardéchoise*, 1982.

Mazollier, Julien, *La Vie quotidienne en Ardèche au début du siecle*, 1983.

Médecin, Jacques, *Cuisine du comté de Nice*, Julliard, 1972, translated as *Cuisine Niçoise*, Penguin Books, 1983.

Mennell, Stephen, *All Manners of Food*, Blackwell, 1985.

Michelin Green Guides: *Vallée du Rhône, Provence, Causses,* etc.

Montagné, Prosper, *Le Trésor de la cuisine du bassin méditeranéen*, 1930.

Montagné, Prosper et Gottschalk, Dr, *Larousse Gastronomique*, Hamlyn, 1961.

Montagné, Prosper, et Salles, Prosper, *Le Grand Livre de la cuisine*, Flammarion, 1929.

Morard, Marius, *Manuel complet de la cuisinière provençale* (1886), Laffitte reprint.

Olney, Richard, *Simple French Food*, Jill Norman, 1984.

Phillips, Roger, *Mushrooms and other Fungi of Great Britain and Europe*, Pan Books, 1981.

Poilâne, Lionel, *Guide de l'amateur de pain*, Robert Laffont, 1981.

Pomiane, Édouard de, *Good Fare*, Gerald Howe, 1932.

Pont, le, *Liqueurs et sirops à faire soi-même*, 1979.

Reboux, Paul, *Plats Nouveaux!*, Flammarion, 1927.

Reyne, Jacky, *Marrons et châtaignes d'Ardèche*, Seilc, 1984.

Roden, Claudia, *A New Book of Middle Eastern Food*, Viking, 1985; Penguin Books, 1986.

Root, Waverley, *The Food of France*, Macmillan, 1983.

Rose, Mademoiselle, *Cent Façons d'accommoder le mouton*, Flammarion, 1931.

Serres, Olivier de, *Le Théâtre d'agriculture et mesnages des champs* (1600).

Stevenson, Robert Louis, *Travels with a Donkey in the Cevennes* (1875).

Stobart, Tom, *Herbs, Spices and Flavourings*, International Wine and Food Publishing Co., 1970; Penguin Books, 1977.

Tosco et Fanelli, *Les Champignons*, Éditions Atlas, 1980.

Les Trucs d'hier et d'aujourd'hui: boissons, Alternative Diffusion, Paris.

Viard, Henri, *Fromages de France*, Dargand, 1980.

Wheaton, Barbara Ketchum, *Savouring the Past*, Chatto & Windus, 1983.

Willan, Anne, *French Regional Cooking*, Hutchinson, 1981.

Young, Arthur, *Travels in France*, 1792.

Zeldin, Theodore, *The French*, Collins, 1983.

INDEX